God's Guidance for TODAY

One-Year Daily Bible Reading
and Prayer Guide

RAYMOND F. CULPEPPER
FLOYD D. CAREY

PATHWAY PRESS

All Scripture quotations, unless otherwise indicated, are taken from the Holy Bible, *New International Version®*. *NIV®*. Copyright © 1973, 1978, 1984 by International Bible Society. Used by permission of Zondervan. All rights reserved.

Scripture quotations marked "NKJV" are taken from the New King James Version. Copyright © 1982 by Thomas Nelson, Inc. Used by permission. All rights reserved.

The Daily Bible Reading scriptures used in this book are taken from *Every Day With the Word*, a publication of the Church of God Department of Evangelism and Home Missions. Used by permission.

Editorial Staff: James E. Cossey, Tom George, Tammy Hatfield, Tammy Henkel, and Esther Metaxes.

Cover Design by Lonzo T. Kirkland
Interior Design by Tom George

Library of Congress Control Number: 2009913259

ISBN: 9781596845015

P

Copyright © 2010 by Pathway Press
1080 Montgomery Avenue
Cleveland, Tennessee 37311

All rights reserved. No part of this publication may be reproduced or transmitted in any form or by any means, electronic or mechanical, including photocopying, recording, or otherwise, or by any information storage or retrieval system, without the permission in writing from the publisher. Please direct inquiries to Pathway Press, 1080 Montgomery Avenue, Cleveland, TN 37311.

Visit *www.pathwaypress.org* for more information.

Printed in the United States of America

MISSION STATEMENT

To maintain, through daily Bible
reading and persistent prayer,
Holy Spirit inspired involvement
in the three initiatives set forth
by the Church of God
to undergird mission
and vision:

PRAYER—
The Heartbeat of the Church

THE GREAT COMMISSION—
The Solution

THE QUEST FOR TRUST—
The Fulcrum of the Future

Contents

Foreword 9

Reading the Bible and Prayer Guidelines 11

One-Year Bible Reading Guide Highlights 13

My Five Goals in Bible Reading and Prayer 15

Prayer Devotionals and Reading Guide 17

Resources 383

FOREWORD

Three initiatives have been set forth by the Church of God in support of fulfilling our mission and vision in changing times:

PRAYER—The Heartbeat of the Church

THE GREAT COMMISSION . . . The Solution

THE QUEST FOR TRUST—The Fulcrum of the Future

This volume, *God's Guidance for Today,* has been designed to undergird active support of these initiatives through daily Bible reading and prayer.

Daily Bible reading will unite us with God's plan and purposes. Prayer will shape us into the likeness of Christ and empower us for visionary and aggressive kingdom service.

When I was growing up, my parents, Frank and Kohatha Culpepper, began each day with Bible reading and prayer. They taught me to hide God's Word in my heart and to memorize scriptures. Before I left for school they would place their hands on my head and pray for God's oversight, "Lord bless and guide our son today. Protect him! Let him be a witness of Your wonderful love by his behavior and by his desire to learn and develop his talents."

Bible reading and prayer has shaped my life—my values, my goals, my relationships, and my ministry.

Bible reading and prayer are the foundation and heartbeat of the church and of the believer:

- Bible Reading Creates Faith
- Bible Reading Nourishes Fortitude
- Bible Reading Prepares for the Future
- Prayer Molds
- Prayer Motivates
- Prayer Equips for Ministry

As you practice reading the Bible every day, you will experience mountain-moving faith and fortitude to stand with boldness and claim God's provisions for the future.

As you personalize the prayers in *God's Guidance for Today*, you will be molded in Christlikeness, motivated to love and learn, and equipped for kingdom-impacting ministry.

In your daily Bible reading and prayer time you will unite with members of the Church of God family around the world. The Holy Spirit will hover over us and empower us to go forward together in Prayer, The Great Commission, and The Quest for Trust. Together, as a spiritual family, we will experience a mighty worldwide flow of supernatural blessings.

My Prayer for You

Lord of remarkable blessings and redeeming love, guide the Church of God family in Bible reading and prayer. May each day in communion with You prompt a closer relationship, a deeper respect for Your holiness, and a clearer understanding of how to live a life of influence. May new beginnings, challenging adventures, and life-changing possibilities be experienced by the inspiration of the Holy Spirit. Amen.

—Raymond F. Culpepper
General Overseer
Church of God

READING THE BIBLE AND PRAYER GUIDELINES

Prepare yourself for an exciting journey! *God's Guidance for Today* will lead you on a trip through the Bible, from Genesis to Revelation, in one year. You will also take a daily personal "walk and talk" journey with God in prayer. The following guidelines will assist you in the journey:

BIBLE READING GUIDE

1. **Read** the One-Year Bible Reading Guide Highlights on the next page.

2. **Goal.** You can take a journey through the entire Bible in one year by reading just a few chapters every day.

3. **Format.** At the bottom of the page of each daily prayer are Bible chapters to read for that day. At the end of one year you will have read the entire Bible. Plus, you will have personalized 365 prayers.

4. **Process.** Read the designated chapters and then place a check mark in the box indicating they have been read.

5. **Insights.** Review mentally or record on paper the personal insights you received from the Bible lesson.

PRAYER GUIDE

1. **Read** the My Five Goals in Daily Bible Reading and Prayer.

2. **Review**. Quickly thumb through the daily prayers. Observe that they include all areas of Prayer, The Great Commission, and The Quest for Trust.

3. **Study**. The format of the prayers contain three subject sections. They are designed to create prayer paths for you to follow.

4. **Observe**. The nature of the prayers contain trigger words to ignite personal petitions, phrases to paint pictures of devotion, and heart-cries to reflect influential commitment.

5. **Personalize**. Relate the prayers to your vision, your desire for spiritual growth, and your determination to live a victorious Christian life.

—Floyd D. Carey

One-Year Bible Reading Guide Highlights

Reading through the Bible from Genesis to Revelation in one year provides an illuminated pathway that:

1. **Leads** to a deeper appreciation and respect for God's leadership and provisions.

2. **Teaches** self-discipline in understanding and following God's plan for life, liberty, and fruitfulness.

3. **Reveals** the magnitude of personal victories that can be experienced by visualizing, trusting, and obeying scriptural truths.

4. **Guides** in developing faith to believe all things are possible in living a victorious life that honors God through uncompromising dedication and unselfish service.

5. **Provides** resources to grow in wisdom, spiritual maturity, and in becoming an honorable witness of God's supreme love and special favor.

6. **Offers** direction and supportive enablement in fulfilling the Great Commission (make disciples) and the Great Commandment (demonstrate love).

7. **Establishes** life on a solid foundation of faith, hope, and love, and how to daily walk with Jesus Christ in total obedience.

My Five Goals in Bible Reading and Prayer

1. To **ESTABLISH** a consistent pattern and place for spending life-transforming time in Bible reading and prayers.

2. To **DEPEND** on the illuminating oversight of the Holy Spirit to comprehend and apply biblical truths.

3. To **PREPARE** mentally and spiritually to make communion with God a life-enriching, compelling priority.

4. To **SHARE** the fulfilling rewards of total lifestyle commitment and obedience with family and friends.

5. To **WITNESS** graciously and verbally of the caring love of God and the promise of abundant life in Jesus Christ.

Name ______________________________

Date ______________________________

DAY 1 — A BALANCED WALK

God of guidance and truth, I want to walk with You today. Like Enoch, I want to walk and talk, walk and work, walk and witness. As I walk with You today, may Your radiant glory cover my countenance and direct my conduct. I ask You to inspire me to:

Walk with a WILLING spirit. I want to be open and honest, not withdrawn or hesitant. May my willing spirit be reflected in an attitude of praise and thanksgiving, and a willingness to support and serve.

Walk with WISDOM that is scriptural. Your Word provides light, liberty, and insights on living a balanced, Christ-centered life. Direct me in reading and applying biblical truths in my relationships and Christian responsibilities.

Walk with WELLNESS that is strengthening. Father, I want to be healthy—spiritually and physically. I want to run the Christian race with a sound body. I will exercise, eat, and rest properly so that I can walk with You, gracious Father, with endurance, excitement, and godly influence.

MY PRAYER NOTES FOR TODAY

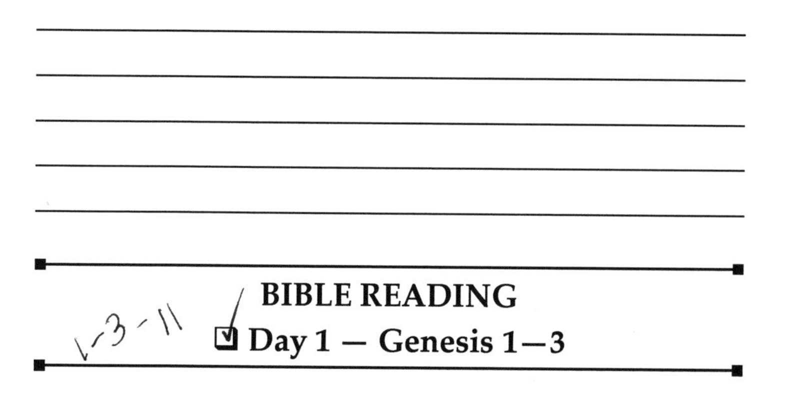

DAY 2 — A BEAMING SMILE

I rejoice because I'm free! I smile because I'm happy! Father, both of these virtues are a gift from You. You have set me free through faith in Jesus Christ and created joy in my heart and a smile on my face. I praise You for this! A smile symbolizes:

SOUL contentment. Lord, I am not looking, longing, or searching for something new. I have found soul contentment in You—upward praise, inner peace, and outward reflections of Your beauty. **I will portray what's in my soul by a smile on my face.**

SEASONED character. My character, molded by Christ, provides comfort, control, and connectivity. A smile opens doors and reveals I'm committed in faith to You and in friendship with others. **I will reflect my character by my smile.**

SELF-ESTEEM confidence. I am more than a conqueror in Christ. Father, You give me confidence to step out in faith, to step up to achieve worthy goals, to step forward in aggressive Christian ministry, and to step into new experiences of fellowship with You. **I will show self-esteem by a convincing smile.**

MY PRAYER NOTES FOR TODAY

DAY 3 — A BOLD FAITH

Great opportunities to learn, grow, and act surround me. I do not want to be idle or fearful. I want to exercise a bold faith and to act with authority to experience and achieve. I want to exhibit a bold faith by:

BELIEVING. Your Word states that I can move the mountains that block progressive thinking and productivity if I believe. Today I believe! I will receive from You and I will act with bold faith in accordance with Your will and work.

BIRTHING. My mind and heart are open to You to birth creative ideas and new patterns to seize possibilities. Today I will walk an uncharted path. I will embrace change and I will act with a bold faith to exalt You and to expand my skills.

BELONGING. I belong to a loving family of believers that are committed to You and to nurturing each member of the family. I will recognize the unity of the family. I will cherish the privilege of belonging and will act with a bold faith to protect and increase the growth of the family.

MY PRAYER NOTES FOR TODAY

____

____

____

____

____

BIBLE READING

☑ Day 3 — Genesis 7—9

DAY 4 — A CARING SPIRIT

Father, You care for me with tender love and caring compassion. I feel Your comforting, protecting, and providing presence. Broken, bruised, and battered people need Your love through me. May I show a caring spirit today to:

The BOUND. Satan holds individuals in captivity through false doctrine, addiction to drugs, and destructive habits. They feel hopeless and helpless. I want to reflect Your tenderness and love through sympathy, understanding, and positive action that leads to transformation.

The BROKENHEARTED. Wayward children, marriage malfunctions, ministry setbacks, disease, and death result in a broken heart crying out for help. I need holy wisdom to help lead others to the path of healing. Infuse me with faith-fuel and Word-wisdom to be a stabilizing force.

The BURDENED. People around me are burdened because of financial, career, and friendship pressures. I bring these people to You in faith, knowing that You will grant them rest, relief, and restoration.

MY PRAYER NOTES FOR TODAY

DAY 5 — A CLOSER WALK WITH YOU

Father of light, liberty, and love, I want to walk closer to You today. I want to know You better, honor You more graciously, and participate in ministry with You more effectively. Touch my spirit to do this by:

Walking directly in the LIGHT of Your Word. You reveal Yourself in the Bible—Your nature, Your plans, and Your affections. I can walk closer to You by being more disciplined in my Bible study—**empower me to do this!**

Walking freely in the LIBERTY of Your forgiveness. You have given me freedom from the power of sin, darkness, and evil. I can walk closer to You by displaying a free spirit and a positive attitude about life—**energize me to do this!**

Walking jubilantly in the LOVE of Jesus Christ. Through Your Son, You have demonstrated the power of love. Your love heals and issues hope. I can walk closer to You by seeking to show the fruit of authentic love in my daily life—**equip me to do this!**

MY PRAYER NOTES FOR TODAY

BIBLE READING

☑ **Day 5 — Genesis 13—15**

DAY 6 — A DYNAMIC CHARGE

All-powerful heavenly Father, I ask You for a dynamic spiritual charge today. Let Your Spirit circulate in my life—in my thinking, acting, and performing. Empower and equip me to be prepared to face obstacles and to endorse opportunities.

Charge me MENTALLY. You have admonished me to think like Christ and to adopt the mind of Christ. I want to do this by thinking righteously, creatively, and progressively. **I am ready for a dynamic spiritual charge today.**

Charge my MOTIVATION. I want to be up and ready to reflect spiritual values today by my walk and my talk. I want to walk with steady steps that denote confidence and conviction. I want to talk with words of wisdom that denote commitment and compassion. **I am ready for a dynamic spiritual charge today.**

Charge my MINISTRY. Like Christ, Father, I want to be about Your business—teaching, encouraging, providing. Anoint me to be both efficient and effective to demonstrate the message and meaning of the Christian life. **I am ready for a dynamic spiritual charge today.**

MY PRAYER NOTES FOR TODAY

BIBLE READING

☑ **Day 6 — Genesis 16—18**

DAY 7 — A FRESH ANOINTING

Father of new life, eternal life, and Scripture-directed life, I am thankful to be part of Your family. I do not want to allow my walk with You to become common, cold, or careless. I want my walk to be close, committed, and colorful. Today, I ask for a fresh anointing:

For ADORATION. I want to sing songs of praise, think thoughts of thanksgiving, and speak uplifting words of adoration. Today, I will make a list of the treasured gifts with which You have blessed me and the promises You have fulfilled in my life.

For an ANCHOR. Master, I need Your anointing as an anchor to hold me steady and to give me security. Satan creates waves of wickedness and sends wild winds of adversity. I trust You alone to be my unmovable anchor.

For ADVANCEMENT. I want to keep spiritual goals before me, Lord—kingdom service, scriptural knowledge, and growth in Christlikeness. Touch me, train me, and tutor me so I can maximize the gifts You have invested in me for Your honor and glory.

MY PRAYER NOTES FOR TODAY

____

____

____

____

____

BIBLE READING

☑ **Day 7 — Genesis 19—21**

DAY 8 — A FRESH FLOW IN PRAYER

Thank you for the opportunity—holy privilege—of close, loving communion with You today. I never want to take this in a casual, "I've got to do it" manner. I want my time with You to be fresh and free-flowing from my heart. So, I ask You to shower me with a creative attitude today so I can:

PRAISE You with fresh words. I often get in a rut saying the same words and going through the same routine. Today I will challenge my will and check my words and open new spiritual windows in praising You and in conveying my deep love.

PETITION You for crucial needs. I will pray for others instead of focusing on my personal needs. I will remember my unchurched neighbors and my friends at church. I will seek You for impact to make my prayers focused and descriptive.

PARTNER with You in ministry. I can do nothing in my own strength. When I partner with You—and this is Your plan—I can be effective in following Your will for my life, in exalting You in worship, and in being a joyful witness.

MY PRAYER NOTES FOR TODAY

____

____

____

____

____

BIBLE READING

☑ Day 8 — Genesis 22—24

DAY 9 — A GOOD SAMARITAN

Father of care and comfort, I desire to exhibit the qualities of a good Samaritan—watchful eyes, a compassionate heart, and helping hands. This does not come naturally. It comes from Your Son living and working in me and through me. So I will be a:

Good SAINT. I am saved and made a saint through the shed blood of my Savior, Your Son, Jesus Christ. I am only made good through Your righteousness. I want to be a good saint bubbling with enthusiasm, maintaining an attitude of thanksgiving, and showing concern for the needs of others.

Good STEWARD. The Good Samaritan in the Bible was a good steward; he had money to help the man who had been robbed and beaten. Teach me the steps to financial security so I can be in a position to assist the needy and to support worthy causes.

Good SOLDIER. Equip me to be prepared to fight against the forces of evil and to protect the weak. Give me courage to stand strong for just causes and for the advancement of Your kingdom.

MY PRAYER NOTES FOR TODAY

____

____

____

____

____

BIBLE READING

☑ **Day 9 — Genesis 25—27**

DAY 10 — A GOOD STEWARD

Gracious and good heavenly Father, I want to be a good steward today, a true and trusted servant. I want my works to be classified as gold, silver, and jewels:

GOLD—Shine with sincerity. I want my service to the church, my acts of kindness to neighbors, and my assistance to the underprivileged to be warm, personable, natural, and covered with unconditional love—as **a trusted servant.**

SILVER—Reflect inward resolve. Whatever I do today, I want it to resonate with a heart committed to You, a head devoted to thinking like Christ, and hands anointed by the Holy Spirit for effective service with impact—as **a trusted servant.**

JEWELS—Sparkle with success. Today I want to show the victory side of being a believer. In You, I have abundant life, conquering power, winning energy, triumphant leadership, and successful achievements—as **a trusted servant.**

MY PRAYER NOTES FOR TODAY

BIBLE READING

☑ Day 10 — Genesis 28—30

DAY 11 — A GREATER VISION

I know what I see is what I will be! This is a combination of vision and faith. Father of new life, I want to see more so I can be more in You and do more in Your kingdom. Let me see:

My POSITION in You. I am a full-fledged member of Your family. I have Your love as a Father and access to the full range of benefits of Your house. **I honor You for this.**

My POTENTIAL in You. I am more than a conqueror in You—totally victorious. Today I want to act and feel like a conqueror. I want to exercise the gifts You have given to me in my relationships, work habits, home life, and Christian witness. **I trust You today.**

My PRAYER position in You. I am able to walk close to You through prayer. Today I want to maintain a prayer on my lips. I will talk to You honestly, openly, and sincerely about commitment, understanding Your commands, and being a compelling, compassionate witness. **I praise You.**

MY PRAYER NOTES FOR TODAY

____

____

____

____

____

BIBLE READING

☑ **Day 11 — Genesis 31—33**

DAY 12 — A GROWING MIND

A mind growing in grace, knowledge, and awareness of believing and achieving is the goal I seek to reach. I depend on Your supervision, holy Father, to achieve this. I am open and ready with a "go" posture:

No FIXED mind-set. My mind is open for You to introduce new thinking patterns and creative thoughts on understanding and applying scriptural truths to my life. Remove any signs of stubbornness, self-will, and self-sufficiency.

No FAITHLESS motives. Father, I want my attention to be focused on bold, aggressive aspirations. I am limited within myself but unlimited in You. I will walk new paths today with great expectations to explore and experience the dimensions of Your power.

No FADED map. Master, I will not let the map You created for me fade. I will study it meticulously and follow it with faith and fortitude. Give me a clear vision in reading the map, wisdom to discern proper directions, and steady, progressive steps in reaching the places and fulfilling the plans You have for me.

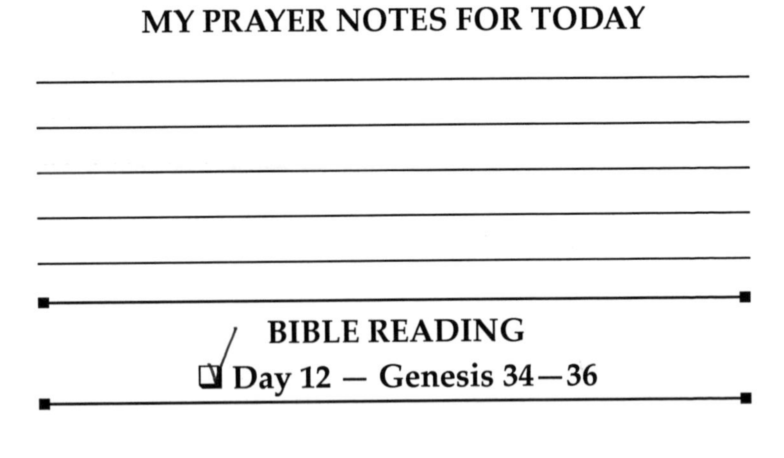

MY PRAYER NOTES FOR TODAY

BIBLE READING

☑ Day 12 — Genesis 34—36

DAY 13 — A HEALTHY CHURCH

Father, I am thankful for my local church. It is a place for coming together to worship and to embrace the work of the Great Commission. I want to be a motivated church member, and I want to perform ministry that will keep my church healthy. I will:

Partner with my PASTOR. The health of my local church requires partnership with my pastor. I will stand by his side and support him, encourage him, and engage in Your work with him.

Team with other PARISHIONERS. I appreciate and respect my church family. I want to show my feelings by being a loyal, trustworthy, and dependable family member. Let the Spirit of Christ be reflected in my relationships and how I perform ministry as a member of the congregational team.

Participate in church PROGRAMS. Lord, I realize I have responsibilities in keeping my church healthy. I need Your instructions and inspiration to maintain a congenial spirit, to be creative in outreach action, and to worship You in spirit and in truth. Anoint me today to be a champion for church health.

MY PRAYER NOTES FOR TODAY

____

____

____

____

____

BIBLE READING

☑ **Day 13 — Genesis 37—39**

DAY 14 — A HOLY HEART

From the heart springs the true values of life. Glorious Father, I realize this and I am committed to developing a holy heart that expresses my deep feelings for You and my faith to engage in Kingdom ministry. As I look up to You, look down on me and anoint my heart to be whole, holy, and fully devoted to You. May my heart represent:

Soul AFFECTION. In all I do—thoughts, words, deeds—may I demonstrate love and soul affection for Your name, Your nature, and the nurturing relationship I have with You. I will make love my theme for today!

Stimulating ATTITUDE. Father, I want my attitude to stimulate positive thoughts, trends, and talk. I want to be upbeat about walking with You and serving in Your Church. I will experience freshness in my faith today!

Spiritual ACTION. From my heart I want to show concern for those in need and to act to meet the needs. I ask for Your supervision and strength. I will be deliberate today in manifesting the nature of Christ—help, hope, healing!

MY PRAYER NOTES FOR TODAY

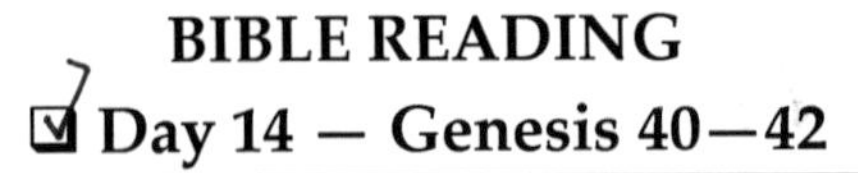

BIBLE READING

☑ Day 14 — Genesis 40—42

DAY 15 — A MEASURE OF FAITH

You have measured out sufficient faith for today. I praise You for this. With this faith I will:

F— **Face** the challenges of life boldly.

A—**Accept** Your oversight to behave wisely.

I —**Invest** in Your Kingdom strategically.

T—**Transact** relationships with others fairly.

H—**Hold** to Your promises firmly.

Your faith will enable me to see You working in my life to fulfill a divine plan that is far beyond my natural capabilities.

Your faith will enable me to taste the fruit of the Spirit and receive spiritual vitamins that will make me healthy, visionary, and progressive. I begin this day with faith, hope, and love.

MY PRAYER NOTES FOR TODAY

BIBLE READING

☑ **Day 15 — Genesis 43—45**

DAY 16 — A NEW COMMITMENT

Revealing Father, every day You show me new aspects of Your nature, new ways to draw closer to You, and new paths to follow to share Your love and peace. These revelations prompt me to make new commitments to develop stronger Christian values.

New commitment to CHRIST. Lord, I recognize the unity of the Godhead—Father, Son, and Holy Spirit. I join this unity in my commitment to Christ, the head of the Church. This commitment prompts me to trust and obey, set higher spiritual goals, and increase my flow of praise.

New commitment to my COMPANION. Thank You for bringing my companion into my life. We walk together in agreement in honoring each other and in serving You. I want my love to grow stronger and to be revealed in growing respect and acts of kindness.

New commitment to my CHURCH. Today I embrace the church's mission and message. I commit to being faithful in attendance, attitude, and actions. By Your leadership and empowerment, I will model commitment to the cause of Christ and my church.

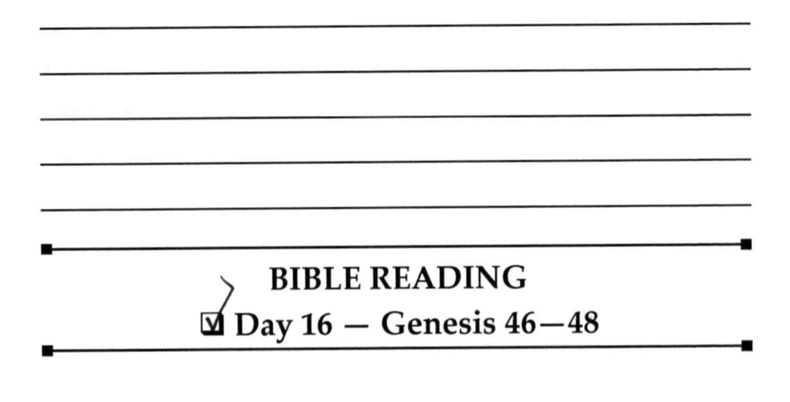

MY PRAYER NOTES FOR TODAY

BIBLE READING

☑ **Day 16 — Genesis 46—48**

DAY 17 — A NEW SONG

In Your Word, Master of music, You have told me to sing a new song. This means to stay in tune and to join You in what You are doing. To be creative. To expect new rays of sunshine from Your throne. In my heart I will be obedient. I will:

Sing a new song of DELIVERANCE. I will not let what you have done in my life fade in my memory. I will keep Your overshadowing fresh in my values and voice by singing a new song of deliverance. I have freedom in Jesus Christ!

Sing a new song of DELIGHT. My heart is filled with surging joy today. I will sing a new song of delight. I have a bright future, steadfast hope, guiding grace, and guaranteed provisions. I have a heart filled with joyful delight today!

Sing a new song of DEDICATION. I want to express my abiding love and heartfelt appreciation by singing a new song of dedication. I will worship intently, serve faithfully, and witness enthusiastically. I am a dedicated member of the worldwide family of God!

MY PRAYER NOTES FOR TODAY

BIBLE READING

☑ Day 17 — Genesis 49—50

DAY 18 — A NEW VIEW

Each day, magnificent Father, is filled with new experiences and opportunities. I don't want to see the same things the same way every day. I ask You to give me a new view so I can grow closer to You and stronger in service with You. I ask you to:

Give me a new view of Your GRACE. Your Word assures me that Your grace is sufficient for every challenge or conflict. I want to experience Your grace in all of its fullness today. I want to stand up and speak up about the abundance of Your unfailing love and grace today.

Give me a new view of Your GLORY. You are infinitely holy, boundless in mercy, and unchangeable in character. You emanate all that is good, holy, and pure. I want to look up, reach up, and touch Your glory today.

Give me a new view of Your GIFTS. You are inexhaustible in Your supply of gifts and unselfish in giving them. I want to store up scriptural gifts to empower me to serve You effectively and far-reachingly today.

MY PRAYER NOTES FOR TODAY

BIBLE READING

☑ **Day 18 — Exodus 1—3**

DAY 19 — A NEW WAY

Creative Father, every day You offer new ways to relate to You, to receive grace, and to renew commitments. I am thankful for the "new way" challenges that you provide. They are filled with explosive opportunities and I want to take full advantage of each one. I will:

RELATE in new ways. Holy Father, I will relate to You with fresh zeal to serve, with driving intensity in prayer, and a more enthusiastic approach to Bible study. This will energize me to relate to others in new ways—understanding, compassion, and support.

RECEIVE deeper understanding. I will be open today to a deeper understanding of kingdom principles and patterns of reaching the unchurched. I will gladly receive, apply, or develop them, and then share with friends and colleagues.

RENEW service commitments. Father, I want to be a giver and an influencer through service in my church, financial stewardship, and ministry in my community. Show me ways to be bold and to make an impact. I honor You, Master, and thank You for the privilege to discover and develop new ways today.

MY PRAYER NOTES FOR TODAY

BIBLE READING

☑ **Day 19 — Exodus 4—6**

DAY 20 — A POWERFUL WITNESS

Every day, Father, Jesus Christ, Your Son, reigns in my life, releases rich blessings, and removes obstacles that hinder spiritual progress. I am grateful for this, and I want praise to flow from my lips consistently and sincerely. Today, I will:

LIFT up Christ. I will lift up Christ with praise in my prayer life. I will lift up Christ with thanksgiving as I go about my daily activities. I will lift up Christ by meditating on His holiness and gifts of grace. I ask, Father, that my expressions and experiences will show Christ in me, the hope of glory!

LEARN to develop Christlikeness. I want You to teach me how to be more like Christ in the way I act and the way I react. I desire to act in ways that demonstrate commitment to Christ and that reflect His character. I want to react with compassion and understanding. Let Your glory shine in my life!

LEAD the lost to Christ. Lord, I want to tell about, and share, the love of Christ—the difference He can make in a person's life. Let Your Spirit prepare me, guide me, empower me, and motivate me. I will be a shining, powerful witness today!

MY PRAYER NOTES FOR TODAY

____

____

____

____

____

BIBLE READING

☑ Day 20 — Exodus 7—9

DAY 21 — A RESPONSIVE DISPOSITION

Father of favor and divine fruit, I always want to be alert and aggressive in responding to responsibilities and opportunities that surround me. I want to see the good, avoid the negative, and accept the challenges. As a ready responder I will:

Respond to RENEWAL. Master, every day is an opportunity to grow in grace, to renew commitments, and to be refreshed by the wind of the Holy Spirit. I will find renewal in my fellowship with You and in reaffirming my allegiance to the cause of Christ.

Respond to RESCUE. People are perishing in the sea of sin. They need to be rescued, shown love, and set on a different course. I will respond to this spiritual emergency. I will be a light, a rescuer in the night.

Respond to RESTORATION. I want to help individuals who have strayed from the straight and narrow way by the traps and temptations of Satan. Guide me in showing concern, demonstrating love, and providing counsel and support. I pray: "And do not lead us into temptation, but deliver us from the evil one: For Yours is the kingdom and the power and the glory forever. Amen" (Matt. 6:13 NKJV).

MY PRAYER NOTES FOR TODAY

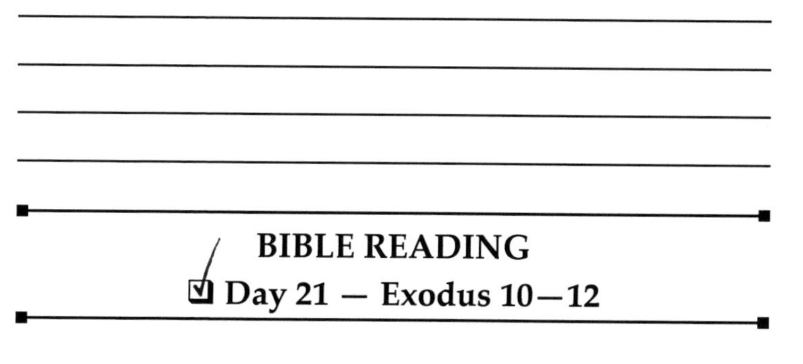

BIBLE READING

☑ **Day 21 — Exodus 10—12**

DAY 22 — A SHARING SPIRIT

Father of favor, I intend to have an upbeat, glowing, Christ-centered spirit today. I also want to share my spirit by being congenial, concerned, and complimentary of the achievements and skills of friends and associates. I want to share by:

LIFTING purposefully. Father, grace me to step out and step up to help lift the load of those under pressure and those facing hardships. Let me do it promptly without backwardness or hesitation and in a way that will spotlight Your righteous goodness.

LOVING intentionally. Love comes straight from You, Master, without conditions or cost. You continually devise ways to convey Your love. Today, I want to follow Your pattern. Energize me to develop ways to show Your love to the unloved, to the untouched, and to be united with other believers.

LEADING graciously. Let me lead today by example and with an attitude of love, acceptance, and appreciation. Also, Father, let me be receptive to Your leadership—learning, growing, receiving.

MY PRAYER NOTES FOR TODAY

BIBLE READING

☑ **Day 22 — Exodus 13—15**

DAY 23 — A MAJOR CONTRIBUTION

I am thankful for my church, community, and country. All three make a major contribution in my life. As a believer, wonderful Savior, I have a duty to make a major contribution to each of them through:

Love for my CHURCH. My church is a place of praise, peace, and protection. I join with other believers in worship that honors You, fellowship that refreshes, and service that provides security. I love my church and ask You to empower me to make a significant contribution.

Love for my COMMUNITY. My community is a place of growing families, friendship, and backyard unity. I want to be a good neighbor by a sharing spirit, a cooperative attitude, and demonstrating Christian character. I love my community and pray I will make a major contribution to community life.

Love for my COUNTRY. I want to be a good citizen by respecting law and order, accepting laws that govern, and supporting leaders. I love my country and pray we will always be "one nation, under God" with life, liberty, and the pursuit of happiness for all people.

MY PRAYER NOTES FOR TODAY

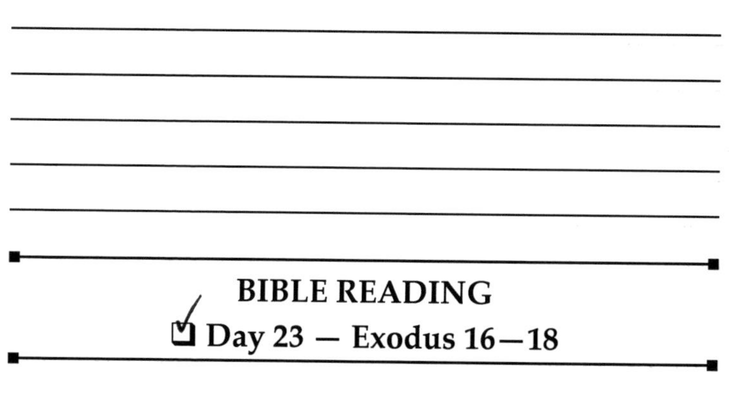

DAY 24 — A STRAIGHT PATH

Lord, it is so easy to go astray, to get off the beaten path into the rough. Today, I ask You to direct me in staying on the right path:

P — The **Personal** path You have designed for my life. I embrace Your will and, like Enoch, I will walk with You.

A — The **Anointed** path of Your love and grace. I need Your closeness and the flow of Your gifts and strength.

T — The **Terrific** path of discovery and adventure in Christ. I recognize Your creative nature and will expect the unusual and the extraordinary.

H — The **Holiness** path of wholeness and mind control. I claim Your presence to develop the qualities of Christlikeness in my life. As I walk with You today, Father, I will observe the path we follow so that I will not stray from it in the future.

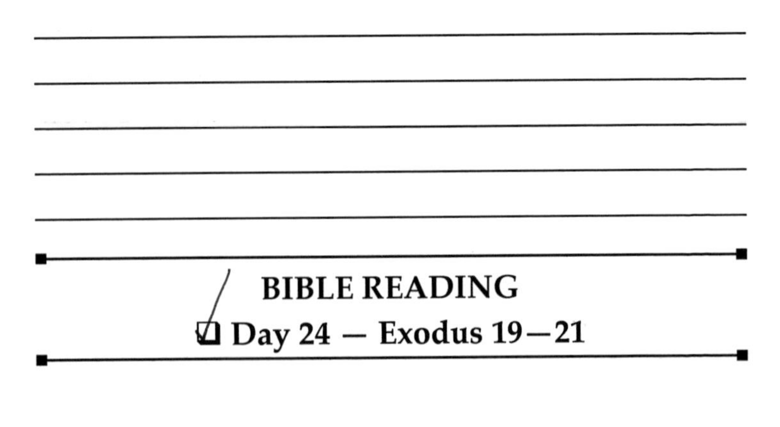

MY PRAYER NOTES FOR TODAY

BIBLE READING

☐ **Day 24 — Exodus 19—21**

DAY 25 — A SUPER FANTASTIC DAY

Today, Father, will be a super fantastic day. Your Spirit will guide me, and faith in You will sustain me. I will enjoy meeting new people. I will experience new wonders. I will be elevated in awareness of the fullness of Your riches. Today is a beautiful day! I praise You and will honor You with my thinking and tasks. Today, I purpose:

To live in Your LOVE. Your love forgives, forgets, and forges companionship. Your love lights the candle of fellowship and friendship. I will let it burn brightly.

To express Your LIBERTY. I am free from bandages, bondage, and binding attitude patterns. I will express my liberty in setting goals, working hard, and relating to others with trust, tenderness, and integrity.

To spread Your LIGHT. I will spread Your light today by my righteous example, by sharing a personal witness, and by showing sincere compassion for the lost. Thank You for a super fantastic day!

MY PRAYER NOTES FOR TODAY

____

____

____

____

____

BIBLE READING

☐ Day 25 — Exodus 22—24

DAY 26 — A VISIONARY PATH

I want to make a difference today! Father of fullness, direct me and develop me to walk a visionary path—a path that is filling, fulfilling, and faithful. I am open, yielded to Your leadership. Let me follow a:

Path of PARTNERSHIP. Lord, I cannot make it on my own strength. I am feeble, faulty, and failing. I depend on You to partner with me—to be my Mentor, my Motivator, and my Master.

Path of PRODUCTIVITY. Master, I want my life to count for You—to influence, inspire, instruct, impact. I do not want to be selfish and keep Your love and liberty to myself. I want to share. And, I will!

Path of PROCLAMATION. Your Word, Father, instructs me to be a witness everywhere, every time—a witness of Your nature and of new life in Your Son, Jesus Christ. Today, I will be a proclaimer. I will proclaim Your love on the mountaintop, in the valley, on main street, and on side streets.

MY PRAYER NOTES FOR TODAY

BIBLE READING

☑ Day 26 — Exodus 25—27

DAY 27 — A WILLING SPIRIT

Believing is the bottom line of receiving. "Lord, if You are willing, you can make me clean" (Matt. 8:1). I know this, Lord, and I want to manifest a willing spirit today.

First, I want to be willing to WORSHIP You in spirit and truth. In spirit, I want to open my heart, release pure praise, and freely express my love to You—in truth, scripturally, openly, and honestly.

Second, I want to WORK willingly to expand your kingdom through the ministries of my church. I want to be available, accountable, and dependable. I want to be a difference-maker.

Third, I want to be willing to be a compassionate WITNESS of Your grace and love. I want to witness for You with love-based words, sacrifice-based works, and Christ-based worship. Today I am willing to be clay in Your hands. Shape me according to Your established will.

MY PRAYER NOTES FOR TODAY

BIBLE READING

☑ **Day 27 — Exodus 28—30**

DAY 28 — A WINNER IN CHRIST

Being a winner in Christ is wonderful, inspiring, nurturing, nobling, enriching, and refreshing. What a way to begin each day! I am grateful! I am thankful! I am awestruck! I am a winner because of:

RESOURCES. You have made me valuable by instilling Your Spirit in me. You have transformed me into the likeness of Your Son, Jesus Christ, so I can walk in newness of life, exhibiting holy characteristics of purity, devotion, and creative power. **I'm a winner!**

REACTION. Today I will react to the religious feelings of my friends. I will establish trust and confidence. Teach me to be patient and to know the right time to say the right thing. **I'm a winner!**

RESPONDING to the physical and emotional needs of my friends and neighbors and showing the true love and kindness of Christ. I want to walk the talk, be a doer of the Word, and build relationships that lead coworkers and people in the community to an acceptance of the message of new life in Christ. **I'm a winner!**

MY PRAYER NOTES FOR TODAY

BIBLE READING

☑ **Day 28 — Exodus 31—33**

DAY 29 — A DEPENDABLE WITNESS

Master, You stated in Your Word that I am to be Your witness—a witness that I believe in You, that I belong to You, and that I help build Your kingdom on earth. Today I want to be a dedicated, delighted, and dependable witness. Equip me, enable me, and energize me to be:

A WORD witness. I will stand firmly on Your Word, the Bible. I will be a witness of the Ten Commandments, the Beatitudes, the promise of Heaven, and Your instructions on living a holy life.

A WORKS witness. I will testify of Your grace and my commitment by my works. I will work to support the ministries of my church. I will work to reach out to the discouraged and needy. I will work to grow my family in Christlikeness.

A WINNING witness. According to Your Word, Father, and by the leadership of the Holy Spirit, I will be "the head and not the tail" (Deut. 28:13 NKJV). I will display the spiritual characteristics of a winner—determination, vision, accountability, endurance, faith, courage, and fortitude. Thank You today for Your unlimited goodness and guiding grace.

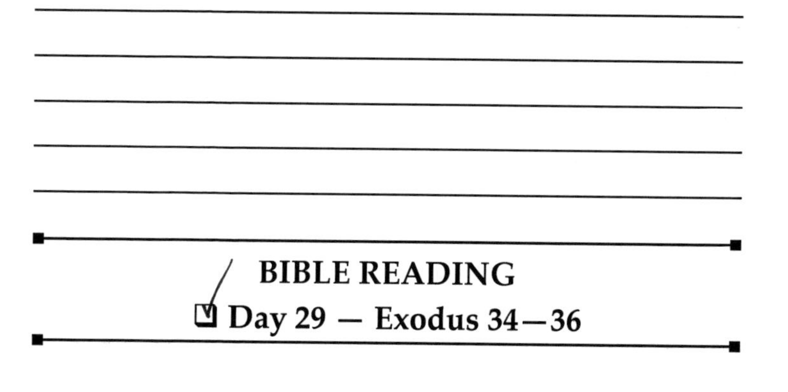

MY PRAYER NOTES FOR TODAY

BIBLE READING

☐ Day 29 — Exodus 34—36

DAY 30 — A GODLY WORLDVIEW

Father, You created the world—land masses, mountains, valleys, and oceans. You also created humankind—families, nations, ethnic groups, and tribes. I desire to have a godly worldview and recognize Your love for all people. I also want to recognize the:

Challenging TASK. To share Your love with everyone, everywhere is a challenge. As I pray, develop a godly worldview in me. Let me see the lost and join forces with other believers in accepting the challenge.

Call for TOGETHERNESS. Father, together, as the body of Christ, combining talents and skills, the challenge becomes achievable. I ask that an overshadowing, inspiring, and motivating spirit would settle over us. I want a godly personal worldview and I want the members of my church to have a united worldview.

Cost of TRIUMPH. Christ paid the cost for my salvation and the salvation for all mankind. Help me to pay the cost for a godly personal worldview—a willingness to see the unreached, a compassionate spirit to intercede for the unreached, and a giving disposition to develop a strategy to minister to the unreached.

MY PRAYER NOTES FOR TODAY

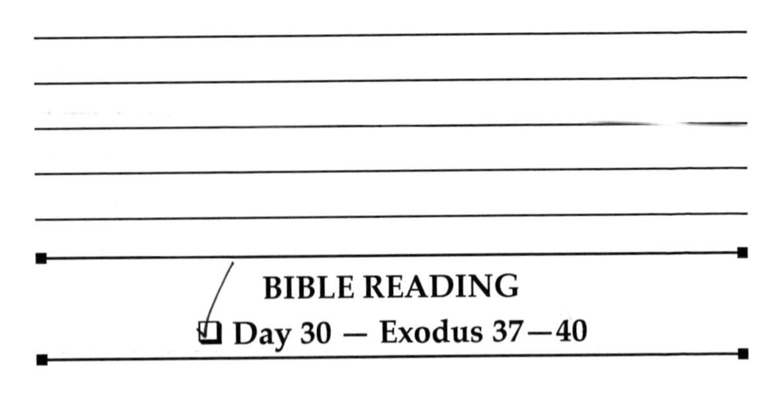

BIBLE READING

☐ **Day 30 — Exodus 37—40**

DAY 31 — A YIELDED SERVANT

Father, I realize Your will for my life can only be carried out as I yield to Your grace and guidance today.

I want to YIELD to You in faith, totally believing that You will accomplish in my life what You have promised. I want to release my faith beyond the "mustard seed" concept to move many mountains—mountains of opposition and obstacles to spiritual maturity.

I want to YIELD to You in service, totally seizing opportunities to be about Your business. I want to work in Your kingdom and I want to witness about Your kingdom.

I want to YIELD to You in Christlike growth, totally applying myself in Bible study and in developing my spiritual gifts. I want to be all I can be in Christ, reflecting His glory in my daily lifestyle.

MY PRAYER NOTES FOR TODAY

____

____

____

____

____

BIBLE READING

☑ Day 31 — Leviticus 1–3

DAY 32 — ABIDING PEACE

Peace comes from Your throne, heavenly Father. You have commissioned Your Son, Jesus Christ, to be the Prince of Peace and to give peace that passes understanding. Today I want to experience and enjoy this peace, and I want to take action steps to make this happen.

First, I want to PROFESS peace. Jesus is the Lord of my life and His love was manifested in giving Himself for me on the cross. **Peace comes through His pardon, affirmation, and care.**

Second, I want to PARTNER with my pastor in peace—joining him in loyalty and allegiance in fulfilling the Great Commission through the local church. **Peace comes through unity in purpose, harmony in actions, and strength in fellowship.**

Third, I want to PROSPER in peace—growing in understanding on how I can be a peace agent. **Peace grows by exhibiting it in lifestyle, sharing it with others, and always focusing attention on it.**

Today I will enjoy abiding peace!

MY PRAYER NOTES FOR TODAY

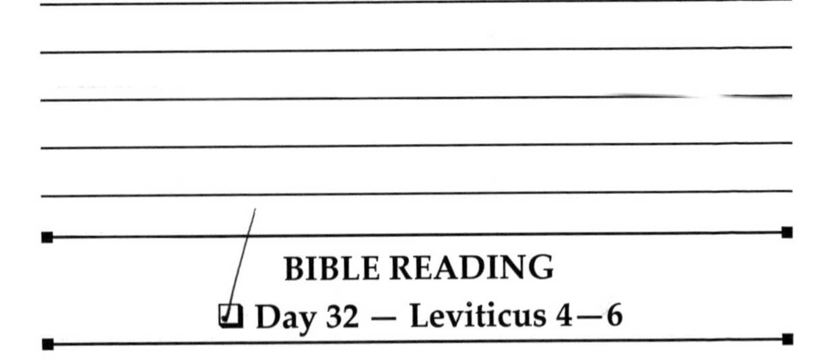

DAY 33 — ABUNDANTLY BLESSED

Father of all blessings, Your blessings surround me, follow me, and are upon me. I am abundantly blessed! I belong to You and You take constant care of me—compassionate, persistent care. You have given me:

Blessed HOPE. Hope is a sustaining blessing. I have hope of Your presence every day, all day. I have hope of the fulfillment of all Your promises. I have hope that Your Word is true, all of it. Hope holds me close to You. **I praise You for blessed hope!**

Sound HEALTH. Master, You have blessed me with a healthy mind—a mind to meditate on Your holy nature, a mind to retain good memories, and a mind to think creative thoughts. You have also blessed me with physical health and avenues for healing when needed. **I honor You for sound health!**

Family HAPPINESS. Father, I am deeply thankful for my biological family, my church family, and my community family. All three families contribute to my happiness, my well-being, my feeling of value and significance, and my Christian testimony. **I exalt You for family happiness!**

MY PRAYER NOTES FOR TODAY

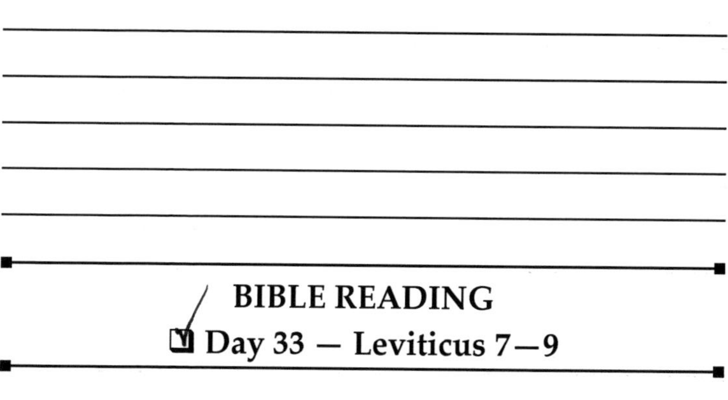

DAY 34 — ACHIEVING BREAKTHROUGH

Every day offers the opportunity to experience a breakthrough that will result in an explosion of faith and turbo energy for ministry. Most of the breakthroughs, I realize, will be mental. This means I must change the way I think. Master, touch my mind to be open and receptive to Your leadership in realizing breaking through opportunities.

I will think POSITIVELY. Father, I will embrace the full scope of Your promises. Today I will lift up the positive and put down the negative. I will look for the good, the beautiful, and the eternal. I will smile, rejoice, and spread cheer and good news.

I will seize POSSIBILITIES. I will walk through every door You open, heavenly Father. Your resources are unlimited and You give freely and abundantly. I will be open and alert to opportunities to share and to serve.

I will focus on PRODUCTIVITY. Lord, I want to make a difference, to make things happen, to achieve, and to influence people for Christ. I will break through barriers in Your name and will claim victory on every front in the power of the Holy Spirit.

MY PRAYER NOTES FOR TODAY

____

____

____

____

____

BIBLE READING

❑ **Day 34 — Leviticus 10—12**

DAY 35 — ADDING VALUE TO LIFE

You add value to my life every day, Father, as I recognize Your unlimited grace and respond with a willing mind and a receiving heart. I rejoice as Your value flows through every area of my life.

Vision—You let me see new wonders in my relationship with You. You overflow my life with achieving vitality.

Affirmation—You let me know that I am an important member of Your family. You overflow my life with assuring acceptance.

Loyalty—You let me feel Your loyalty to me by Your Spirit that guides and guards. You overflow my life with binding love.

Uniqueness—You reveal that You have made me special and gifted. You overflow my life with unparalleled advantages.

Excitement—You touch me with Your joy that gives laughter and a merry heart. You overflow my life with exhilarating happiness.

MY PRAYER NOTES FOR TODAY

____

____

____

____

____

BIBLE READING

☑ **Day 35 — Leviticus 13—15**

DAY 36 — ADVANCEMENT TODAY

Father, Your kingdom is continually moving onward, forward, and upward. I want to be in step with Your move, always motivated, always alert, and always aggressive. I want to advance in manifesting a true Christlike spirit in all I do. Empower me:

To LEAN forward. I will not stand still. I will stand up against any force that hinders my spiritual growth. Father of progress, I look to You for strength to not bow or bend and for stamina to stand firm and faithful, and to lean forward.

To LEARN eagerly. Every day with You, Master, is an opportunity to learn about righteousness, love, peace, and opportunities to grow in grace and fellowship with You. Father of unlimited wisdom, touch my mind to be open and fertile for learning and creative thinking.

To LOOK excitedly. There is beauty all around me—people, places, things. Father of possibilities, anoint my eyes to see the good, the holy, and the valuable; to live with excitement and great expectations in sowing and reaping in Your harvest fields.

MY PRAYER NOTES FOR TODAY

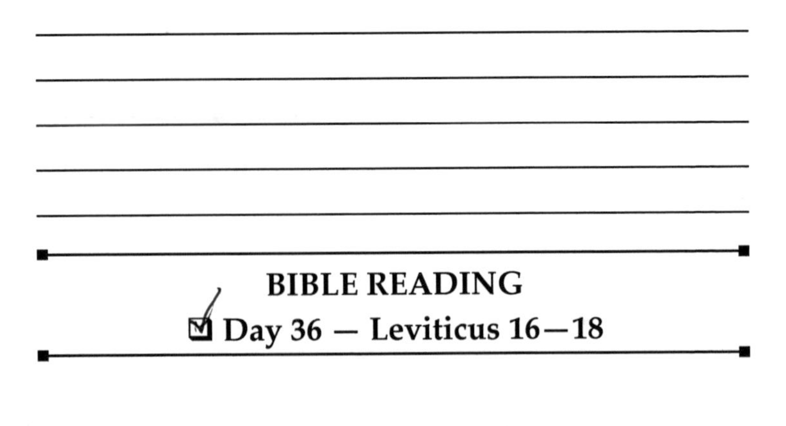

BIBLE READING

☑ **Day 36 — Leviticus 16—18**

DAY 37 — ADVENTURE TODAY

Lord, every day is filled with adventure in my relationship with You. So, today I pray this prayer.

Let me …

See You more clearly,

Embrace You more tenderly,

Walk with You more closely,

Stand for You more boldly,

Show Your love more readily,

Serve You more effectively,

Praise You more joyfully,

Thank You more energetically.

I want to do this because You are worthy, because it is Your will, and because I will become richer in faith, stronger in witness, and fuller in fellowship.

MY PRAYER NOTES FOR TODAY

____

____

____

____

____

BIBLE READING

☑ **Day 37 — Leviticus 19—21**

DAY 38 — AGGRESSIVENESS TODAY

Vision bestowing Father, I need aggressiveness today to face the besetting influences that confront me. There are many forces that will attempt to trip or turn me in maintaining a steady walk with You. Give me aggressive power to face:

Spiritual FATIGUE. Home and work duties can zap and sap my energy to perform spiritual duties. I want to be on guard against this. As I look up to You, send down power to lift You up in worship and to reach out to witness with aggressive zeal and fervor.

Enemy FORCES. Satan attacks and tries to sidetrack my spiritual vision. I want to defend my faith but I also want to come against the strongholds of the Evil One. Help me to put on Your full armor and to be aggressive in resisting evil influences.

Fractured FEELINGS. Truth is powerful and penetrating. It condemns! It causes hurt feelings! Truth also shows a better way to relate, to walk a straight course in life, and to win friends and influence people. Birth an aggressive spirit in me to help heal fractured feelings with Your uplifting and soothing grace.

MY PRAYER NOTES FOR TODAY

____

____

____

____

____

BIBLE READING

❑ **Day 38 — Leviticus 22—24**

DAY 39 — ALL-SUFFICIENT GRACE

God of unlimited, unrestricted, and all-sufficient grace, I live today with the full assurance that You walk with me to make my life complete, productive, and sufficient by Your all-sufficient grace. I trust in Your grace:

To maintain my FAITH. I realize that Satan is at work in the world to destroy my faith and the faith of all the members of Your family. Surround me with Your matchless grace so I can maintain an undiluted faith in Your protection, promises, and peace.

To live by FAITH. I want my faith to be the guiding force for all my actions, my relationships, and my approach to life. I want to cherish Your protection, rejoice in Your promises, and reflect Your peace. Cover me with Your matchless grace to achieve these goals.

To share my FAITH. I do not want to be selfish or self-centered with my faith; I want to share it in love openly and honestly. Cover me with Your matchless grace so I can be light in the darkness, a helper in the time of need, and a caring, compassionate, Christian friend at all times.

MY PRAYER NOTES FOR TODAY

____

____

____

____

____

BIBLE READING

❑ **Day 39 — Leviticus 25—27**

DAY 40 — AMAZING LOVE

Compassionate Father, You are the fountain of amazing love that flows to me today. Your love is amazing because it is pure, providing pardon, peace, and protection.

Without Your love there is …

- **Isolation,**
- **Frustration,**
- **Condemnation,**

With Your love today I can …

- **Walk** in fellowship with You,
- **Worship** in spirit and truth,
- **Work** in harmony with other believers,
- **Witness** with sincerity and boldness,
- **Wait** on You with expectation,
- **Willingly** perform kingdom ministry.

I praise You, Father, for Your amazing love. I will stay submerged in the sanctifying flow of Your love today. I will enjoy it, share it, and be guided by it.

MY PRAYER NOTES FOR TODAY

____

____

____

____

____

BIBLE READING

❑ Day 40 — Numbers 1—3

DAY 41 — AN OPEN DOOR

God, You have set before me an open door today. An open door to experience new relationships, expand my skills, and impact others with convincing Christian witness.

I want to walk through the open door but I need Your instructions, insights, and inspiration. Your Word gives me instructions — I will read it. Your Word gives me insight — I will trust You. Your Holy Spirit gives me excitement — I will respond with an open mind and heart. I don't have to knock or ring the doorbell. The door is open. Today I will:

- **Remember** Your promises.
- **Rejoice** in Your provisions.
- **Reject** negative patterns.
- **Refuse** to be swayed by problems.
- **Refuel** with Your power.
- **Refresh** with Your peace.

Yes, yes, yes! I am walking through the open door today!

MY PRAYER NOTES FOR TODAY

____

____

____

____

____

BIBLE READING

❑ **Day 41 — Numbers 4–6**

DAY 42 — AN OPEN HEART

Revealing Father, I want open eyes and an open heart today. I want open eyes to see You at work in churches and kingdom ministries. I want an open heart for You to work in my life—revealing, revitalizing, restoring. My heart is open for:

HEALING. Healing emotional damage, hard feelings, physical pain. I do not want anything to block open communication with You or fellow believers. Let Your Spirit dissolve any feelings or relationship friction that impedes spiritual freedom or growth. I accept Your divine healing today!

HOPE. All things are possible with You, matchless Master. I want to maintain hope for lost loved ones and do my part to influence them. I want to maintain hope for transformation to take place in churches and in my county and community. I will spread divine hope today!

HEALTH. Let me be aware of maintaining a healthy lifestyle. My body is the temple of the Holy Spirit and I will treat it with respect, watch care, and proper nourishment. I will guard divine health today!

MY PRAYER NOTES FOR TODAY

____

____

____

____

____

BIBLE READING

❑ **Day 42 — Numbers 7—9**

DAY 43 — AN OVERFLOWING LIFE

This is a beautiful day. You have placed sunshine in my heart. And, today, I want this sunshine to be reflected in what I do, what I say, and how I relate. I ask You to guide me in three specific areas:

1. I desire to be FAITHFUL. I want to be faithful in biblical doctrine, in performing Christian duties, and in career dedication. Therefore, I ask for insight, zeal, and performance strength.

2. I desire to be FRUITFUL. Your Word often talks about harvest fields and instructs believers to go forth believing for results. In my life today I want to be results-oriented, to achieve noteworthy goals in my home life, social life, and church life.

3. I desire to be FRIENDLY. Let me show friendliness in my attitude and speech. I also want to be a friend—a friend that encourages, meets a crisis need, and fosters a zeal to be visionary and creative. I will live a life of overflowing joy today.

MY PRAYER NOTES FOR TODAY

BIBLE READING

❑ **Day 43 — Numbers 10—12**

DAY 44 — ASSURANCE OF HEAVEN

Father, Your promises are steadfast, unmovable, and permanent. I rejoice today in the assurance of heaven and the promise to spend eternity in Your presence. Thank You for:

The PURITY of heaven. No sin in heaven! Absolute purity. An environment void of carnality, confusion, or conflict. Perfect harmony—togetherness, undiluted trust, love that is endless! Thank You, Master of purity, for Your promises!

The PROVISIONS of heaven. No sickness in heaven! No homeless. No broken hearts. No regrets. Absolute contentment and perpetual happiness. Today I will keep a picture of heaven in my mind to generate delight and endurance. Thank You, Master of provisions, for Your grace.

The PEOPLE of heaven. No strangers in heaven! Only kingdom family members. A glorious eternal reunion—meaning, belonging, rejoicing, fulfilling God's perfect will. Today I will think about the people in heaven and their fellowship with You. Thank You, Master of eternity, for the people in heaven and for the people who will be in heaven.

MY PRAYER NOTES FOR TODAY

____

____

____

____

____

BIBLE READING

❑ **Day 44 — Numbers 13—15**

DAY 45 — ASSURANCE OF VICTORY

I have steady steps today, Lord and Master, because I have assurance of victory in my spiritual life. Satan comes against me in many forms—deception, darkness, dazzling overtures of fame and fortune. I look to You! I trust You to be my defender and deliverer. Guide me to:

RECOGNIZE mentally the schemes of Satan. My visual perception is not always accurate. Satan paints colorful, enticing pictures. Father, let the mind of Christ work in my mind so I can detect and stand against his advances. Also, as I read the Bible, reveal to me the nature and characteristics of Satan so I can be fully prepared for victory.

RESPOND courageously to Satan's challenges. In Christ I will not back up, bow down, or blow up. I will look up, stand up, and speak up, and show that I am certified by You for total victory.

RELY wholeheartedly on divine strength. Father, I yield to the infilling of Your power to defeat the attacks of Satan and to be a living witness of kingdom grace, gifts, and goodness. Today I will live a victorious life and sing a song of praise and thanksgiving.

MY PRAYER NOTES FOR TODAY

___

___

___

___

___

BIBLE READING

❑ **Day 45 — Numbers 16–18**

DAY 46 — ATTITUDE ADJUSTMENT

Father, I am thankful You are changeless in Your attitude toward me—every day the same, in every situation, always trustworthy. People, problems, and projects often get next to me and my attitude changes. I become distant, rigid, and sometimes unkind in spirit and words. I am open to attitude adjustments today:

Adjust my attitude toward the ATTITUDE of others. I do not want to respond to individuals with a negative attitude. Give me insight to understand their circumstances and the reasons behind their anxiety and actions.

Adjust my attitude toward the ANOINTING of others. Sometimes it seems that others receive all the attention and accolades in Christian service. Let me rejoice when each member of the body of Christ is effective in ministry.

Adjust my attitude toward my ACHIEVEMENTS. Father, You have endowed me with skills and abilities for the mission You have assigned me in kingdom ministry. I want to show appreciation for the manner in which You are fulfilling Your will in my life!

MY PRAYER NOTES FOR TODAY

____

____

____

____

____

BIBLE READING

❑ Day 46 — Numbers 19—21

DAY 47 — AVOIDING FEAR

Fearless Father, the goal of Satan is to fill my heart and mind with fear. Your will for me is to be filled with faith that flows with freedom to think creatively, and to love unconditionally. I trust You to avoid fear today because:

Fear BAFFLES. Lord, the devil wants me to be confused about my values, beliefs, and trust. Today, I will not be baffled by his attacks or impressions. **I will look up and receive my strength from You!**

Fear BLOCKS. I do not want to be blocked in my spiritual growth, witness, or service. I will not allow Satan to stand in the way of my vision or progress. **Today, I will look out and map directions based on instructions from Your Word!**

Fear BLINDFOLDS. Master, You have set forth promises in the Bible for my peace, protection, and prosperity. The Evil One desires to dim and distort my vision. He does not want me to see the path of success You have set before me. **Today, I will look around and keep my eyes open to the beautiful experiences You have for me!**

MY PRAYER NOTES FOR TODAY

____

____

____

____

____

BIBLE READING

❑ **Day 47 — Numbers 22—24**

DAY 48 — BLESSED TODAY

Father, Your will is to bless me. In all my ways today I will look for, and receive, Your unlimited blessings. I will be open to receive, quick to offer thanksgiving and praise, and be unselfish in sharing with family and friends. I will:

Believe that You desire to prosper me.

Lean on Your Word for guidance.

Engage in praise for stability in Christ.

Stay tuned in to positive imaging.

Stand tall to see the possibilities around me.

Experience innovative involvement in ministry.

Develop and use my skills to maximum levels.

MY PRAYER NOTES FOR TODAY

____

____

____

____

____

BIBLE READING

❑ **Day 48 — Numbers 25—27**

DAY 49 — BALANCED PROSPERITY

Lord of untold and unlimited riches, You have prospered me in so many different ways. Often I zero in on only one area—material prosperity. However, I want to be balanced in my approach to prosperity.

Let me be balanced in MATURITY prosperity. I do not want to be lopsided in my Christian growth, emphasizing only what I like best. Give me guiding grace and balance in digesting Your Word so that it will make me a total, influential person in life.

Let me be balanced in MESSAGE prosperity. I want to share the message of the love of Christ and the liberty found in Him in a way that is respectful and that will bear fruit. Let me be aggressive in establishing friendships with the unchurched so I can model Christlikeness and be a fruitful witness.

Let me be balanced in MONEY prosperity. You give me daily bread and I want to be content, not always wanting more. With financial prosperity I am able to do more, give more, and see more results. In all I do, I want to honor You and be a believer that reflects love, appreciation, and thanksgiving.

MY PRAYER NOTES FOR TODAY

____

____

____

____

____

BIBLE READING

❑ **Day 49 — Numbers 28—30**

DAY 50 — BEGINNING AGAIN

Yes, Lord, today I can begin again. There will never be another yesterday. The things I want to do, but didn't do, can be done today. You give me a new beginning today.

Yes, Lord, today I will seize the day with grace and gusto and begin again with noble dreams, undeterred determination, and glowing enthusiasm. Today will be beautiful—people, places, projects. I will release a refreshing spirit as I relate to others and join them in making a difference.

Yes, Lord, today I can begin again.

I will **LEAN** on You for strength.

I will **LEARN** from Your Word in order to receive guidance.

I will express **LOVE** that reflects a commitment to Christ and His Church.

I will forget the things behind me and press forward to achieve excellence as a disciple of Jesus Christ.

MY PRAYER NOTES FOR TODAY

____

____

____

____

____

BIBLE READING

❑ **Day 50 — Numbers 31—33**

DAY 51 — BINDING RELATIONSHIPS

Above all, Father of acceptance and forgiveness, my relationship with You is priority number one. I am committed to a worshiping, receiving, giving, serving, and rewarding relationship. I am also thankful for relationships with friends and neighbors. Give me wisdom to:

ACCEPT people where they are. Regardless of what level of life they are on—socially, financially, spiritually—I want to accept people where they are. This is the pattern Christ set. His relationship formula was love, acceptance, and forgiveness. Today, I will embody His formula!

ACKNOWLEDGE differences. Father, I want to be an effective witness for You. I want to make an impact on others regardless of their personality, habits, work ethic, or living standards. Today, I will exhibit the attitude of Christ!

ACT with integrity. I want to be open and honest in what I say, how I act, and the standards I maintain. I need the illuminating and guiding work of the Holy Spirit. Today, Father, I will show trust in Your care and oversight.

MY PRAYER NOTES FOR TODAY

____

____

____

____

____

BIBLE READING

❑ **Day 51 — Numbers 34—36**

DAY 52 — BELIEF AND BEHAVIOR

It is pivotal, Master, that I back my beliefs with positive, Christlike behavior. My friends will not listen to my testimony if I do not practice what I profess. I must walk the talk! Today, let me be responsive and yielded to the Spirit through:

Calculated COMMITMENT. There is a price to pay for total obedience. When the price is calculated, and accepted, a firm, grounded commitment is established. Father, I will pay the price! But, I need the strength and supportive ministry of the Holy Spirit.

Controlled CONDUCT. Conduct flows from commitment. Since I am committed, Master, I look to You for divine power to control my conduct and to set an example of trust and obedience. The CODE of my conduct will be **C**hrist, **O**thers, **D**edication, **E**nthusiasm.

Creative COMMUNICATION. Today I want to inspire and encourage through creative communication—kind words, helpful insights, motivating comments, uplifting counseling, and stimulating statements. This will create a receptive atmosphere to influence, make a difference, and share the message of love, hope, and freedom in Jesus Christ.

MY PRAYER NOTES FOR TODAY

____

____

____

____

____

BIBLE READING

❑ **Day 52 — Deuteronomy 1—3**

DAY 53 — BLESSING LEADERS

Mighty Master, You have told me to respect those occupying positions of leadership. I want to do this both as a command and as a privilege. I want to be a supporter and a follower with integrity and disciplined support. Bless:

COUNTRY Leaders. You bless the nation who upholds You as Ruler and Lord. May our leaders seek You, rule righteously, and maintain Biblical standards. May our country truly operate by our motto, "In God We Trust."

CHURCH Leaders. You have set rulers over me in the Lord—overseers, bishops, pastors. They lead by example, teaching, preaching, and encouraging. Provide them with strength to serve and give me a submissive spirit to be a supportive follower.

COMMUNITY Leaders. You want me to connect with my community and to be an influential citizen. Inspire me to participate with my church in sponsoring activities that touch my community, city, and county. I ask You to bless local leaders with pure motives, creative ideas, and projects that assist and establish hope and peace.

MY PRAYER NOTES FOR TODAY

____

____

____

____

____

BIBLE READING

❑ **Day 53 — Deuteronomy 4—6**

DAY 54 — BLESSING MY PASTOR

Lord, Your Son is the Great Shepherd—protecting and watching over Your people. My pastor is a shepherd under His guidance to care for me—teaching, feeding, nurturing. I ask You to bless my pastor's:

Personal FAMILY. My pastor's family pays a high price for his total commitment—demanding expectations, 24/7 duties, nurturing responsibilities. I ask You to bless them today! Surround them with loving support and appreciation. Guide church members in creating an atmosphere of security and significance for them.

Church FAMILY. There are many ideas and opinions about Your work among church members. Personal feelings often divide and block the free flowing of Your Spirit in the mission of the church. I ask You to bless my pastor's church family with a spirit of loyalty, unity, harmony, and binding love.

Community FAMILY. Give my pastor favor in the community—leaders, organizers, workers. Bless my pastor as he or she reaches out and supports projects that lift up the broken and betrayed and advance social concerns and educational opportunities. Bless him or her with influence that advocates community involvement.

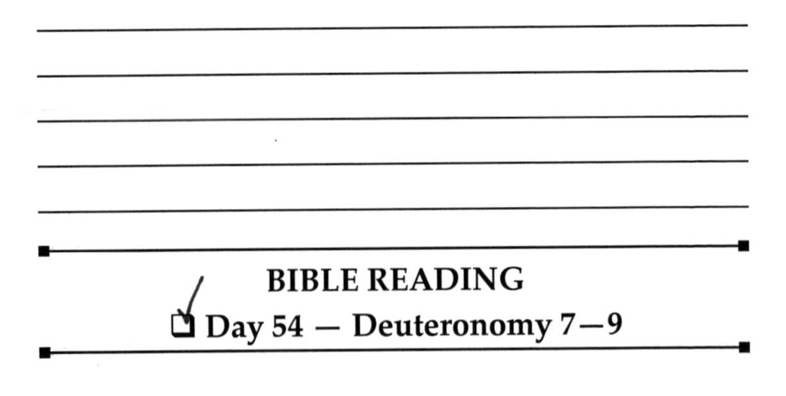

DAY 55 — BLESSING OTHERS

Other people impact my life in many different ways. There is both the good and the bad. I am thankful for those who set an example for me, those who encourage me, and those with whom I experience the joys of life. Holy Father, I ask you to bless all of these with gifts of grace.

Bless my FAMILY. Keep my family ties tight. Touch each one of them with guiding grace to live rich, abundant lives. Let them understand and follow Your plan of wellness and wholeness.

Bless my FRIENDS. Keep my ties tight with friends. Let me show respect and appreciation for their uplifting input in my life. Touch each one of them with protecting grace to live full, enriched, and Christ-exalting lives.

Bless my FOES. Keep me from condemning so I can establish spiritual ties with them. Let me set an example of love, faith and forgiveness. Touch each one of them with saving grace so they can follow the path of scriptural righteousness that gives hope, peace, calmness and security.

MY PRAYER NOTES FOR TODAY

____

____

____

____

____

BIBLE READING

❑ **Day 55 — Deuteronomy 10—12**

DAY 56 — BLESS THE LORD

Father, Your Word tells me to "bless the Lord at all times" (34:1 NKJV) and with "all that is within me" (Ps. 103:1 NKJV). I want to fulfill these privileges today. To bless You with "all that is within me" includes how I **love,** how I **give**, and how I **live.**

Today I want to exhibit a LOVE that glows, goes and gives. I want to glow with Christlikeness—being a good friend, neighbor, and coworker—showing respect, understanding, and appreciation. I want to go out of my way to make a difference in the lives of others and to give of myself in creative, productive ministry.

Today I want to GIVE, to invest in the lives of those close to me, and to give companionship that encourages and lifts up.

Today I want to LIVE life to its fullest through explosive faith, spiritual fireworks, and Spirit-produced fruit. Today will be a beautiful day and I will bless You with my lifestyle.

MY PRAYER NOTES FOR TODAY

BIBLE READING

❑ **Day 56 — Deuteronomy 13—15**

DAY 57 — BLESSED HOPE

I am thankful today, Father, for a blessed hope. In the world there is turmoil and strife, the devastating work of the devil. Your will is peace and harmony, but sin created a gulf that can only be crossed over on the bridge built by Your Son Jesus Christ. Salvation, redemption, and restoration give me a blessed hope.

My blessed hope HEALS. My spirit, my mind, my soul is healed and I can live free and whole. I am not burdened with guilt or fear. Thank You that I can walk upright, secure, spiritually strong, and healthy.

My blessed hope INSTILLS. Your Spirit within me gives stability. It instills a bold confidence to face life head on, to stand on Your Word, and to live with goals that bring calmness and point to Your majesty.

My blessed hope THRILLS. Everyday with You, mighty Master, is sweeter and greater than the day before. Today is filled with adventure and You will reveal new paths for me to follow and new promises for me to embrace. I will experience **HOPE** today—Happiness, Order, Prosperity, Excitement.

MY PRAYER NOTES FOR TODAY

____

____

____

____

____

BIBLE READING

❑ **Day 57 — Deuteronomy 16—18**

DAY 58 — BREAK IN, LORD

There are many things vying for my attention and affection today. I ask You, God of wonder, break into my planned schedule and business. Break in and let's have a show-and-tell day.

Show me PATHS of new adventure that explore heaven-sent values. Tell me how I can join You in what You are doing in the world today.

Show me PROMISES that I have overlooked that are available to me. Tell me about spiritual secrets that bring new revelations of Spirit-anchored miracles.

Show me PARTNERSHIP principles to unite with You, with church leaders, and with other believers to reveal the relevancy of Your Word in daily encounters. Tell me again how I can walk with You and be a true show-and-tell of Christlikeness.

MY PRAYER NOTES FOR TODAY

____

____

____

____

____

BIBLE READING

❑ **Day 58 — Deuteronomy 19—21**

DAY 59 — BREAKING BARRIERS

Father of overcoming power, Satan erects barriers to block my spiritual progress. Manifest Your power in my life today to break barriers. Anoint my thinking to be positive, creative, and aggressive. Give me directions and discipline to face and break through barriers.

SHARING the good news. Father, help me to develop tact in sharing the good news of new, full, abundant life in Jesus Christ. Let me break barriers of resistance and hostility by radiating warmth, compassion, and kindness. I desire to walk the talk!

SEPARATING the church from the community. Often barriers separate the church from the people we are trying to reach—judgmental attitudes, internal activities, and strictness before service. May our church have open hands, hearts, and doors!

SPOILING fulfilling relationships. Barriers of selfishness and self-centeredness spoil relationships and hinder unity, harmony, and progress. Master, by Your guidance, I want to be open, honest, congenial, and a true friend. May the Spirit work in my life to break barriers that block the flow of Your grace!

MY PRAYER NOTES FOR TODAY

____

____

____

____

____

BIBLE READING

❑ **Day 59 — Deuteronomy 22—24**

DAY 60 — BREAKING HABITS

Father of majesty and might, I praise You for giving me liberty through the love of Your Son, Jesus Christ, for taking away my sinful nature, and directing my steps in paths of righteousness. I don't want habits in my life that hold me back from becoming all You want me to be. Let me face habits that would:

HINDER achievements. You have set before me open doors for personal achievements in my Christian walk and in my career. Today, I open my heart and hands. Touch them with Your guiding grace and give me freedom from any hindering habits.

HANDCUFF relationship. Lord of love, I don't want to be limited in my relationships by unproductive thinking and behavioral habits. I want to be a true friend at all times. Give me a spirit of openness and honesty that leads to trust and confidence.

HOLD back healthy growth. For physical health I must eat right, exercise, and avoid dangerous habits. For spiritual health I must read the Bible, pray, and avoid habits that hold back worship and praise. Father, undergird my attitude and actions so I will grow stronger in spiritual understanding and kingdom service.

MY PRAYER NOTES FOR TODAY

BIBLE READING

❑ **Day 60 — Deuteronomy 25—27**

DAY 61 — BRING CHANGE, LORD

Steadfast Father, You are changeless in Your holiness, righteousness, and majesty. I depend on Your consistent oversight of my life and to guide me in becoming more like You. I want to be steadfast, devoted, and dependable. This, I understand, requires change. Bring change today in:

My COMMITMENT. I do not want any loose ends or loopholes in my surrender to You or service in Your kingdom. Check my commitment. Guide me in changing anything that weakens my spiritual stance or strength.

My CONDUCT. Father, empower me by Your Spirit to stand firm, speak in faith with compassion, and love without reservations. I want to check my conduct daily so I can walk the Christ walk!

My CAREER. Whatever I do I want to do it for Your honor and glory. In my career I want to model a strong work ethic, to encourage co-workers, and to strive for superior performance. Lead me in manifesting the fruit of the Spirit so I can be an influential witness of the majesty of Jesus Christ!

MY PRAYER NOTES FOR TODAY

BIBLE READING

❑ **Day 61 — Deuteronomy 28—30**

DAY 62 — BUILDING RELATIONSHIPS

Thank You, wonderful Father, for the life-giving relationship that I have with You through the new birth and adoption into Your heavenly family. I receive Your guidance daily, feel Your love, and enjoy Your resources. Give me the pleasing know-how to show my friends how they can have a transforming relationship with you. I will:

REVEAL my relationship with You by prudently displaying the fruit of salvation in wholesome conversations, biblically-based conduct, and inspirational church activities.

RESPECT the religious feelings of my friends and build strong ties that establish trust and confidence. Teach me to be patient and to know the right time to say the right thing.

RECOGNIZE the physical and emotional needs of my friends and neighbors. I will show the true love and kindness of Christ. I want to be a doer of the Word and to build relationships that lead coworkers and people in the community to accept the message of new life in Christ. Glory!

MY PRAYER NOTES FOR TODAY

BIBLE READING

❑ **Day 62 — Deuteronomy 31—34**

DAY 63 — CARE FOR TODAY

Thank You, compassionate Father, for caring for me today and for giving me CARE:

Connect. You permit me to connect with You through prayer and to talk, listen, and learn of Your nature, purposes, and plans.

Affirm. You affirm me as Your child and accept me into Your storehouse of unlimited grace and gifts.

Respond. You respond to my needs and make alive the gifts with which You have endowed me.

Energy. You energize my mind and spirit with positive thoughts of duty, development, and discipleship. I will run the Christian race and relax in Your oversight because I know You CARE for me.

MY PRAYER NOTES FOR TODAY

BIBLE READING

❑ Day 63 — Joshua 1—3

DAY 64 — CARE FOR NEIGHBORS

Today I want to show a spirit of care and respect for my neighbors by demonstrating the characteristics of a committed Christian. I cannot influence people outside my community if I do not impact people inside my community. I will:

Show HOSPITALITY. Lord of love, I want Your love to show forth through me to my neighbors—awareness, kindness, appreciation. This will require deliberate action on my part—to speak, to encourage, to show care.

Provide HELPS. Direct me in displaying an attitude of action—observing, visiting, asking. This means that I must take the lead by offering assistance, going the extra mile, and demonstrating care.

Demonstrate HONESTY. Father, You are dependable and consistent—available, approachable, responsive. I want these qualities to be a part of my life. This requires me to examine how I act on a daily basis, how my neighbors view me, and how I can communicate with them. Today, by Your oversight, I will convey an authentic attitude of care.

MY PRAYER NOTES FOR TODAY

BIBLE READING

❑ **Day 64 — Joshua 4—6**

DAY 65 — CARING AWARENESS

Throughout the day I want to be aware of the opportunity to show a caring disposition. I desire that my attitude and actions would reflect sincere love, openness, and a willingness to assist. But I need help, Your anointing, merciful Father. I want to reflect Your nature:

By sharing COMPASSION. Master, You identify with my needs and show compassion and provide a path of assistance. Today, I want to follow Your pattern, and show compassion to those suffering and facing difficult situations. Your pattern also calls for me to act and provide support.

By uplifting CONVERSATIONS. In talking with friends and associates, I want my conversations to be laced with uplifting words—words that spark vision, stimulate excellence, and fosters security. I will spread the good news today!

By managing CONTROL. Lord, I want You to be in control of my life—my steps, my service, my sanctification. Today I will be open to Your oversight and control. I will also be a friend to others rather than a controller.

MY PRAYER NOTES FOR TODAY

BIBLE READING

☑ **Day 65 — Joshua 7—9**

Sun 3-6-11

DAY 66 — CARING SPIRIT

Father of care and comfort, I desire to manifest Your characteristics of care and comfort in my life today. I need an infusion of Your strength to do this. I need the indwelling of the Holy Spirit to guide me. I need the inspirational love of Christ to motivate me. Direct my activities so a caring spirit will be visible and influential in the:

Control of my TEMPER. Christ carefully weighed every situation and knew when to refresh or rebuke, comfort or cast out, lift up or put down, instruct or pass judgment. Touch my temper so I can show care and comfort or act to correct or condemn.

Comfort of TALK. In my speech and conversations today, I want to speak words that trigger creative thoughts, inspiration to achieve, and peace of mind. As Your Spirit energizes me I want to energize my family and friends with a caring spirit.

Content of TRANSACTIONS. In all my business transactions I want the contents to be honest, fair, and mutually beneficial. This approach will reveal a caring spirit that is founded on Christian values. Father, I will honor You with my caring spirit today.

MY PRAYER NOTES FOR TODAY

____

____

____

____

____

BIBLE READING

❑ **Day 66 — Joshua 10—12**

DAY 67 — CHOICES TODAY

Father of daily companionship, "This is the day the Lord has made; let us rejoice and be glad in it" (Ps. 118:24). However, I will be confronted with many choices. Guide me in making correct, positive choices so I can rejoice and be glad.

I will choose to **SMILE** to show that I have a contented, friendly spirit.

I will choose to **SING** to show that I have a thankful, grateful heart.

I will choose to **SURRENDER** to show that my life is committed to Your will.

I will choose to **SHARE** to show that I am an authentic, unselfish Christian.

I will choose to **STAND** to show I have guiding values for my life.

I will choose to **SERVE** to show I am loyal and support my church.

I will choose to **SHINE** to show I am learning, loving, and leading.

MY PRAYER NOTES FOR TODAY

BIBLE READING

❑ **Day 67 — Joshua 13—15**

DAY 68 — CLAIMING POWER

Almighty, all-powerful Father, You have promised power to live a dedicated life, to develop ministry talents, and to defend against the assaults of Satan. I claim this power in the name of Your Son, Jesus Christ. I will go forth today with a victorious attitude because of Your promise of:

MIGHTY Power. Power from above! That's mighty power! That's power beyond human performance, reasoning, or understanding. Father, I will depend on Your mighty power to make wise decisions and to demonstrate Christ-centered loyalty.

MENTAL Power. I desire to embrace the admonition to have the mind of Christ. The thinking of Christ revolved around helping people, healing people, and giving people hope. Guide me in displaying these same thinking qualities in my life.

MINISTRY Power. I want to be an illuminating example and to display enthusiasm in performing ministry. To do this I need ministry insight, ministry innovation, and ministry initiative. Touch me, teach me, and train me to be an impacting servant that is pleasing in Your sight.

MY PRAYER NOTES FOR TODAY

____

____

____

____

____

BIBLE READING

❑ **Day 68 — Joshua 16—18**

DAY 69 — CLEAR GOALS

Goals are foundational for growing faith and moving forward in spiritual maturity. Master, I need clear goals and I need You to inspire me and lead me. I also want to embrace demanding convictions to achieve goals.

GUIDANCE Goals. Lord, motivate my thinking and touch my heart so I can develop goals to guide me in maintaining influential integrity in my loyalty to church involvement, in strong relationship values, and in utilizing talents for a successful career. I **will honor You with my goals!**

GLORY Goals. Whatever I do or say, Father, I want You to receive glory and honor. I want to be faithful in worship, in witnessing, and in kingdom work. May my countenance show forth Your glory. **I will serve you with my goals.**

GIVING Goals. I want to be a giver of encouragement, assistance, unconditional love, and hope in Christ. Father, tie me to these giving goals, make them compelling, yet sincere and soft. **I will spotlight Your love and advance Your kingdom with my goals.**

MY PRAYER NOTES FOR TODAY

____

____

____

____

____

BIBLE READING

❑ **Day 69 — Joshua 19—21**

DAY 70 — CLEAR OUT THE CLUTTER

Clutter in the mind can block clear communication and hinder communion with Christ. Clutter dilutes convictions and redirects commitment. It is a tactic used by Satan to sap joy and victory achievements. The excuses of clutter, and how they can be eliminated, must be faced head on:

Ministry Mistakes. Mistakes made in serving God can be faced, forgiveness accepted, the future embraced, and faith applied. Don't look back, look up, and look out! God has wonderful plans! Positive possibilities are before you!

Mind Management. Kick out the clutter by managing thoughts. Think on true, noble, just, pure, lovely, and good things (Phil. 4:8). Turn negative thinking into positive thinking. Adopt the promise, "I can do all things through Christ who strengthens me" (v. 13).

Mercy Motivation. You are not alone—God's mercy and love are always present to clear out the clutter. He will replace clutter with comfort, control, and creative impressions. You are now on the move, motivated by God's mercy to think new thoughts, to make new plans, and to live with new enthusiasm.

MY PRAYER NOTES FOR TODAY

____

____

____

____

____

BIBLE READING

❑ **Day 70 — Joshua 22—24**

DAY 71 — CLIMB MOUNTAINS

Mighty, magnificent, heavenly Father, I want to climb mountains in my life today—steep mountains, unexplored mountains, mountains of success, and mountains of significance.

Today, let me **SURVEY** mountains of opportunity with extraordinary zeal and bubbling anticipation, knowing You have set them before me.

Today, give me **STRENGTH** to climb with driving determination and faith-based dedication to reach lofty heights in my spiritual life, in my family, and in my career.

Today, let the magnificent **SCENERY** capture my undivided attention. Let me see the beauty of growing relationships, the glow of sterling values, and the grandeur of striving for excellence.

Today, I want to **SEE** my potential from the top of the mountain—a full view of Your boundless blessings that surround me, sustain me, and send me forth in the triumphant power of the Holy Spirit.

MY PRAYER NOTES FOR TODAY

___

___

___

___

___

BIBLE READING

❑ **Day 71 — Judges 1—3**

DAY 72 — CLOSE TO YOU, LORD

I want to be close to You today, my Lord. Close to You:

Through **C**onfidence in Your Word and presence.

Showing **L**ove in expressing myself to You.

Including **O**thers in enjoying the richness of Your grace.

Singing **S**ongs that reflect faith, courage, and trust.

Showing **E**nthusiasm in my walk with You, my talk about You, and my witness for You.

Yes, today I want to be **CLOSE** to You, Lord!

MY PRAYER NOTES FOR TODAY

BIBLE READING

❑ **Day 72 — Judges 4—6**

DAY 73 — CLOSENESS TODAY

I want to feel, touch, and respond to Your presence today, loving Father.

Your presence brings assurance, peace, and joy. You can feel all three of these. I want to be open and sensitive so I can recognize and feel Your presence in all my activities today and reflect Your assurance, peace, and joy in my personality.

I want to reach out and touch You today. You are a friend, partner, helper, and coworker. I need a friend to share with, a partner to plan with, a helper to lean on, and a coworker with whom I can be productive. You release energy and excitement when I touch You.

Today I want to be responsive to Your presence, Your power, and Your promises. Today, by faith and grace, I will be filled with divine guidance and a flow of gifts that make life glow and sparkle with the unusual, the extraordinary.

MY PRAYER NOTES FOR TODAY

____

____

____

____

____

BIBLE READING

❑ **Day 73 — Judges 7—9**

DAY 74 — CLOSER UNITY

Unity brings people together in understanding, fellowship, and spiritual purpose. Unity with You, Father, represents salvation, security, and abiding significance. My first responsibility is total unity with You. This keeps me on the right path and in a right relationship with You. I want greater unity:

With my LOVED ones. Father, I love my family, relatives, and friends. I want to establish closer unity with them—calling, visiting, praying. This will strengthen me and provide opportunities to share, nurture, and enjoy their company.

With my LEADERS. I am thankful for my pastor and church leaders. I want to bond with them by blessing them with support and partnership. Let me encourage them by being dependable, trustworthy, and visionary.

With the LOST. Guide me in forming genuine relationships with my lost friends and neighbors. I want to see the good in them and respect them so I can make a difference in their values and spiritual direction. Let Your Spirit teach, train, and guide me in how to lead them in knowing Christ.

MY PRAYER NOTES FOR TODAY

____

____

____

____

____

BIBLE READING

❑ **Day 74 — Judges 10—12**

DAY 75 — COMPLETELY INVOLVED

Today, Master of mercy, I am determined to be completely involved in making a difference with my heart, head, and hands. I cannot do this without Your guiding grace and the energizing force of the Holy Spirit. I want to make a difference by how I value my relationship with You and how it impacts my life today. I will do this:

By a HEART of love. Father, I ask You to let Your love shine through me in the form of a friendly smile, faithful service, and fruitful spiritual growth. I want to communicate true compassion and be a person others trust.

By a HEAD of worshipful thoughts. Father, I ask You to let the mind of Christ direct my thoughts and plans. I want thoughts that honor You and plans that help to establish Your kingdom. I want to think holy, creative, and honorable thoughts today.

By HANDS that are clean and active. Father, I ask You to anoint my hands for honest labor in my career, for helping others in reaching their goals, and for lifting up those suffering and seeking answers to perplexing problems. I will be completely involved!

MY PRAYER NOTES FOR TODAY

____

____

____

____

____

BIBLE READING

❑ **Day 75 — Judges 13—15**

DAY 76 — COMPLETELY OPEN

Father, You reveal, instruct, and guide. You do not withhold "good tidings of great joy" from me. Every day Your love flows openly, freely, and completely. I receive Your love with gratitude, humility, and thanksgiving. Today, I want to have an:

Open HEART to receive, love, and give. Father, Your heart is open for all people and to show care and compassion. Work through me to have an open heart filled with love that embraces, concern that provides, and empathy that consoles. **Love through my heart today!**

Open HEAD to see, think, and hear. Master, I do not want to limit my capacity to see clearly, think deeply, and to hear wisely. I am open to Your leadership today. Lead me as Your child and representative to be open to new opportunities, to draw closer to You, and to manifest the virtues of grace. **Dwell in my thoughts today!**

Open HANDS to touch, work, and unite. I want to be busy today in work that makes a difference, holds up, brings together, and results in productivity. **Anoint my hands to serve!**

MY PRAYER NOTES FOR TODAY

____

____

____

____

____

BIBLE READING

❑ **Day 76 — Judges 16—18**

DAY 77 — CONNECTING WITH OTHERS

Saints, sinners, the separated, the suffering, the sick, and the successful—I will come into contact with them today. Let me connect with them in a significant, life-enriching manner. Let me relate to them in three specific ways:

FIRST, let me be a reflector of Your love. I know love dissolves doubt, fear, hard feelings, and misunderstandings. I know love builds up, binds together, and brings forth the best in others. **Let me be a love-vessel, a love-reflector, and a love-spreader today.**

SECOND, let me build solid relationships. I know some people are bashful and backward in forming relationships. **Let me smile, step forward, and initiate the process of interacting and becoming personally involved in establishing relationships.**

THIRD, let me make a difference in the lives of other people today. I want to worship You, put in a full day's work, and be a witness by the way I act and what I say. **Let me build relationships today that will help me, my friends, family, and associates.**

Today will be a rich and rewarding day in building relationships.

MY PRAYER NOTES FOR TODAY

____

____

____

____

____

BIBLE READING

❑ **Day 77 — Judges 19—21**

DAY 78 — CONSISTENT DETERMINATION

Reaching spiritual goals requires consistent determination. By Your guidance and grace, mighty Father, I want my commitment to You to be consistent today and everyday. I want to be explosive in service and an example in lifestyle by:

CONDUCT that is Christlike. The fruit of the conduct of Christ matched what He stood for and advocated. There were no loopholes or questionable practices in His walk or talk. Lord of glory, grace me so I can model the qualities of consistent determination in living a balanced, devoted life.

COMPASSION that is authentic. Christ exhibited compassion in helping people—healing, feeding, comforting, and delivering. I want the nature of Christ to be reflected in my life through authentic service by supporting just causes, lifting up the fallen, and caring for the bruised and bewildered.

CONVERSATIONS that encourage. I will talk to a lot of people today. I want my conversations to be inspiring, encouraging, informing, uplifting, and motivating.

MY PRAYER NOTES FOR TODAY

____

____

____

____

____

BIBLE READING

❑ **Day 78 — Ruth 1—4**

DAY 79 – CREATING INSPIRATION

Father of all creation, I am inspired every day by Your holy virtues, Your acts of grace, and the promises of Your Word. Your actions create an environment of inspiration. I want to follow Your model. I want to share hope and happiness by my:

VALUES. I want to inspire others by the values I maintain and advocate. I will build my social and spiritual values around what is holy, good, and honorable. I can only do this by your indwelling, purifying, and equipping Spirit. **I will shine with sterling values today!**

VISION. Master, I want to see You high and lifted up, working wonders, and endowing me with the capabilities to reflect the characteristics of Christ. I want a far-reaching vision of evangelism reaching the destitute, and of education searching the Scriptures. **I will glow with a penetrating vision today.**

VITALITY. I want to be an upbeat, energetic messenger of peace. I want people to be affected by my vibrant spirit. I yield to, and depend upon, Your shaping and strengthening Spirit. **I will impact people and projects by my contagious vitality today!**

MY PRAYER NOTES FOR TODAY

BIBLE READING

❑ **Day 79 – 1 Samuel 1–3**

DAY 80 — STRONGER RELATIONSHIPS

Strong, affirming relationships are valuable assets. They bring individuals together for spiritual fortification, provide combined strength for service, and offer refreshing times for sharing faith, hope, and love. Today, Lord of glory, I want to build strong relationships by:

Reducing RELATIONSHIP barriers. Sometimes different viewpoints about serving You create barriers that hinder uplifting fellowship. Today, I want to reduce anything that restricts positive, growing relationships—judgmental attitudes, preconceived concepts, or cultural misunderstandings.

Increasing RELATIONSHIP values. Every person is valuable in Your sight. I want to treat every person in my life with honor, respect, and dignity. I want to show I value them by my talk and the way I treat them.

Maintaining RELATIONSHIP connections. I want to stay in touch with those I love and value. I can do this by praying for them, scheduling fellowship times with them, and affirming their importance to me.

MY PRAYER NOTES FOR TODAY

BIBLE READING

❑ **Day 80 — 1 Samuel 4—6**

DAY 81 — CREATING TRUST

I want my trust in You, faithful Father, to increase every day. Trust locks out doubt and opens the door to confidence-building understanding. Guide me today in expanding and displaying my trust in You.

During TRIALS I will trust You. Satan will try my faith and plant trials on the path I walk. I will look straight ahead in holy trust and depend on You for overcoming grace and guidance.

Amid TENSION I will trust You. In my career, as well as in church work, there will be tension as a result of different viewpoints and styles. I will trust You for an agreeable spirit and a "let's come together attitude."

Experiencing TRIUMPHS. I will honor You for trusting me. I know that in Christ I am more than a conqueror; that I will experience victories as a result of Your all-sufficient power and Your trust in me to represent You with bold faith. I will give You the glory and I will continually praise You!

MY PRAYER NOTES FOR TODAY

BIBLE READING

❑ **Day 81 — 1 Samuel 7—9**

DAY 82 — DELIVERANCE TODAY

Throughout history, Master, You have delivered Your people from the forces of evil. The goal of Satan is to oppose and oppress those who are committed to following You. Every day he is at work to block, belittle, and beat down believers. Today, I rely on You for deliverance from:

Distracting THOUGHTS. Satan desires to invade my mind with distracting thoughts—suspicion, doubt, anxiety. Let Your Spirit build a shield around my mind so my thoughts can focus on love, acceptance, forgiveness, and strength to achieve and shine in my spiritual journey.

Disruptive TRAPS. Satan will set traps in my path to disrupt progress in Christian service. Give me penetrating eyesight to detect and avoid these traps. Also, I want to be a watchman to help steer others around Satan's evil devices.

Divisive TEMPTATIONS. Satan will try to make tough decisions look easy by colorful temptations. Let me recognize his tactics and give me grace to make sound decisions. I will depend on Your delivering power to be a true, faithful, and fruitful follower.

MY PRAYER NOTES FOR TODAY

____

____

____

____

____

BIBLE READING

❑ **Day 82 — 1 Samuel 10—12**

DAY 83 — DEMONSTRATING TRUST

Trust opens the door to Your storehouse of abundant grace and unlimited gifts. I want to demonstrate radical trust today, mighty Master! I want to trust You in every area of my life.

I want to demonstrate trust in my FAITH. My faith is anchored in You! Today I want to speak with faith-filled words, act with faith-directed integrity, and relate to others with faith-based love.

I want to demonstrate trust in my FAMILY. My family is a precious gift from You. Today I want to touch each member of my family with inspiring words, with respect for their special uniqueness, and with support for fulfilling their dreams.

I want to demonstrate trust in my FRIENDS. I am surrounded with caring friends. Today I want to be a friend who understands their problems, stands with them during difficult times, and shares spiritual and material resources with them.

MY PRAYER NOTES FOR TODAY

___

___

___

___

___

BIBLE READING

❑ **Day 83 — 1 Samuel 13—15**

DAY 84 — DEPENDING POWER

Father of action, I don't want to try to defend the way I am thinking. I want to depend on what You think and the way You think.

Today, I will depend on You for DIRECTIONS. You know the path that is before me; I ask You to direct my steps. Father, let my steps be Spirit-anointed and Scripture-based. I know Your directions will be accurate and will provide me with the resources to journey successfully.

Today, I will depend on Your oversight in the DEVELOPMENT of the spiritual gifts in my life. Gifts that will honor You and advance Your kingdom. I want to be open, sensitive, and yielded so I can respond to Your decisions with faith and bold fortitude.

Today, I will depend on You for holy DETERMINATION. The devil seeks to destroy my walk with You. He will create confusion and conflict and try to destroy the influence of the local church. Clothe me with fierce faith to stand up, speak out, and bring together leaders and people to perform Your work with love, unity, and joy.

MY PRAYER NOTES FOR TODAY

____

____

____

____

____

BIBLE READING

❑ **Day 84 — 1 Samuel 16—18**

DAY 85 — DEVELOPING COMMITMENT

I'm committed, Father, and I want to develop characteristics that broadcast my commitment—by my values, by my vision, and by my vitality. I need enlightenment, endurance, and energy to fully develop my commitment. Overshadow me to maintain:

VALUES not shaken by situations. I will face situations that will challenge me to circumvent my values, to bypass standards that highlight my commitment to You. Give me spiritual stamina to stand tall, speak with authority, and serve You with integrity.

VISION not dimmed by setbacks. You have given me a vision of reaching up to You in worship and reaching out in evangelism. I want this vision to remain clear, challenging, and compelling. Give me strength not to doubt, not to take detours, or to be divided in my love and loyalty to You and my church.

VITALITY not diluted by negativism. I will be met with criticism, controlling spirits, complaining, and competition today. I will remain upbeat, unflappable in my spirit and disposition. I will keep peace in my mind and joy in my heart by recognizing Your presence, promises, and all-sufficient power. Glory to Your name!

MY PRAYER NOTES FOR TODAY

____

____

____

____

____

BIBLE READING

❑ **Day 85 — 1 Samuel 19—21**

DAY 86 — DISCIPLINED BEHAVIOR

Father, I want to be under Your control today so I can be in control of my conduct, my commitment, and my career. I know if I am to be an authentic witness I must practice disciplined behavior. I will depend upon the directing power of Your Word and the equipping power of the Holy Spirit to:

Be disciplined in my CONDUCT. My conduct, Lord, includes both my attitude and my actions. A happy, upbeat attitude reveals internal calmness and peace. I want Jesus on the inside to shine forth on the outside. I will guard my words and monitor my disposition so my conduct will display love, acceptance, and harmony.

Be disciplined in my COMMITMENT. My commitment, Master, includes both my love and my loyalty. Expressions of love in worship reveal gratefulness and thanksgiving. I will focus on my commitment to show vision, courage, and dependability.

Be disciplined in my CAREER. My career, Creator, includes both my skills and time. When I do my best You are pleased and honored. I will develop my career to show balance, innovation, and stability.

MY PRAYER NOTES FOR TODAY

____

____

____

____

____

BIBLE READING

❑ Day 86 — 1 Samuel 22—24

DAY 87 — DIVINE LEADERSHIP

I need divine leadership today, Holy Father! There are so many paths from which to choose. But, only You know the right ones—the ones that lead to purity, peace, and prosperity. I ask You to lead me and I will follow. Lead me in:

The path of LOVING my neighbor. I want to love my neighbor as myself in relationship to salvation. Lead me to be an example in lifestyle so I can invest and then give a verbal witness of Your grace to forgive, mend, and motivate.

The path of LEARNING more about You. I want to read and study Your Word more so I can better understand how to walk close to You. Lead me to serve with "turned-on" power.

The path of LONG-SUFFERING. I want to be both kind and patient. Lead me to keep my cool so I can be even-tempered and help friends and family members to be spiritual, rational, and Bible-based in their thinking.

MY PRAYER NOTES FOR TODAY

BIBLE READING

❑ Day 87 — 1 Samuel 25—27

DAY 88 — DREAM FANTASTIC DREAMS

Father of the present and the future, I want to dream eye-opening dreams that impact today and the future—dreams that are heaven-sent, heart-anchored, and mind-quickening. Direct me in employing the gifts You have invested in me to dream:

Dreams that DEVELOP. I want to grow in Christlikeness daily. Empower me to develop dreams that increase spiritual integrity, the pursuit of righteousness, and the bravery to serve with compassion and boldness. I will dream dreams that develop today!

Dreams that DEMONSTRATE. I want to reflect Christlikeness every day. Energize me to demonstrate unquestionable love in building relationships, witnessing to the unchurched, and fulfilling duties as a believer. I will dream dreams that demonstrate today!

Dreams that make a DIFFERENCE. I want to show Christlikeness today that influences people I associate with. Equip me to convey that serving Christ results in personal fulfillment, peace of mind and heart, and a positive outlook about the future and happiness. I will dream dreams that make a difference today!

MY PRAYER NOTES FOR TODAY

____

____

____

____

____

BIBLE READING

❑ **Day 88 — 1 Samuel 28—31**

DAY 89 — EAGER READINESS

Lord of unspeakable gifts, I know You are ready to bless me today; to send me grace gifts. The only condition is that I be ready to receive. I will condition myself to be ready today:

Responsive. Today, I will be responsive to Your will and openness to bless me.

Eager. Today, I will glow with eagerness to join You in receiving, giving, sharing.

Attuned. Today, I will stay attuned to Your Word, Your Spirit, and Your desire to bless.

Determined. Today, I will reflect a spirit of determination to stand, speak, and stick.

Yielded. Today, I will yield to You in everything I do; ready to receive.

Father, I know You stand at the door of my life, ready to lead, give, and bless. Today I am ready to receive.

MY PRAYER NOTES FOR TODAY

BIBLE READING

❑ **Day 89 — 2 Samuel 1—3**

DAY 90 – EMBRACING GOD'S WORD

Father, You reveal Yourself through Your Word, the Holy Bible. I desire to know You in all Your splendor and to receive daily strength from Holy Scripture. I will read, study, and apply what You reveal to me because Your Word:

Gives me WISDOM. Your wisdom gives me the ability to weigh thoughts and to make wise decisions, quickens my mind and makes me alert, and provides me with insights that motivate me to take action. **Let Your wisdom direct my decisions today!**

Reveals Your WILL. Father, I want to abide in Your ideal will today. You have a purpose for my life. You have a path for me to follow. You have power to equip me to know and do. Abiding in Your will gives me peace and spiritual prosperity. **Let Your will be reflected in my life today!**

Teaches me how to WALK. Master, You have instructed me to walk worthy of my identification with You. I want to represent You with a holy heart, a motivated mind, and helping hands. I want to be an example of a committed, joy-filled believer. **Let Your will determine my walk today!**

MY PRAYER NOTES FOR TODAY

____

____

____

____

____

BIBLE READING

❑ **Day 90 – 2 Samuel 4–6**

DAY 91 — EMBRACING GOOD THINGS

Everything about You, gracious Father, is good. You are good in all things, all the time, and in all circumstances. Today I want Your nature of goodness to be reflected in my life.

I want to embrace GOOD PEOPLE. Good people make life pleasant and enriching. They inspire and create an atmosphere of love, acceptance, and adventure. Your love on the inside of a person makes the outside beautiful, warm, and inviting for fellowship.

I want to embrace GOOD PROGRAMS. In addition to church activities, there are good programs designed to help the hurting, hungry, and homeless. I pray for the support and success of these programs—bless them!

I want to embrace GOOD PLACES. Father, You created a beautiful world. I want to enjoy good places of scenery, relaxation, activities, and fun—mountains, lakes, parks, and hiking trails. Thank You for Your rich, full, and abundant blessings. I honor You today!

MY PRAYER NOTES FOR TODAY

BIBLE READING

❑ **Day 91 — 2 Samuel 7—9**

DAY 92 — THE GREAT COMMISSION

Father, the Great Commission is Your love for the world! It reflects the giving of Your Son for lost humanity. It embodies going, giving, and guiding in making disciples. I will embrace the Great Commission and all that it embodies by:

GUIDING through building relationships. I realize that I must build relationships with the unchurched in order to influence them for Christ. I want to be a good neighbor by modeling Christlikeness, providing assistance, and showing compassion and affirmation.

GIVING hope through kindness. I can also embrace the Great Commission by taking part in acts of kindness—community projects, assisting the needy, and supporting causes to help the homeless and hurting. Everywhere Christ went He made an impact by doing good. Lord, I want to follow His example.

GOING with the good news. Praying for pastors, missionaries, and church leaders is important. But, Father, I must go with the good news by inviting people to church, sharing my testimony of faith in Christ, and participating in outreach campaigns. Equip me and empower me to be a Great Commission champion.

MY PRAYER NOTES FOR TODAY

____

____

____

____

____

BIBLE READING

❑ **Day 92 — 2 Samuel 10—12**

DAY 93 — ENERGY AND FOCUS

Energy flows with focus! Lord, I want to be focused in my relationship with You—to be obedient, to live with great expectations, and to contribute to kingdom enlargement. As I remain focused, Your divine energy will flow into and from my life. I will maintain:

Focus on FOUNDATION. "On Christ the solid rock I stand, all other ground is sinking sand." Father, Jesus Christ, Your Son, is my foundation. I will focus on this foundation. I will stand on it, build on it, and base my plans on it. **A sure foundation!**

Focus on FRAMEWORK. Father, I have a sure foundation; I will erect a framework of faith on it. I will build a house that is warm with hospitality, that has a nurturing spirit, and that cultivates kindness and security. **A sturdy framework!**

Focus on FUTURE. You know the future, Master, so I will focus on the future by trusting You and walking with You. My trust will empower me to live without fear. My walk with You will give me clear directions, holy companionship, and revealing communication. **A sterling future!**

MY PRAYER NOTES FOR TODAY

BIBLE READING

❑ **Day 93 — 2 Samuel 13—15**

DAY 94 — ENJOYING BEAUTY

I am surrounded by beauty, creative Father. There are captivating, swirling, blue clouds, flowers, trees, and vegetation! There are beautiful, good, kind, generous people. There are churches, agencies, and programs that give hope, help, and emotional healing. Today, I want to enjoy and experience the beauty that surrounds me.

I want to enjoy Your BOUNTIFUL love. Your love touches every area of my life—family, church, and career. It is sufficient for every situation, every need, and every challenge. **Therefore, I will rest in Your love and apply it to my life.**

I want to enjoy Your BLESSINGS. Your Word is filled with promises of peace, protection, and spiritual prosperity. I will enjoy emotional peace, divine protection, and prosperity in ministry and materially. **Also, I realize I am blessed to bless others.**

I want to enjoy BONDING with friends. Friends are a gift from you. I want to bond with them in trust, fellowship, and sharing. **May my life be an example and a road map to reaching God-size goals.**

MY PRAYER NOTES FOR TODAY

____

____

____

____

____

BIBLE READING

❑ **Day 94 — 2 Samuel 16—18**

DAY 95 — ENJOYING GOD'S HANDIWORK

What a beautiful day! I am surrounded by majestic, awe-inspiring beauty—trees in brilliant color, uniquely designed flowers, and birds chirping a message of "wake up, look up, and live the high-flying life."

I will enjoy the motivating beauty that You have created around me. I will enjoy it, express love for it, and plan experiences to surround it.

Father, Your power in nature says to me that You have a noble purpose in life for me. You want me to succeed, to feel significant, and to see the resources that are available to me in You.

I embrace Your message and will live a motivated life today. I will take new steps that lead to discovery, adventure, and self-improvement. I will attempt great things to demonstrate my commitment to You. I will make the people and projects I touch glow with expecting the unexpected and going beyond the norm.

MY PRAYER NOTES FOR TODAY

____

____

____

____

____

BIBLE READING

❑ Day 95 — 2 Samuel 19—21

DAY 96 — ENJOYING LIFE

Father, You have set a beautiful day before me—a day filled with opportunities, adventure, and inspiring experiences. Under Your banner of love I will enjoy life today! I will elevate the positive and eliminate the negative. I am set to:

LIVE with enthusiasm. Master, You live within me. Let Your nature be reflected in my lifestyle by a positive attitude, a warm smile, a generous disposition, and a connecting spirit. Whatever I do, wherever I am, I will charge the atmosphere with great expectations!

LOOK for the best. I will look for the best in people, places, and things. I will compliment the good! I will speak about unique characteristics! I will be a fountain flowing with helpfulness, encouragement, and excitement!

LEARN something new. Father, You have given me a heart to love, hands to do service, and a mind to think and learn. Today, I will learn something new about Your Word! I will look at new ways to worship and work! I will stay close to You to learn more about Your will and majestic nature!

MY PRAYER NOTES FOR TODAY

____

____

____

____

____

BIBLE READING

❑ **Day 96 — 2 Samuel 22—24**

DAY 97 — EQUIP ME, LORD

Father of transforming grace, I welcome You to work in my life today. I want to experience and express Your nature. Touch me, turn me, tutor me so I can know, grow, and show Your characteristics in my life.

I want to KNOW in a deeper measure Your plan for my life, the developmental process, and the path I am to follow. Equip me as I seek You and submit to Your guidance. Invest Your knowledge in me today so I can know Your perfect will.

I want to GROW, deeper and stronger, in biblical revelation, biblical faith, and biblical works. Equip me as I study and apply Your instructions to witnessing with zeal and working with consistent impact.

I want to SHOW deeper and more convincingly the blessings and benefits of a life anchored in the love of Christ. Equip me so I can meditate, circulate, and radiate the gifts of grace, Your goodness, and the guiding force of the Holy Spirit.

MY PRAYER NOTES FOR TODAY

BIBLE READING

❑ **Day 97 — 1 Kings 1—3**

DAY 98 – EXCELLENCE IN MINISTRY

Lord of eternal glory, I recognize You are excellent in all Your ways—holiness, mercy, judgments, righteousness. Creation is a magnificent display of Your perfection and excellence. As an adopted member of Your family, You have placed deep within me an intense craving to show forth excellence in my:

EXPERIENCE in Christ. The new birth makes all things new—self esteem, assurance, values, and goals. I want to do my very best today in whatever I do to reveal that my experience is an authentic life commitment. Christ in me is the hope of glory.

EXPRESSIONS of commitment. People around me, Lord, will know that Christ dwells within me by the manner in which He is expressed in my lifestyle and how I demonstrate His likeness.

EXAMPLES of compassion. I know people judge me by what I do, not what I say. Empower me to serve unselfishly, to support willingly, and to stand firmly for You, my family, and church.

MY PRAYER NOTES FOR TODAY

BIBLE READING

❑ **Day 98 – 1 Kings 4–6**

DAY 99 — EXCELLENCE IN MY LIFE

A grand and glorious day is before me! I want to seize it with enthusiasm, faith, boldness, and a spirit of excellence. I ask for insight and energy to make today impacting, fun, and fruitful.

I want to be an EXTENSION of Your love. I will treat others with dignity and respect. I will seek to understand their personality, recognize their gifts, and honor them for who they are.

I want to reflect a spirit of EXCITEMENT. I will emphasize the positive, praise the good, and promote open communication. I will be joyful and express thanksgiving for my many blessings.

I want to EXPLORE new possibilities. I will walk new paths, try new techniques, and seek new ways to be more effective. In You, Father, all things are possible. I believe this and will trust You for results!

MY PRAYER NOTES FOR TODAY

BIBLE READING

❑ Day 99 — 1 Kings 7—9

DAY 100 — EXERCISE SPIRITUALLY

Flabby spiritual muscles! I don't want this to happen to me. I want to exercise spiritually so I can possess an active faith, aggressive vision, and a healthy growth attitude. I want to maintain a desire to run the Christian race with endurance. To achieve this I will:

EXERCISE spiritually. Today I will feed on the enriching vitamins of Your Holy Word—to be a hearer and a doer of Your Word. I will keep my feet on paths of righteousness, my heart filled with Your love, and my mind active with pure thoughts.

EXPAND my influence. My talk will influence people but acts of kindness and concern will influence them more. Stabilize my spiritual stance so I can model the characteristics of Christ—compassion, understanding, and a willingness to sacrifice to assist those in need.

ENVISION new horizons. Father of new days, You have many exciting adventures in store for me. Open my eyes to see them, my hands to seize them, my mind to comprehend them, and my heart to enjoy them. I will walk with You today, mighty Master, in health, hope, and happiness.

MY PRAYER NOTES FOR TODAY

____

____

____

____

____

BIBLE READING

❑ **Day 100 — 1 Kings 10—12**

DAY 101 — EXPRESSING EXCITEMENT

What a beautiful day! A day filled with challenging opportunities and brimming with potential. Thank You, Father, for the gift of today! I want to show my appreciation by expressing excitement in my walk, in my worship, and in my work.

Expressing excitement in my WALK. I want to walk close to You today, so close that Your graceful characteristics will be reflected in my life. I want colleagues and friends to see You in my lifestyle.

Expressing excitement in my WORSHIP. Talking to You, singing songs of praise to You, and exalting Your name is a glorious, exciting privilege. I want to show this excitement with an upbeat attitude and uplifting expressions of joy and thanksgiving.

Expressing excitement in WORK. You give me strength and thinking power to work. I want my work to honor You and to be a contributing force to the faith and welfare of others. I want my work to be impacting and inspiring.

MY PRAYER NOTES FOR TODAY

___

___

___

___

___

BIBLE READING

❑ **Day 101 — 1 Kings 13—15**

DAY 102 — EXPRESSIVE CONTENTMENT

Contentment in life is a set of beliefs in full operation. Father, I understand and embrace this statement. Today I want to show contentment as a balanced believer. I want to:

Show contentment to my FAMILY—to practice what I profess in words, deeds, and actions. I love my family and I want them to see Christ in me every day and to be a testimony to my honest, real-life commitment.

Show contentment in my FAITH—to rejoice in God's promises and to live by them without doubt or hesitation. I want to be ready to give an answer to questions concerning what and why I believe.

Show contentment in the FUTURE—to be happy and growing in my vocation and in the assurance of an eternal home in heaven. I want to live every day with great expectations—relating, dreaming, and experiencing total life in Christ.

MY PRAYER NOTES FOR TODAY

____

____

____

____

____

BIBLE READING

❑ **Day 102 — 1 Kings 16—18**

DAY 103 — EXTRA PERFORMANCE

I need extra strength today to live successfully, significantly, and to shine as a believer. Thank You, Father, for the extra strength available from You. By faith and with thanksgiving, I accept your loving gift of extra strength. This strength comes in the form of:

Positive ATTITUDE. Father, You have replaced fear in my life with faith. I believe! My positive attitude today energizes me to be optimistic and to expect top-notch results. My positive attitude is based on scriptural promises, Your omnipresence, and the equipping power of the Holy Spirit.

Principle-anchored ACTION. I want my actions to always be straightforward, without inciting questions about motive. Whatever I do, I want to be guided by scripturally and morally grounded principles.

People-centered ACTIVITIES. Lord, I don't want to be selfish in my Christian profession or practices. I want to be mindful of others' needs and participate in activities that relieve the pain and anxiety of family conflict, career difficulties, and financial pressure. I am depending on You, Master, for extra strength to represent You with compassion and authority.

MY PRAYER NOTES FOR TODAY

BIBLE READING

❑ Day 103 — 1 Kings 19—22

DAY 104 — EXTRA STRENGTH

Almighty, all-sufficient heavenly Father, I need strength from You to live a life that makes a difference. I am often stressed, and sometimes I stumble and fall. Give me strength from You to stand tall and to speak with conviction and authority. I need:

Strength to SHINE. Today I want to reflect Your nature—love, long-suffering, liberation. Work in my mind and heart to develop these distinguishing characteristics. Work in my actions and activities to demonstrate these characteristics.

Strength to SERVE. Today I want to show forth Your goodness—giving, going, serving. Touch my thoughts and dreams to understand these unselfish qualities. Empower me to practice them with generosity and consistency.

Strength to SEPARATE. Today, I want to separate myself from anything that would weaken my commitment to You—lukewarmness, laziness, idleness. Guide me away from these inhibiting traps. Energize me to be alert and productive, to step out and step forward to shine and serve in ways that focus on Your kingdom.

MY PRAYER NOTES FOR TODAY

____

____

____

____

____

BIBLE READING

❑ **Day 104 — 2 Kings 1—3**

DAY 105 — EYES WIDE OPEN

Lord of all glory and beauty, I want to keep my eyes wide open today to observe what You are doing and how I can join You in it. As I walk with You, great and wonderful things are in store for me. In meditation and motivation I will keep my eyes wide open:

To see OPPORTUNITIES. You have set opportunities before me to mature in Christ, mentor young believers, and motivate church workers. Let me possess a positive attitude and show positive action in making these opportunities fruitful. **I will have clear vision today!**

To see OBSTACLES. Satan will set obstacles before me today to try to block my closeness with You and to detour my spiritual progress. Anoint my eyes to see these obstacles, to go around them, and to become stronger and more alert in the process. **I will have commitment vision today!**

To see OVERFLOW. Your blessings are abundant, full, free, and overflowing. I receive these blessings with admiration and appreciation. Yes, I will share them with others and testify of Your supreme kindness. **I will have celebration vision today!**

MY PRAYER NOTES FOR TODAY

____

____

____

____

____

BIBLE READING

❑ **Day 105 — 2 Kings 4—6**

DAY 106 — FACING CHANGE

Lord, You invented change! You changed nothing into something and changed the world. You changed me from a dying wanderer to a living witness of transformation in Christ. There are many change situations I will face today. Guide me to:

Change to enhance CREATIVITY. Your Spirit gives creative energy to view things differently, consider options, and be more effective. I don't want to be locked into a mold of sameness, dullness, lukewarmness. I look to You for a spirit of innovation.

Change to avoid CONFLICT. Your Spirit gives insight to let go of the habits and confrontational dispositions that generate conflict. I don't want to be locked into a mold of "I'm right, you're wrong, you need to change." I want to be open to new ideas and ways of performing ministry. I look to You for a spirit of openness and opportunities to dialogue and agree.

Change to foster COMMITMENT. Your Spirit gives directions on dedication and growing in grace. I don't want to be locked into a mold of "one way, the only way." I want to be yielding and submissive. I look to You for a spirit of renewal and refreshing.

MY PRAYER NOTES FOR TODAY

____

____

____

____

____

BIBLE READING

❑ **Day 106 — 2 Kings 7—9**

DAY 107 — FACING CRISES

I will face discomforts, undesirable circumstances, and seemingly unconquerable habits in life. I will face some type of crisis today! I need both push and pull power to survive, to shine, and to feel significant. Give me:

Power to CONTROL. Lord, touch me with drive and desire to control my thinking, my response to negative impulses, and my reaction to criticism. You are the Master controller. Let Your controlling power saturate my pursuits and practices.

Power to CONFRONT. Today, give me boldness to confront perplexing problems and problem people. Let me stand firmly for truth, righteousness, and fairness. Give me strength to confront weaknesses and lack of wisdom in my life and to make constructive changes.

Power to CREATE. Father, You are the author of all creation. I ask You to let Your creative energy flow in my life to think big, act wisely, and to plan creatively. I always want to be a pacesetter in kingdom ministry.

MY PRAYER NOTES FOR TODAY

BIBLE READING

❑ **Day 107 — 2 Kings 10—12**

DAY 108 — FACING GIANTS

Problems that appear as giants to me are like grasshoppers to You, all-powerful Father. You have assured me that Your grace issues grit to stand in faith—to fight, defend, and overcome. I will face issues and events today with strength and victorious strategy from You. I will face the:

Giant of GLOOM. I am surrounded by gloom—people out of work, crisis in politics, financial collapse. There are divided homes—divorce, death, children separated from parents. Satan is at work! Where Satan works, Your grace works more—revealing, restoring, energizing, fortifying, and rolling back the clouds of doom. **I trust You!**

Giant of GUILT. Lord, sometimes mistakes of the past rise up to haunt me. They stand like a giant to block inner peace. I accept Your forgiveness, Your joy, and Your abiding presence. **I trust You!**

Giant of GRUDGES. Hard feelings toward others deprive me of closeness with You. By faith I will forgive, forget, and forge forward. I will form new relationships and be a healer, not a divider. **I trust You!**

MY PRAYER NOTES FOR TODAY

____

____

____

____

____

BIBLE READING

❑ **Day 108 — 2 Kings 13—15**

DAY 109 — FACING SPIRITUAL FOES

Many enemies, sustaining Father, seek to interfere with my connection with You. I want to face them head on, deal with them, and overcome them through the guidance of Your Holy Spirit. I depend on heavenly help:

To overcome DOUBT. When Satan raises questions in my mind about the authenticity of Your Word, my allegiance to Your Church, or the reality of Your promises, I will dispel them through praise, prayer, and the promises I have been blessed with.

To harness DISTRACTIONS. The enemy will try to distract me from Bible reading, church attendance, and sharing my faith by a packed personal schedule, unproductive projects, and time-wasters. I will stay on course by remembering my priorities as a child of the King and the gifts You have invested in me.

To unify DIVISION. The Evil One will attempt to divide the body of Christ and create conflict and disorder. I will be a helper, a healer, and a herald of positive news. I will emphasize unity in Christ, teamwork in the church, and partnership with each other.

MY PRAYER NOTES FOR TODAY

BIBLE READING

❑ **Day 109 — 2 Kings 16—18**

DAY 110 — FACING YESTERDAY

Yesterday is over! Memories of yesterday can be motivational or cause misery. Today, Father, I want yesterday, today, and tomorrow to come together and bring balance, perspective, and focus into my life. Give me faith and fortitude to:

MANAGE memories. Some memories resurface grief and pain—bad decisions, the deaths of loved ones, and missed opportunities. Some memories bring joy and strength—educational achievements, finding true love, and dynamic spiritual experiences. Quicken my memory to be strengthened by the positive and to focus on Your power to overcome.

MOVE into tomorrow. You have exciting things in store for tomorrow—action, adventure, and accomplishments. I want to be prepared to move into tomorrow with spiritual plans, a productive disposition, and guiding principles. Anoint my eyes so I can see clearly the path You want me to follow.

MULTIPLY the present. Opportunities to learn, grow, serve, and acquire surround me. I want to put on Your spiritual armor. I want to cultivate the mind of Christ to multiply my influence and effectiveness.

MY PRAYER NOTES FOR TODAY

____

____

____

____

____

BIBLE READING

❑ **Day 110 — 2 Kings 19—21**

DAY 111 — FAITH FOR TODAY

Lord, Your Word says, "According to your faith will it be done to you" (Matt. 9:29). I need Your assistance today. I need Your guidance on how to release faith to receive.

Let me release faith to overcome SELFISHNESS. I want to relate to family and friends with genuine interest, care, and understanding. I want to reflect unconditional and unselfish love, compassion, and care.

Let me release faith to confront SUFFERING. Suffering comes in many forms and degrees—sickness, grief, conflict, unfulfilled dreams. In all things I know You give grace to be a victorious champion.

Let me release faith to SERVE. I want to make a difference in the effectiveness of my church by supporting my pastor, discovering and developing spiritual gifts, and participating in projects that extend the influence and impact of my church.

MY PRAYER NOTES FOR TODAY

____

____

____

____

____

BIBLE READING

❑ **Day 111 — 2 Kings 22—25**

DAY 112 — FAVOR IN MY FUTURE

Father, You are by my side today—upholding me, steadying my steps, and directing me in the right direction. I feel Your nearness and place my hand in Yours. I will enjoy today as a result of the security You provide. I will enjoy today because I have Your favor in my future.

You have a PLAN for my future. Your Word states that You have a plan for my future— a plan filled with hope, prosperity, and happiness. Your favor is in my future, and I purpose to live with confidence and courage because You are in control of my life.

You have a PURPOSE for my future. I am so thankful I am included in Your kingdom plans. I am committed to Your plans. I will seek Your instructions and follow the route You have outlined for me.

You have a PATTERN for my ministry. Master, You have invested gifts in my life. These gifts form a pattern for me to use in ministry—touching the unchurched, teaching scriptural truths, training for effective service. Anoint me, empower me, equip me to faithfully and effectively follow the pattern You have designed for me.

MY PRAYER NOTES FOR TODAY

____

____

____

____

____

BIBLE READING

❑ **Day 112 — 1 Chronicles 1—3**

DAY 113 — FEARLESS CONFIDENCE

Almighty Father, You dispel fear and respond to biblical faith. Today, I desire to be fearless in what I say and what I do. This fearless position will be founded on fearless confidence in Your power, what You have promised, and Your provision for extraordinary achievements. I will display:

Confidence to EMBRACE. I will embrace Your commands and instructions outlined in the Bible. You have given guidelines on how to worship, how to treat others, and how to witness with Holy Spirit authority. **I will show fearless confidence today!**

Confidence to ENDURE. I will endure the hardships of living a separated life and the evil attacks of Satan. You have told me to "hold out" and to "hold on" and that You will see me through. **I will demonstrate fearless confidence today!**

Confidence to EMBARK. I will embark on new avenues of discovery and adventure in my Christian walk. Thank You for the privilege to learn, grow, share, and receive from You. **I will display fearless confidence today!**

MY PRAYER NOTES FOR TODAY

____

____

____

____

____

BIBLE READING

❑ **Day 113 — 1 Chronicles 4—6**

DAY 114 — FEELING YOUR PRESENCE

Lord of all comfort and grace, I want to feel Your presence today. Your Word assures me that You are by my side. Teach me how to reach out and touch You, to trust You to solve problems, to stand firm in faith, and to feel significant in kingdom ministry.

Your presence gives PEACE. You said, "I am with you always" (Matt. 28:20). Therefore, I will be free in my spirit and rejoice in Your protective care and companionship.

Your presence grants POWER. You promised, "I have given you power to trample on snakes and scorpions and to overcome all the power of the enemy; nothing will harm you" (Luke 10:19). Therefore, I will act wisely, forcefully, and fearlessly and put on the full armor You have provided.

Your presence guarantees PRODUCTIVITY. You proclaimed, "You will bear fruit and more fruit" (John 15:5). Therefore, I will cultivate, plant, and water in the garden of service and harvest fruit that will honor You and support growth in Christlikeness.

MY PRAYER NOTES FOR TODAY

BIBLE READING

❑ Day 114 — 1 Chronicles 7—9

DAY 115 — FILLED WITH THANKSGIVING

Father, I want to begin every day with thanksgiving. But today I am filled, running over with thanksgiving because of Your overflowing grace and gifts to me. I want to show my spirit of thanksgiving in three specific ways:

A VOICE of praise. I lift my voice with words, songs, and expressions. Words share my deep love, songs convey the joy in my heart, and expressions reveal my commitment to serve.

A VALUE system of devotion. I know what is important in my relationship with You—reading Your Word, claiming Your promises, and sharing my faith. You give me grace and guidance in doing this.

A VICTORY stance of celebration. I know that I am a certified conqueror in You. Today I wave the banner of victory over sinful influences and the unsuccessful attacks of the enemies of righteousness.

MY PRAYER NOTES FOR TODAY

BIBLE READING

❑ **Day 115 — 1 Chronicles 10—12**

DAY 116 — FINDING WEALTH

Wise Father, You have made me wealthy in faith, family, and friends. I want to be wise in utilizing my faith, protecting my family, and showing appreciation for my friends. I will do this in specific ways:

Charming ATTITUDE. I will show my inner wealth—peace, contentment, values—with warm facial expressions and a charming smile. I will be positive in my praise, in facing problems, and in dealing with difficult people. **Father, I will do this today through Your uplifting power.**

Constructive ACTIVITIES. I will show my outer wealth—opportunities, work ethic, contributions—with creativity and accountability. I will be selective in how I apply my talents, in utilizing my strength, and in advancing the cause of Christ. **Master, I will do this today through the guidance of Your Spirit.**

Creative ADVANCEMENT. I will show my future wealth—stewardship, training, testimony, maturity—with self-discipline and a compelling vision. I will be aggressive in service, building relationships, and discovering new ways to support my church. **Lord, I will do this today through Your equipping grace!**

MY PRAYER NOTES FOR TODAY

____

____

____

____

____

BIBLE READING

❑ **Day 116 — 1 Chronicles 13—15**

DAY 117 — FIRED-UP FAITH

Limitless loving Father, I want my faith to be on fire today—sizzling, flowing, glowing! I believe this is Your will! You want me to be active and aggressive in applying faith in worship, in my work, and in witnessing. Today, give me:

FULLNESS of Your favor. My goal today is to please You. I cannot earn Your blessings, but You have promised me the fullness of Your favor if I trust You, obey You, and embrace Your precepts.

FRESHNESS in my friendships. Father, I want Your love in me to be reflected through me to my friends. I want to be a friend that shows care and that shares love, laughter, and learning experiences.

FIRE in my faith. Today, Lord of glory, I want my faith to accept challenges, solve problems, and establish standards. Your touch will make this happen! I am open, ready, and willing. I want to make things happen, to turn things around, to see the good and positive. Fire me up today with the igniting strength of Your Spirit.

MY PRAYER NOTES FOR TODAY

____

____

____

____

____

BIBLE READING

❑ Day 117 — 1 Chronicles 16—18

DAY 118 — FLOWING FAITH

I know faith will empower me to see the invisible and to reach out and touch the yet to be formed. I know this, trusting Father, but I want it to be a part of my daily life in You.

I want my faith to flow consistently FORWARD. I do not want to be stuck in a rut or to be in bondage to the past. I want to face each day with expectations, excitement, and plans to experience and grow.

I want my faith to flow without FRICTION. I do not want to get bogged down in actions or discussions that divide loyalty, dampen relationships, and disrupt constructive dialogue. I want my faith to invite inquiries and stimulate Word-based thinking.

I want my faith to bear FRUIT. I want to be a source of inspiration and encouragement. I want my faith to reveal the fruit of the Spirit in plans, approaches, and partnership in ministry.

MY PRAYER NOTES FOR TODAY

BIBLE READING

❑ Day 118 — 1 Chronicles 19—21

DAY 119 — FLOWING IN ABUNDANCE

Your Word, abiding Father, states that I can have abundant life in and through Your Son, Jesus Christ. This abundant life is fresh, fulfilling, fruitful, and anchored in faith. I look to You to enjoy the abundant life today.

Let me stay in the FLOW of the abundant life and the stream of Your favor. Today, I will embrace the guidance of Your Word, stand for the authority of Your Word, and enjoy the enriching benefits of Your Word.

Let me GROW in the abundant life and reflect the characteristics of Christ. Today, I will show love to the unlovely, compassion to the confused, and hope to the destitute.

Let me SOW the abundant life and share with others a life-changing testimony. Today, I will look for ways to share the good news of cleansing, forgiveness, and freedom through an experience with the Author of Life, Jesus Christ.

MY PRAYER NOTES FOR TODAY

BIBLE READING

❑ Day 119 — 1 Chronicles 22—24

DAY 120 — FLOWING POWER

There are many types of power—political, positional, or personality power. I realize, Father, You are the true source of all power. Your power transforms, trains, and tutors. I need Your power. I seek Your power. I yield to the infusion of Your power. Today, guide me to:

EXERCISE spiritually. I want to stay in shape by focusing on active faith! I want to stand firmly on Your Word and build muscles for ministry. I want to run the Christian race with endurance and to keep the finish line in clear view.

EXPAND my influence. I need Your power, equipping Father, to expand the strength of my influence. I want my influence to be character-building, hope-giving, and life-motivating. Anoint my influence to impact the lifestyle of my friends.

ENVISION new horizons. Today, by holy inspiration, I will look up and look out to see new spiritual adventures and opportunities. Every day in You, life-changing Father, is filled with privileges to walk closer to You and to grow stronger, deeper, and wider in reflecting Your grace and will.

MY PRAYER NOTES FOR TODAY

BIBLE READING

❑ **Day 120 — 1 Chronicles 25—27**

DAY 121 — FOLLOWING GOD'S PATH

Lord of life and liberty, I want to follow the path You have outlined for me today. You have plans for me, great and glorious plans.

I will rejoice in Your plan for PEACE. Your plan takes away fear and gives me peace of mind and peace in performing ministry. Your peace gives me contentment and happiness in worship, witness, and work.

I will accept your plan of PARTNERSHIP. I understand I am in partnership with You, with my pastor, and with the members of my church. We are all gifted, under You, to perform kingdom ministry in love, truth, and harmony.

I will endorse Your plan for PRODUCTIVITY. If I go forth with loving compassion, with seeds of concern and care, You have promised that I will be productive in fulfilling the Great Commission and in impacting the outreach of my church. Today, I will follow Your plan and will wave the banner of Your righteousness and rule.

MY PRAYER NOTES FOR TODAY

____

____

____

____

____

BIBLE READING

❑ **Day 121 — 1 Chronicles 28—29**

DAY 122 — GOD'S COMMANDMENTS

Your Word instructs me how to please You and how to follow a path of productivity in living successfully. You give clear instructions on how to relate to You, my family, my church, and my neighbors. You also offer support and strength to be faithful and consistent in following Your plans. Today I want to:

OBEY Your commandments. I cannot do this by myself—I need Your oversight and Your enabling power. I want to embrace and obey all Your commandments and to honor You with a willing spirit, an open mind, and a submissive attitude.

ORCHESTRATE my activities around Your commandments. I want my head, heart, and hands to be in sync with what I believe and profess. I want my life—attitude, actions, and activities—to reflect my commitment and obedience to Your will.

OFFER assistance to others. I want to assist others in understanding and keeping Your commandments through modeling, teaching, and encouraging. I want to do this in the power of the Holy Spirit and with a tender, compassionate spirit.

MY PRAYER NOTES FOR TODAY

____

____

____

____

____

BIBLE READING

❑ **Day 122 — 2 Chronicles 1—3**

DAY 123 — FOCUS ON LOVE

Christianity is based on love. Your love, life-giving Father. You love me. You love the lost of every generation to the degree that You gave Your only Son, Jesus Christ, as a sacrifice for sin and separation from You. I love You for this and desire to express my love in worship and service. I want this love to extend to:

My FAMILY. Father, I want Your love to flow from me to my family. I want family members to feel my love by the way I respect them, treat them, and add value to their lives. I will show a loving spirit and set an example of faithfulness in fulfilling home duties.

My FRIENDS. I am thankful for friends. I enjoy them! They add zest and adventure to my life. Today, I want my friends to both feel and see my love for them by demonstrating a life anchored in the love of Christ—compassion, courtesy, and compliments.

My FAITHLESS Neighbors. My unsaved neighbors need a witness. I will be that witness by being a loving friend—showing interest, sharing inspirational fellowship, and inviting them to attend church activities.

MY PRAYER NOTES FOR TODAY

____

____

____

____

____

BIBLE READING

❑ **Day 123 — 2 Chronicles 4–6**

DAY 124 — FORGIVENESS TODAY

Lord of love, You are the Father of forgiveness. I need Your grace and guidance every day to keep my feet on the path of purity and my mind focused on ministry. I confess that I am weak and I often slip and slide in my devotion and duties. I ask for forgiveness for:

My FAILURES. Father, I want to represent You with pride and excellent performance. Forgive my failures and build up my faith today so I can model Christlikeness and the fruit of the Spirit. Show me the traps and tricks of Satan so I can be prepared to overcome them and stand firm in faith.

My FRIENDS. Sometimes my friends stumble and fall. This causes doubt, division, and depression. As You have forgiven me, I will forgive them. I will also stand with them on the path of recovery and assist in restoring self-esteem and scriptural commitment.

My FOES. According to Your Word, Master, I will pray for my enemies and those who abuse me and forgive their damaging actions (see Matt. 5:44). I pray for their salvation—to understand and accept Your love to become a new creation in Christ.

MY PRAYER NOTES FOR TODAY

____

____

____

____

____

BIBLE READING

❑ **Day 124 — 2 Chronicles 7—9**

DAY 125 — FREEDOM IN CHRIST

Father, I know You forgive and forget. You give freedom from past mistakes and power to move forward. Thank You for freedom from fear, failure, and for freedom to think clearly, constructively, and creatively. Freedom in You issues an attitude of contagious contentment and peace of mind. I realize all of this flows from You based on three principles:

CONVERSION—becoming a new creation in Christ. I express love today for the sacrificial death of Christ that grants eternal hope and the assurance of heaven.

COMMITMENT—being personally committed to following You according to the route and rules outlined in Your Word. Every day I want to view and renew my commitment to following You in love and devotion.

COMPANIONSHIP—walking with You in faith and energized by the fruit of the Spirit. Thank You for all the spiritual fruit—such as love, joy, peace, long-suffering, gentleness, kindness, and goodness—that You freely give. Today I will enjoy freedom and the abundant life in Christ!

MY PRAYER NOTES FOR TODAY

____

____

____

____

____

BIBLE READING

❑ **Day 125 — 2 Chronicles 10—12**

DAY 126 — FRIENDSHIP IN FOCUS

Friendships are important in shaping my character and testimony. I want my life to impact the lives of my Christian friends and to influence the life of my unchurched friends. Today, I recognize the:

REWARDS of friendship. Friendship yields rewards—sharing of experiences, assisting each other, dreaming together, and unifying in Christian service. Father, I am thankful for my friends! Bless me to be a trusted friend. Bless my friends and surround them with supportive grace.

RESPECT for friendship. Respect is developed in the mind recognizing personality traits, appreciating skills, and developing behavior insights; and in the heart loving without fear, conveying admiration, and sharing values. Father, let my faith grow and join forces with respect for friendship.

RESPONSIBILITIES of friendship. Responsibilities are a vital aspect of maintaining fruitful friendships, and include protecting confidences, giving emotional support, and contributing to spiritual growth. Father, I want to represent You to my friends by exhibiting integrity and confidence.

MY PRAYER NOTES FOR TODAY

BIBLE READING

❑ **Day 126 — 2 Chronicles 13—15**

DAY 127 — SUCCESS TO SIGNIFICANCE

Lord, I am thankful for the open path You have set before me. It is a path of personal achievement, adventure, and advancement. My goal is success in work, worship, and witness. I want my success to be anchored in significance—exalting You, rendering service, and making an impact in kingdom ministry. I will:

Formulate a personal MISSION. My mission is to honor and worship You. I will formulate a personal mission code to guide my devotion to You, my dedication to my family, and my duties to my church. **My mission will direct my life!**

Serve as a MODEL. I need Your wisdom to serve as a model of commitment to Christ. I ask You to mold me into the image of Your Son so I can demonstrate the qualities of loving kindness and Christian grace. **I will let modeling Christlikeness direct my life!**

Focus on MINISTRY. Today, I want to be a worker and a witness. I realize, Master, I must follow the pattern of Christ who said, "I must be about my Father's business" (Luke 2:49). Your business is to love, teach, lead, feed, and disciple. **I will let involvement in ministry direct my life!**

MY PRAYER NOTES FOR TODAY

____

____

____

____

____

BIBLE READING

❑ **Day 127 — 2 Chronicles 16—18**

DAY 128 — FRUITFULNESS TODAY

Lord of abundant increases, I want to plant, prune, and produce fruit today. I want to "show and tell" about the fruit of a godly life in a way that will result in transformation—new creations in Jesus Christ. I will do this through:

Demonstrations of HOLINESS. Father, I want to do the right things the right way with scriptural motives. Let Your Spirit clothe and cover me. Keep my thoughts Christ-centered so I can model the fruit of purity and a daily walk with You.

Acts of HELPFULNESS. On the Jericho road of life, there are people in need—discouragement, debt, and depression. I do not want to walk past them. I want to give encouragement, financial assistance, and spiritual inspiration. Work through me to do this!

Expressions of HOPEFULNESS. Today I want to share a spirit of hope and happiness. Whatever the situation there is hope, a future through Jesus Christ! I want to express this in my attitude and actions. Let the Holy Spirit inspire me and anoint me to be a person of influence.

MY PRAYER NOTES FOR TODAY

____

____

____

____

____

BIBLE READING

❑ **Day 128 — 2 Chronicles 19—21**

DAY 129 — FULLNESS IN LIFE

Father, You have set today before me. It is filled with beauty, potential, and opportunities to discover and experience. I want to live life in its fullness. Let Your creative power flow in my life so I can:

Live in PRAISE, displaying a positive spirit of thanksgiving, thankful to You for salvation and security, for family and friends, for faith and freedom, for opportunities to grow spiritually, and for grace to overcome. **I will live with a heart of praise today!**

Live my PASSION, following the path of the dreams You have placed in my heart, being a faithful follower of Your Son, Jesus Christ, being an influential witness of Your love for the lost and lonely, and utilizing my talents to be productive and successful. **I will live with a commitment to my passion today!**

Live in PARTNERSHIP, joining forces with You and others to achieve worthy objectives. Father, I will partner with You in walking the Christian walk, with my pastor in fulfilling the ministry of my church, and with family and friends in a fruitful lifestyle. **I will live a life of trustworthy partnership today.**

MY PRAYER NOTES FOR TODAY

____

____

____

____

____

BIBLE READING

❑ **Day 129 — 2 Chronicles 22—24**

DAY 130 — FULLY COMMITTED

It is vital to my spiritual health and integrity, Father, to be fully committed. I want to live a committed life and harvest the fruit of commitment. I need divine intervention, a heaven-sent infusion of wisdom, and an infilling of supernatural strength. I pray for this. I will display a willing and open spirit by:

Being DEDICATED to dependence on You, to righteous living, and to my church. Dedication is the key to wholeness and balance in living the life of Your Son and in walking the Christian walk. **I will demonstrate dedication today!**

Being DETERMINED not to back up in service, back down in convictions, or back out of ministry. Determination gives dreams wheels and builds a road to drive on. **I will publicize determination!**

Being DEPENDABLE in reflecting Christlikeness in daily behavior, in performing ministry responsibilities, and in cultivating the qualities of binding friendship. Dependability is the foundation for trust and confidence. Trust and confidence open doors to influence to lead and for Christ-exalting impact. **I will magnify dependability today!**

MY PRAYER NOTES FOR TODAY

___

___

___

___

___

BIBLE READING

❑ **Day 130 — 2 Chronicles 25—27**

DAY 131 — GIFTS FOR TODAY

Lord of graciousness and goodness, I praise You for gifts that make my life great. I want to recognize the scope of these gifts, receive them into my life every day, and watchfully guard them.

Thank You for the gift of GRACE. Through Your grace I have been redeemed and set free to live, love, and experience. Your grace keeps good things flowing into every area of my life at church, home and work.

Thank you for the gift of angels that GUARD. You tell me in Your Word that You have appointed angels to watch over me—to protect from danger, harm, and the Enemy of my soul.

Thank You for the gift of divine GOODNESS. Food, clothing, and lodging are united with peace, significance, and purpose through You. I am a complete person in You, equipped for every good work and to experience the best in You.

MY PRAYER NOTES FOR TODAY

BIBLE READING

❑ **Day 131 — 2 Chronicles 28—30**

DAY 132 — GIVE A SHOUT

Lord, You reign supreme over all the kingdoms of the earth. Your reign is marked by unlimited love, unmatched grace, and unstoppable advancement. I praise You for the honor to be a soldier in Your heavenly army and I have a shout today, a shout of:

TRUTH. Your Word is truth. I stand on solid ground today. I stand on the solid Rock, Christ Jesus. I stand for and with Jesus, the Rock of my salvation. **I will shout forth truth today!**

TRIUMPH. Your power produces victory. I will not be defeated because I have the forces of heaven backing me, supporting me, and encouraging me. **I will experience victory after victory!**

TESTIMONY. Your Word needs to be shared. I want to be a living, walking, speaking testimony. I will share truth, victory, and the glory of heaven. **I will shout testimonies of mighty blessings!**

MY PRAYER NOTES FOR TODAY

____

____

____

____

____

BIBLE READING

❑ **Day 132 — 2 Chronicles 31—33**

DAY 133 — GIVE ME A DREAM

God of sparkling light, birth a dream in me today. As I read Your Word, I observe that You gave dreams to Your followers—dreams about physical deliverance, spiritual gifts, and personal victories. Wonderful, dazzling dreams. Out of sight dreams.

Give me a fresh dream today. I want a dream that will activate creativity in my mind, a stirring in my soul, and a moving by the Holy Spirit to see and to achieve.

Set a green light before me. Let me press the accelerator that ignites power, passion, and productivity in mission and message. Zoom! New dream! New scenery! New, bold action!

As you gave dreams in the past to excel in kingdom ministry, I claim a dream from You today! I am open to receive—mind, heart, and hands. And I promise, I will honor You with the dream.

MY PRAYER NOTES FOR TODAY

BIBLE READING

❑ **Day 133 — 2 Chronicles 34—36**

DAY 134 — GIVE ME A SUNSHINE SPIRIT

Today, Father, I want the sunshine of Your love to radiate in my life. I want a glow to show through my disposition and the manner in which I face life—both the opportunities and the obstacles. I want Your sunshine to be reflected in my heart, head, and hands.

I want to show forth the sunshine of SERVICE. Selfishness separates and causes individuals to doubt my sincerity. Let me be a servant today, serving You with true devotion and serving others through acts of kindness and encouragement.

I want to beam with the sunshine of SHARING. Your Word, Lord, is a record of sharing joy, contentment, and love. So, I want to share Your peace today and point people to Jesus Christ, the Prince of Peace!

I want to reflect the sunshine of STEADFASTNESS. As I serve and share, I want my family and friends to see my steadfast devotion to You and Your Church. I want to be an example of a true follower of Jesus Christ in all I do. I receive Your sunshine today!

MY PRAYER NOTES FOR TODAY

BIBLE READING

❑ **Day 134 — Ezra 1—3**

DAY 135 — GIVE ME CONFIDENCE

Conditions and circumstances often undermine my confidence. May I always look to You and be ready to meet challenges and enjoy new adventures. Whatever I need is available from You!

I look to the CROSS for victory. Christ overcame death, hell, and the grave. The Cross represents victory over the power of Satan to deceive, destroy, and discourage. I embrace the power of the Cross today, **heavenly Father!**

I look to CHRIST for inspiration. Because He overcame, He empowers me to overcome. He walked and talked with authority and fulfilled His Father's will and work. I will visualize the presence of Christ with me today, **heavenly Father!**

I look to the CHURCH for support. The church is structured by Christ to guide His people in living the "abundant life" and in fulfilling the Great Commission. I will stay close to my church, enjoying strengthening fellowship, and engaging in love-directed evangelism today, **heavenly Father!**

MY PRAYER NOTES FOR TODAY

____

____

____

____

____

BIBLE READING

❑ Day 135 — Ezra 4—6

DAY 136 — GIVE ME UNDERSTANDING

Father of grace and wisdom, I need understanding today to build my faith and to find direction to experience Your fullness in doctrine, development, and duties. Teach me today:

To understand DOCTRINE. Your Word is truth. It is my guidebook to understanding You—Your nature, will, and actions. As I read Your Word, open my mind and illuminate Your truths to transform doubt into discovery.

To understand DEVELOPMENT. I want to be a complete disciple. I want to reflect Christlikeness in all my ways and works. Let Your Holy Spirit work in my mind and spirit to conform to Your holy purposes.

To understand DUTIES. Like Christ, I must be about Your work. How can I best serve You? In what areas can I make the greatest impact? I yield to Your will.

MY PRAYER NOTES FOR TODAY

BIBLE READING

❑ **Day 136 — Ezra 7—10**

DAY 137 — GLORIOUS GIFTS

What a wonderful day! Thank You, loving Father, for the beauty and bountiful blessings that You give me today. What excitement! What adventure! Today is jam-packed with majestic wonder and multiple opportunities.

Thank You for the gift of GRACE. Grace flows from Your throne. It is unmerited and undeserved. Your grace releases from sin, refreshes the soul, and restores wholeness. There is grace for every need!

Thank You for the gift of GRACIOUSNESS. This gift flows from grace. It is an attitude of respect, love, and appreciation. It is a genuine spirit of caring and helpfulness. I want to share this gift today!

Thank You for the gift of GROWING. Today I will grow in my relationship with You. I will grow stronger in Your Word, witnessing, working in the church, and winning the battles against the temptations of Satan. Today is a glorious day filled with gifts from You. I am exceedingly grateful!

MY PRAYER NOTES FOR TODAY

BIBLE READING

❑ **Day 137 — Nehemiah 1—3**

DAY 138 — GOD'S WORD ACTIVE

Lord of purity and power, I thank You that Your Word is alive and active in my life. It is my foundation for a growing faith. It outlines plans on how to please You. It gives directions for future security. It is the source of my energy and strength. Today:

I ACCEPT the promises of Your Word. Your Word, Father, is filled with glorious promises of comfort, hope, healing, care, protection, and provision. Your promises cover every area of my life and grant me freedom to love, grow, and enjoy unlimited blessings.

I will APPLY the principles of Your Word. Your Word outlines principles for victorious living, honoring You, raising my family, treating my neighbors kindly, expanding Your kingdom, and reflecting the image of Christ. Today, by the guidance of Your Spirit, I will diligently seek to apply the principles of Your Word.

I ACKNOWLEDGE the power of Your Word. Your Word, Lord, sets forth power to overcome, to withstand the assaults of Satan, to stand firmly for truth, and to be visionary and productive. I honor and praise You for making Your power available to me.

MY PRAYER NOTES FOR TODAY

____

____

____

____

____

BIBLE READING

❑ **Day 138 — Nehemiah 4–6**

DAY 139 — GRACE TODAY

Growing, giving, glowing grace—I need all three. Lord, You have given me the grace of credibility and cleansing. I walk in confidence today because I know, without reservations or restrictions, that Your grace is sufficient. I praise You for this. I also ask You to continue to meet my need for:

Grace for GROWTH. Guide me to grow daily in the likeness and love of Your Son, Jesus Christ. I want to grow stronger in faith, in fulfilling the Great Commission, and in producing the fruit of a righteous, fully devoted disciple.

Grace to GIVE. Give me discipline to keep my body on Your altar as a living sacrifice—submissive, receptive, and obedient. As I have received from You, lead me to give to others love, acceptance, and support.

Grace to GLOW. Father, I ask You to give me power to maintain a bright, dazzling spiritual glow. As people see this glow they will understand the inward peace and outward possibilities of a life built on the Rock, Jesus Christ.

MY PRAYER NOTES FOR TODAY

____

____

____

____

____

BIBLE READING

❑ Day 139 — Nehemiah 7—9

DAY 140 — GRACE UPON GRACE

Your grace, Holy Father, flows continually and abundantly in my life. I lift my voice in adoration, praise, and thanksgiving because You do not withhold Your presence, promises, or Your provisions from me.

You give me grace to GROW in Your likeness by Your Word and Spirit, and to grow in wisdom, knowledge, and understanding so I can live free and balanced.

You give me grace to GIVE myself to You in prayer and daily communion, in the service of others by the example of Christ, and by expressions of care.

You give me grace to GO forward in my relationship with You so my life will be rich and full, and in my career so I can make a difference in my family, my church, and my world. Thank You for grace upon grace.

MY PRAYER NOTES FOR TODAY

BIBLE READING

❑ **Day 140 — Nehemiah 10—13**

DAY 141 — GRAND PROMISES

Lord, Your promises are full, free, and forever. Today I want to grip Your grand promises and personally apply them to my life.

The grand promise of PRAISE. I honor the promise today of being able to enter into Your presence with praise—for salvation, for the Savior, living within me, and for the fruit of the Holy Spirit.

The grand promise of PROTECTION. I cling to the promise of Your presence in the valley of the shadow of death and know that even a host encamped against me will not be able to harm me That gives me assurance today.

The grand promise of PROVISION. I depend on the promise that You will give me "daily bread" and finances sufficient to sustain my needs, to support Your church, and to "take the gospel into all the world." Thank You for Your generous, grand, and glorious promises.

MY PRAYER NOTES FOR TODAY

____

____

____

____

____

BIBLE READING

❑ **Day 141 — Esther 1—3**

DAY 142 — GREAT BLESSINGS

Loving life-giving Father, You have told me to think about blessings today—true, noble, pure, and lovely things. Every day You open the windows of heaven to bless me. I am thankful and grateful for:

PROVISIONS. You abundantly supply my needs. Day in and day out You give me food, shelter, clothing, affirmation, and opportunities to apply the skills You have invested in me. **I convey my deepest respect and appreciation for Your abundant blessings!**

PROTECTION. Satan, the Enemy of my soul and all that is true, noble, pure, and lovely, seeks to destroy my faith and to lead me astray. You form a wall of protection around me and give me the grace and grit to stand strong. **Thank You for Your abundant blessings!**

POSSIBILITIES. You surround me with possibilities to learn, grow, and experience. Every day I have the opportunity under your guidance to explore heavenly gifts and to relate them to earthly service and spiritual growth. **Thank You for Your abundant blessings!**

MY PRAYER NOTES FOR TODAY

____

____

____

____

____

BIBLE READING

❑ **Day 142 — Esther 4—6**

DAY 143 — GREAT JOY

After the return of Christ to heaven, His followers returned to Jerusalem with "great joy." Today, Father, we have "great joy" for the same reasons they embraced:

We have the PROMISE of the Holy Spirit. Today I want to be led and fed by Your Spirit—led in being obedient and fed by understanding and applying Your Word.

We have the PROMISE of the return of Your Son, Jesus Christ. I want to be ready and steady—ready to meet Christ with open arms and steady in performing His work until He returns.

We have the PROMISE of the abundant life in Christ. I want to shine and serve—shine with the fullness of fellowship with You and serve others to show that Your nature is love. Great joy is mine!

MY PRAYER NOTES FOR TODAY

____

____

____

____

____

BIBLE READING

❑ **Day 143 — Esther 7—10**

DAY 144 — GREAT MERCY

Father, great mercy flows from You. Your grace encircles me in all areas of life. I thank You today that Your grace is not based on my goodness, grit, or gifts. If it were, I would be hopeless and helpless. In loving grace You transformed me and provided (see 1 Peter 1:3-5):

NEW BIRTH. I am not what I used to be. I'm different, transformed in thinking, walking, talking, acting, and setting goals. I am a new creation in an old world. Guide me in reflecting my new birth with new behavior and new avenues of communion with You.

NEW HOPE. I am not boxed in or living behind closed doors. I am free in body, soul, and spirit to live life in Jesus Christ to its fullest. I am thankful, grateful, and appreciative. I have a firm hope for future security and success.

NEW INHERITANCE. In Christ, I have a present inheritance of forgiveness, righteousness, and peace. I also have a future inheritance of heaven, a glorious reunion, and eternal bliss. I relax in Your grace! I will rejoice in Your grace! I will live as an overcomer in Your grace today!

MY PRAYER NOTES FOR TODAY

___

___

___

___

___

BIBLE READING

❑ **Day 144 — Job 1—3**

DAY 145 — GRIPPING POSSIBILITIES

I want to have "open eyes" today, heavenly Father, to see the magnificent possibilities You have set before me.

I want to LOOK UP to You and receive the opportunities You want me to grip today. I want personal growth, spiritual awareness, and assistance in contributions.

I want to WAKE UP to gifts You have placed within me to support Your kingdom cause. I want mental motivation, soul sensitivity, and relationship skills.

I want to STAND UP and stand out to achieve maximum results in living the overcoming Christian life. I want winning witness, results-oriented involvement, and triumphant celebration. I praise You and receive by faith all the possibilities You have set before me today.

MY PRAYER NOTES FOR TODAY

____

____

____

____

____

BIBLE READING

❑ Day 145 — Job 4—6

DAY 146 — GUIDANCE TODAY

Father of light and liberty, I need divine guidance today, like the man in the Bible who said, "Lord, I believe; help my unbelief" (Mark 9:24 NKJV). I proclaim that I believe, but I need your guidance to believe more clearly, persuasively, lovingly, and insightfully.

Guide me today to see Your will for my life more **CLEARLY.** I want to walk the path of perfect harmony and personal fulfillment with You.

Guide me today to live and witness more **PERSUASIVELY** of Your laws and grace.

Guide me today to reflect Your nature more **LOVINGLY** in my relationships with others and in demonstrating Christian care and concern.

Guide me today to live more **INSIGHTFULLY** in building Your kingdom with others respecting their gifts and ministry. Amen.

MY PRAYER NOTES FOR TODAY

____

____

____

____

____

BIBLE READING

❑ **Day 146 — Job 7—9**

DAY 147 – GUIDING PATHS

You are by my side as I walk the paths You have laid out before me. I want to walk these paths briskly with my eyes wide open to see the wonders of Your love. Direct me to walk in harmony with You.

I want to walk the path of PARTNERSHIP with You. You have a plan for my life and I must join You as a partner in fulfilling that plan. **I will seek You to understand my responsibilities as a partner.**

I want to walk the path of PEACE. Your love in my heart generates peace that keeps me happy, shows concerns for the happiness of others, and creates a happy atmosphere. **I will live a life of peace today.**

I want to walk the path of PROSPERITY. You supply all of my needs and for this I am extremely thankful. You want me to prosper with a growing faith, financial gains, and grounded relationships with others. **I will praise You continually for Your unlimited gifts.**

MY PRAYER NOTES FOR TODAY

____

____

____

____

____

BIBLE READING

❑ Day 147 – Job 10–12

DAY 148 — GUIDING POWER

I do not seek power for position or for prestige. I need power to perfect my walk with you and to be spiritually productive. I need power from You to exercise spiritual possibilities—worshiping, working, witnessing, and winning. Mighty Father, I seek You and ask for the:

Power to POSSESS. Like the Israelites, who were instructed "to possess the Promised Land," I want to possess the promises You have extended to me—communion in prayer with You, partnership with my pastor and other believers in kingdom ministry, and personal spiritual gifts of the Holy Spirit.

Power to PROCLAIM. I want to proclaim the provisions of the Gospel of Jesus Christ—pardon from sin, peace of mind, purity of purpose, and the assurance of a heavenly paradise.

Power to PARTNER. To be an effective witness I must partner with the Holy Spirit—His guidance, anointing, and empowerment. I request this partnership and the power that goes with it. I praise You today for power to possess, to proclaim, and to partner.

MY PRAYER NOTES FOR TODAY

____

____

____

____

____

BIBLE READING

❑ **Day 148 — Job 13—15**

DAY 149 — HALLELUJAH TODAY

Father, whatever comes or goes or stays, I will say hallelujah anyway! I will praise You! I will praise You for spiritual opportunities and for strength to overcome obstacles. I will praise You for a solid foundation of faith that empowers me to say:

Hallelujah to HEAVEN. Heaven is a home You have prepared for Your family. I praise You today, Master, for the assurance, the beauty, and the eternal bliss of heaven. **Today I will look up and maintain a clear view of the promise of heaven. Hallelujah!**

Hallelujah to HOLINESS. Father, You are holy in all Your ways. Your love and laws are governed by purity. I want to live a holy life in honor of You, in respect for saving grace, and in order to set high standards of conduct. **Today I will look in and search my soul to stay holy. Hallelujah!**

Hallelujah to HEALTH. My desire is to stay healthy spiritually, focused in faith, devoted in discipline, and steady in service. I also have a desire to stay healthy physically by sleeping, eating, and exercising properly. **Today I will look around and capitalize on opportunities to stay healthy. Hallelujah!**

MY PRAYER NOTES FOR TODAY

____

____

____

____

____

BIBLE READING

❑ **Day 149 — Job 16—18**

DAY 150 — HAPPY LIFE TODAY

I begin today with spiritual health, great expectations, and a vision of Your glory, heavenly Father. Thank You for the glowing opportunities you have set before me. I will walk with steady steps. I will lift my voice in praise to You. I will:

ENJOY Your love. Your love, Father, surpasses all we can think or ask for. I will enjoy Your love. It liberates, activates, and elevates. It provides, protects, and creates. It gives me security and significance. Eternal Master, I will enjoy Your love today!

EXPERIENCE Holy Spirit power. The strength of the Holy Spirit equips me to live a power-driven life. It upholds, controls, and molds. It changes, challenges, and comforts. I will move forward with boldness and assurance today!

EXPRESS Christ in me. Christ in me is the hope of glory (see Col. 1:27). Your work in me, Jesus, gives me purpose, potential, and guiding principles. I will express my admiration and Your anointing through worship, thanksgiving, witness, and service in my life today.

MY PRAYER NOTES FOR TODAY

____

____

____

____

____

BIBLE READING

❑ **Day 150 — Job 19—21**

DAY 151 — HEALING FOR FRIENDS

Your Word tells us "by His wounds we are healed" (Isa. 53:5). This promise includes emotional and physical healing. Today I pray for my friends who need both of these. On the steady structure of Scripture, I offer petitions for them today!

Give physical HEALING. For friends who are sick and suffering, visit them with Your presence that brings comfort and healing. Let them feel Your touch in their spirit and body, a touch that brings relief from pain and dissolves sickness.

Give spiritual HOPE. Your Word gives assurance and victory over mind-twisting problems such as sickness, financial pressure, and family stress. Let hope arise and a vision birthed that generates trust, transformational life patterns, and truth-anchored solutions.

Give personal HAPPINESS. You give peace through Your Son who is the Prince of Peace. Let there be calmness, strength to focus on holy promises, and abiding faith that gives satisfaction and assurance.

MY PRAYER NOTES FOR TODAY

BIBLE READING

❑ **Day 151 — Job 22—24**

DAY 152 — HEALING TODAY

Father of life and energy, hope and healing come from You. All of us need healing in some way. I look to You for a flow of divine healing today.

Provide healing for MEMORIES. Memories of death, divorce, and disaster cause pain and heartache. Give healing and allow me to remember the good, pleasant, and inspiring.

Provide healing for MOTIVATION. I do not want the sickness of fatigue and boredom to stifle my walk with You. Give healing so I can serve with excitement, face challenges with boldness, and find adventure in creating new ways for new days.

Provide healing for MENTAL and physical difficulties. Let the mind of Christ operate in my life with thoughts of health, wholeness, and wellness. Give healing so I can be strong in body, soul, spirit, and conveying my love to You.

MY PRAYER NOTES FOR TODAY

____

____

____

____

____

BIBLE READING

❑ **Day 152 — Job 25—27**

DAY 153 — HEALING RELATIONSHIPS

Lord, I know wholesome, healthy relationships are a plus factor. Sometimes, however, personality traits and unguarded expressions damage relationships. I want to be the one who takes the initiative to bring about healing. I will do this by:

Facing FACTS. Some people have "hot buttons." I must avoid pushing them. I must also accept differences in lifestyles, habits, and routines and focus on strengths and areas of agreement. This builds harmony in relationships and church ministry.

Asking for FORGIVENESS. Father, I make mistakes. Sometimes I offend with words or decisions. When I do, I want to be quick and sincere in asking for forgiveness. I also want to forgive others for unkind deeds. Master, You set the example for forgiveness. I will follow Your pattern.

Moving FORWARD. Every day I have the opportunity to strengthen and make my relationships stronger. I can do this by praying for my friends, affirming their value, encouraging them in developing and utilizing talents, and moving forward in relationships that enrich and advance Your kingdom.

MY PRAYER NOTES FOR TODAY

____

____

____

____

____

BIBLE READING

❑ **Day 153 — Job 28—30**

DAY 154 — HEART CONTENTMENT

Heart joy! Heart happiness! Heart hope! It all means heart contentment! I have it in You, heavenly Father. I am grateful, thankful, and fulfilled. I'm blessed! Today I ask You to work in and through me, empowering and shaping me to always have a:

HAPPY heart. The contents of my heart are reflected in my countenance. My heart is filled with happiness because Your Spirit is working to shape me, to give me security, and a feeling of significance. **I honor You for a happy heart!**

HOLY heart. My heart is pure and holy as a result of Your cleansing power. I speak, display, and advocate the contents of my heart. I am committed to keeping my heart holy so I can abide in Your presence and enjoy abundant life in You. **I praise You for a holy heart!**

HEALTHY heart. Master, I want to keep my heart healthy by proper spiritual eating, exercising, and rest. A healthy heart will give me the strength and endurance to run the Christian race swiftly and steadily and to cross the finish line with honor and dignity. **I worship You for a healthy heart!**

MY PRAYER NOTES FOR TODAY

____

____

____

____

____

BIBLE READING

❑ Day 154 — Job 31—33

DAY 155 — HEART HAPPINESS

Father of grace, goodness, and favor, I have heart happiness today through the redemptive ministry of Your Son, Jesus Christ. I want to openly reveal this happiness by my actions and activities, spiritual growth, and a gleaming personality. My happiness:

Flows from Your GOODNESS. You are good all the time, all the time You are good to me. I'm thankful! In every event of life You plan the best for me. Father, gracious gifts are a part of Your nature. You give, and give, and give. **I have heart happiness as a result of Your goodness.**

Provides for spiritual GROWTH. Life in and with You, Master, is a life of discovery, adventure, and growth. I'm thankful! As I meditate and study your Word, I want to grow in wisdom, righteousness, and understanding. **I have heart happiness as a result of spiritual growth.**

Creates a victorious GLOW. I want Jesus on the inside to show on the outside. I am thankful and I want a glow on my face to show it. I want the glow to be visible, vivacious, and to signify victory. **I have heart happiness as a result of a victorious glow.**

MY PRAYER NOTES FOR TODAY

BIBLE READING

❑ **Day 155 — Job 34—36**

DAY 156 — HEART HARMONY

Lord of love, You steadfastly display Your love in acts of kindness, divine protection, and daily care. All of Your mighty works are in harmony with Your nature and attributes. Today I want my actions to be in harmony with what's in my heart.

Heart harmony in HOLINESS. Father, I want what is in my heart to be reflected in pure deeds, honest actions, and unquestionable expressions. I want the products of my nature to be holy and authentic.

Heart harmony in HABITS. Today, direct me in forming habits that are in line with my commitments to You and to practice what I profess. Holy habits will keep me balanced and growing spiritually.

Heart harmony in HELPFULNESS. Father, release Your love through me in overt acts of helpfulness to those who need assistance and affirmation. I desire to be active and aggressive in both telling about the good news and in touching lives with the message of love, acceptance, and forgiveness.

MY PRAYER NOTES FOR TODAY

BIBLE READING

❑ **Day 156 — Job 37—39**

DAY 157 — HEART TRUST

Faithful Father, I want to be open and honest in my prayer expressions today. Being open and honest requires trust. In the United States we have "In God We Trust" printed on our currency. The actions of our citizens do not always match this slogan. In my life, I want my trust to be a partner with my actions. So, I ask You:

Help my trust to be HOLY. I want my trust to be true, tough, tested, and founded on Your Word. I want my attitude and actions to point to Your purity and holiness, and to reflect an open heart commitment.

Help my trust to be HONORABLE. I want my friends and foes to be able to say that I am honorable, trustworthy, and that I keep my word.

Help my trust to be HEALTHY. I want to grow daily in wisdom, knowledge, and understanding. This will aid me in making the right decisions, eliminating the wrong decisions, and maintaining accountability for my decisions. I want to wear the label of a honest and trustworthy disciple of Jesus Christ.

MY PRAYER NOTES FOR TODAY

____

____

____

____

____

BIBLE READING

❑ **Day 157 — Job 40—42**

DAY 158 — HEAVEN ON MY MIND

Father of love, light, and liberty, I lift my voice in praise for the promise of an everlasting life with You in heaven. You walk and talk with me every day on earth. In heaven, I will be in Your presence and sing songs of redemption with the saints of all ages. Thank You for the assurance of:

Blessed HOPE. Master, my hope of heaven has been blessed by You with an irrevocable, solid-rock guarantee. I praise You for a deed to a home in heaven and a protection policy against the damaging work of the devil.

Eternal HEALTH. On earth I live under the curse of disobedience by Adam and Eve. This curse incurs sickness, weakness, and frailty. In heaven there will be total deliverance, perfect health, perfect wholeness, and perfect mobility. Accept my praise and thanksgiving!

Family HAPPINESS. Heaven is a home where all your children will be a member of Your happy family, restored to Your likeness, abiding in Your presence, and enjoying the eternal pleasures of Your provisions.

MY PRAYER NOTES FOR TODAY

____

____

____

____

____

BIBLE READING

❑ **Day 158 — Psalms 1—9**

DAY 159 — HELP ME BE A MENTOR

Thank You, Father, for the mentoring work of the Holy Spirit. I feel divine leadership and development. I feel support from the many mature believers who surround me with encouragement and enrichment. I want to be a helper and a mentor also. Guide me in:

MODELING Christian character in my relationships at home, work, and church. I realize I cannot influence others with the fruits of being a Christian if I do not exhibit the fruit in my daily lifestyle.

MINISTERING with vision and dedication in Christian work that really makes a difference. I want to serve in both the church and the community, helping to heal the wounded and establishing hope.

MOTIVATING individuals to a higher level of fellowship with You and with others. I want to show the power of believing and building a life of great expectations and grace adventure. Mentor me so I can mentor others.

MY PRAYER NOTES FOR TODAY

BIBLE READING

❑ **Day 159 — Psalms 10—17**

DAY 160 — HELP ME BE DISCIPLINED

Mighty Father, I want my life to reflect disciplined behavior, commitment, control, and action that is Christ-centered. I cannot do this without your oversight and enabling. Therefore, I turn to You! I trust You! I need Your touch!

I **TURN** to You for grace, guidance, and spiritual gifts. I want to keep my eyes on You and my mind open to receive direction.

I **TRUST** You because Your Word is steadfast and true, tested and proven. You are always near. I will trust You for my needs and for directions to be Your witness.

I need Your **TOUCH** for cleansing and for power to be productive as a Christian and as a citizen. Your touch will give me a holy glow and a flow of energy to be a disciplined and devoted disciple. Thank you!

MY PRAYER NOTES FOR TODAY

____

____

____

____

____

BIBLE READING

❑ **Day 160 — Psalms 18—22**

DAY 161 — HOLDING STEADY

Lord of strength, I want to be steady in my relationship with You today. There will be distraction! Satan will try to divert my attention and dilute my testimony. I need Your strength! I need Your oversight! I need stabilizing faith to be:

COURAGEOUS in conflict. The forces of evil will create conflict and tension, weakening relationships and blocking progress. My goal is to exalt Christ and to generate peace. Father, give me the courage to be a mediator and show your scriptural plan for walking together in love. **Guide me to be steady in conflict.**

COMPLETE in devotion. In Christ, I am a new person. I want to act like a new person by being complete in my devotion. This includes Bible reading, a consistent prayer life, involvement in worship, and financial faithfulness. **Let Your Spirit surround me to be steady in devotion.**

COMMITTED to service. My neighbors see that I am committed to You by my service to You in assisting the needy, caring for the distraught, supporting care ministries, and relating to others in love. **Empower me to honor You by being steady in service.**

MY PRAYER NOTES FOR TODAY

____

____

____

____

____

BIBLE READING

❑ **Day 161 — Psalms 23—31**

DAY 162 — HOLY GUIDANCE

There are many paths I can take today. Some will have dangerous pitfalls; others will beckon me with unsurpassed potential and spiritual prosperity. Give me holy guidance to take the right path and to keep in step with Your will. Give me guidance for:

GODLY demonstration. I want to demonstrate love, acceptance, and forgiveness in my actions and thoughts to best represent You and reflect Your nature. As I demonstrate godly virtues, people will see Christ in me and will show forth true life and love in You.

GRACE application. I want to apply Your unmerited, undeserved, unlimited, and unstoppable love and grace in my relationships and thoughts. This is how I can effectively convey the good news and share it with others. As I apply grace to my work and walk, people will see the true essence of Christianity.

GIFTS utilization. I want to utilize joy, patience, understanding, and goodness in my habits and lifestyle to convincingly impact the lives of friends and associates. As I utilize my gifts, I will strengthen my influence and extend the influence of my church.

MY PRAYER NOTES FOR TODAY

____

____

____

____

____

BIBLE READING

❑ **Day 162 — Psalms 32—37**

DAY 163 — HOLY LEADERSHIP

Faithful Father, I am in need of Your divine guidance today.

Guide me in staying close to You in thought, practice, and witness.

Guide me in learning from, encouraging, assisting, and upholding others.

Guide me in dreaming and visualizing Your unlimited power and resources, and connecting to them honestly and thankfully.

Guide me in expressing my deep feelings of love, my desire to please You, and my determination to run the Christian race with boldness.

Guide me today in understanding how to minister to the lost, hurting, and lonely, and to give comfort, hope, and cheer.

A thousand thank-Yous!

MY PRAYER NOTES FOR TODAY

BIBLE READING

❑ **Day 163 — Psalms 38—44**

DAY 164 — HOLY SPIRIT LEADERSHIP

Father, You have instructed me that the Holy Spirit will lead me in all truth about You, Your Word, and the way of righteousness. I am responding to the leadership of the Spirit today. I'm leadable:

Lead me to LOVE. I need guidance to love the lovable and the unlovable. Lead me in accepting those who are different in culture or creed. Lead me to demonstrate love to my family, friends, and faith partners. **I'm open to instructions on love!**

Lead me to LABOR. I want to work in the church and in the harvest field surrounding the church. However, I need to be led, motivated, and empowered. Your Holy Spirit can do this. **I'm ready to be taught lessons on labor!**

Lead me to LEAD. I want to be a submissive follower and an effective leader. I want to lead by example, by accepting positions of leadership, and by maintaining unquestionable integrity. **I'm dependent on divine power to lead!**

MY PRAYER NOTES FOR TODAY

____

____

____

____

____

BIBLE READING

❑ **Day 164 — Psalms 45—51**

DAY 165 — HOLY STRENGTH

I need strength today that only You can give, Holy Father. Yes, I need physical strength, but more importantly, I need spiritual strength to shine and to serve. Let me receive strength from:

Holy SCRIPTURES. Your Word is filled with promises of supernatural power, glowing grace, and rare gifts. I believe the Bible is God's Word and that its contents can be counted on in every area of my life.

Holy SPIRIT. You have outlined that the Holy Spirit is our guide. He will lead us in knowing the truth and in living the truth by His undergirding, unlimited strength.

Holy SERVICE. As I obey You and serve the church and those around me, You will bless me with performance-power and sustaining strength. I will stand on this fact. I know that You will always fulfill Your promises.

MY PRAYER NOTES FOR TODAY

____

____

____

____

____

BIBLE READING

❑ **Day 165 — Psalms 52—59**

DAY 166 — HONOR GOD

Father God, I want to honor You today. How can I, a chunk of clay bound by fading flesh, honor You and bring attention to Your immeasurable grace? In a feeble way, let me express myself:

By living a HOLY life. I understand that holy means pure. A life with purpose entails discipline and conduct restrictions. I want to walk hand-in-hand with Your Word that provides grace and guidelines for focusing on Your exalted nature.

By living a HELPING life. I do not want to be selfish and self-centered in my pursuits and practices. I want to help others, sharing to meet needs and to find new life in Christ.

By living a HEALTHY life. I can stay healthy physically by eating properly and exercising. I stay healthy spiritually by daily prayer, Bible reading, and letting my light shine. Both of these honor You and speak of a convincing lifestyle dedicated to Jesus Christ.

MY PRAYER NOTES FOR TODAY

____

____

____

____

____

BIBLE READING

❑ **Day 166 — Psalms 60—67**

DAY 167 — HOLY HAPPINESS

The framework of happiness is commitment to a great cause. With commitment comes contentment through the manifestation of Christ in me, participation in the mission of the church, and the fulfillment of my career responsibilities. I will emulate happiness by:

Motivating CONVERSATIONS—uplifting, edifying, and stimulating. Father, in my conversations today I want my words to be warm, loaded with value, and to create a desire to excel. My witness for Christ is elevated when I radiate happiness.

Maximizing my CAREER—relating, learning, and advancing. I want to show that I enjoy what I do and work at developing my skills, enabling me to establish relationships based on integrity and trust that position me to have a witness in the marketplace.

Moving forward in CHRIST—learning, receiving, and giving. As I grow in grace my happiness intensifies, increasing my influence. As my influence increases, my opportunities for service increase. I will relate with respect, impress with convictions, and advance the cause of Christ with authority.

MY PRAYER NOTES FOR TODAY

____

____

____

____

____

BIBLE READING

❑ **Day 167 — Psalms 68—71**

DAY 168 — I AM THANKFUL

My heart is filled with thanksgiving. Holy Father, I am so thankful that I know Your Son, Jesus Christ, belong to Your Church, and enjoy enriching relationships with other believers. I have so much to praise You for and to express my thanksgiving.

I am thankful for SALVATION provided through Your love and manifested through the sacrificial death of Jesus Christ. I am saved from the bondage of sin and freed to live an abundant and victorious life. **I raise my voice in thanksgiving!**

I am thankful for SIGNIFICANCE and transformed into a new creation through the price paid by Jesus Christ. Glorious Father, I feel valuable in Your sight. You have endowed me with gifts to make a difference in the lives of my family and friends. **I raise my hands in thanksgiving!**

I am thankful for the opportunity to SERVE equipped by the power of the Holy Spirit. I want to share good news today about life in Christ. I want to serve in my church as a model of commitment. I want to assist others to express the love of Christ. **I raise the banner to serve in thanksgiving!**

MY PRAYER NOTES FOR TODAY

____

____

____

____

____

BIBLE READING

❑ **Day 168 — Psalms 72—77**

DAY 169 — I AM WILLING

Father, You have given me a free will to change, to conqueror, and to chart a course of action for ministry. The impact of my choices will be determined by my willingness to know and to do Your will. Therefore, today:

I am willing to let go of any desire, pursuit, or commitment that would strain my relationship with You. I will let go of any person, doctrinal position, or power strategy that would limit my spiritual growth or ministry effectiveness.

I am willing to give in, to give my support to people or programs that have Your approval and that will advance Your cause. I will not be stubborn or selfish.

I am willing to go out as Your Word directs, to invite people in to have fellowship with You, with Your people, and to become a member of Your family. I'm willing today to follow Your leadership and to grow in grace, love and peace.

MY PRAYER NOTES FOR TODAY

____

____

____

____

____

BIBLE READING

❑ **Day 169 — Psalms 78—81**

DAY 170 — I BELIEVE!

I believe that today is full and running over with possibilities and opportunities.

POSSIBILITIES to discover new paths of productivity, new procedures to be more effective, and new patterns to express praise and thanksgiving.

OPPORTUNITIES to develop new skills, new insights to live bolder and higher, and new principles to express compassion and congratulations.

I believe that tomorrow is packed and brimming with sights and privileges.

SIGHTS that create fresh respect for hard work; sights that inspire fresh creativity; and sights that stimulate fresh desire and drive to attempt staggering feats.

PRIVILEGES to be a dynamic person of honor and integrity to systematically display grace and to honor God in dynamic worship and in sharing the joys of walking with Jesus.

MY PRAYER NOTES FOR TODAY

____

____

____

____

____

BIBLE READING

❑ **Day 170 — Psalms 82—89**

DAY 171 — I DECLARE!

Father of dazzling plans, You want every day of my life to be filled with action that edifies, uplifts, and challenges me to experience a life of sublime success. I realize I must do my part and be ready to receive from You. Therefore, today:

I declare strengthening PEACE. You give peace that strengthens and supports during trying times, conflict, and the attacks of the Enemy. Today I will have security, grow spiritually, and stand in Your peace.

I declare spiritual PROSPERITY. You want me to prosper spiritually because this will result in fruitfulness in all areas of my life—family, finances, and friends. Today I will embrace Your plan for prosperity and share with others how to experience it.

I declare soul and mind PURITY. You offer power to remain pure in my heart, mind, and actions. Today I will dream big, demonstrate the qualities of a champion, and declare my allegiance to Your Son, Jesus Christ, and the advancement of Your kingdom.

MY PRAYER NOTES FOR TODAY

BIBLE READING

❑ **Day 171 — Psalms 90—97**

DAY 172 — I PRAISE YOU!

Faithful Father, You are always faithful in Your promises and provisions to me. I am so thankful and I want to be faithful in praising You and exalting Your life-giving name. Every day I want my praise to be pure, powerful, and consistent.

I want to praise You PERSONALLY. I want to praise You in worship services at church. I also want to praise you personally as a lifestyle—meditation, expression, and intercession. I want praise to be on my lips at all times.

I want to praise You in PUBLIC. I want my life in public to reflect a spirit of praise—thanksgiving, joyfulness, and connection with You, wonderful Father. I want praise to be visible in my life at all times.

I want to praise You in my PERFORMANCE. I want my work to be marked by excellence—consistency, efficiency, and dependability. Father, You are excellent in all Your ways and I want to follow Your pattern. I want praise to be witnessed in my life at all times.

MY PRAYER NOTES FOR TODAY

____

____

____

____

____

BIBLE READING

❑ **Day 172 — Psalms 98—104**

DAY 173 — I RAISE MY HANDS TODAY!

Faithful Father, You are worthy of all praise and honor. Your hands symbolize mercy, healing, and daily protection. My hands represent commitment, worship, and Christlike witnessing. Today I raise my hands to You:

In life SURRENDER. I Surrender all! I surrender my will for Your will. I surrender my goals for Your kingdom goals. **I ask You for faith and fortitude to keep my hands raised in total yieldedness to You.**

In worshipful SINGING. I sing because I'm happy. I'm happy because I have been freed from bondage and sinful guilt. I sing songs of thanksgiving, of love, and of peace. **I ask You for oversight to keep my hands raised with a pure heart so I can sing vibrantly and sincerely.**

In consistent SERVICE. I serve to model the example of Christ. Jesus, Your Son, came into a wayward world to serve, not to be served. He taught, encouraged, and gave sustaining hope. **I ask You for insight and inspiration to keep my hands raised to serve You, my church, and the unchurched with a loving heart and pure motives.**

MY PRAYER NOTES FOR TODAY

____

____

____

____

____

BIBLE READING

❑ **Day 173 – Psalms 105–110**

DAY 174 — I RECEIVE TODAY!

I don't want to appear selfish, giving Father, but I receive today the things You want to give to me. I receive them with thankful hands, a rejoicing heart, a concerned mind, and a growing sense of awe.

I will receive Your GRACE. Your grace represents Your undeserved and unrestricted attention to the many needs of my life—salvation, security, and satisfying success. Whatever conditions surface, Your grace is there to delight, defend, or develop.

I will receive Your spiritual GIFTS. Your gifts represent Your plan for fulfilling ministry in the local church—serving, sharing, and supporting my pastor. Whatever skills you have invested in me I will maximize their use to honor You and expand Your kingdom.

I will receive Your GREATNESS. Your greatness represents Your unlimited power to overcome every obstacle, fulfill every dream, and defeat every enemy. Whatever the challenge in my Christian walk or my career, Your miracle working power will enable me to be in control, to stay committed, and to be a Christ-exalting conqueror.

MY PRAYER NOTES FOR TODAY

BIBLE READING

❑ **Day 174 — Psalms 111—118**

DAY 175 — I WILL BE OPTIMISTIC

Today, I will be optimistic because I know You have a plan for my life, a beautiful plan that will stretch my imagination, stir my spirit of expectancy, and solidify my faith to believe and receive.

Today, I will look for and seize the opportunities You set before me. I will endeavor to relate to others with confidence, advance personal skills, perform with excellence, and make a difference in the lives of friends and neighbors.

Today, I will be obedient to Your call and promises. Father, guide me in becoming a mature disciple and a convincing witness, and in supporting the ministries of my local church.

Today, I will be optimistic. I will seize opportunities, practice obedience, and honor You with my lifestyle and devotion.

MY PRAYER NOTES FOR TODAY

____

____

____

____

____

BIBLE READING

❑ **Day 175 — Psalms 119**

DAY 176 — I WILL DECLARE

Within my own strength, Holy Father, I cannot declare anything or achieve anything. But, in You, by the power of the Holy Spirit, I can declare my dedication, determination, and discipleship intentions. Today, that is what I want to do.

I will declare my DEDICATION to Jehovah God. Lord, You are my life, my hope, and my future. Without You I am absolutely nothing. I want You to know I am totally dedicated to worshiping You, reading Your Word, and witnessing about Your loving grace.

I will declare my DETERMINATION to live righteously. By Your guidance I will walk, talk, relate, and model Your love righteously. I am determined to stand tall in embracing the truth of Your Word.

I will declare my DISCIPLESHIP intensions. I understand a dedicated, determined disciple must practice consistent stewardship of time, tithes, and sharing truth. By Your infusion of zeal and strength, I will display all three of these characteristics in my daily lifestyle.

MY PRAYER NOTES FOR TODAY

____

____

____

____

____

BIBLE READING

❑ **Day 176 — Psalms 120—127**

DAY 177 — I WILL RELEASE FAITH

Father, I need Your guidance on releasing faith and receiving blessings. "According to your faith will it be done to you" (Matt. 9:29).

Let me release faith to overcome SELFISHNESS. I want to relate to family and friends with genuine interest, care, and understanding. I want to reflect unconditional and unselfish love, compassion, and care.

Let me release faith to confront SUFFERING. Suffering comes in many forms and degrees—sickness, grief, conflict, and unfulfilled dreams. In all things, I know You give grace to be victorious, to be a champion.

Let me release faith to SERVE. I want to make a difference in the effectiveness of my church by supporting my pastor, discovering and developing spiritual gifts, and participating in projects that extend the influence and impact of my church.

MY PRAYER NOTES FOR TODAY

____

____

____

____

____

BIBLE READING

❑ **Day 177 – Psalms 128–136**

DAY 178 — I WILL SOAK IN SONSHINE

Jesus Christ is the Sonshine that warms, empowers, and enables me to radiate authentic love.

Today I will walk in Sonshine. Great opportunities and exciting challenges are before me—new scenery, new experiences, and new relationships.

Today I will bask in Sonshine. Father, I will use my God-given gifts to be productive in work duties, fulfilling assignments and learning new methods for maximum achievement.

Today I will work in Sonshine. Whatever I do, I want the qualities of Christlikeness to be released through me to impact, enlighten, and encourage.

Today I will reflect Sonshine.

MY PRAYER NOTES FOR TODAY

BIBLE READING

❑ **Day 178 — Psalms 137—142**

DAY 179 — I WILL WORSHIP

Everyday is an opportunity to worship You, Father, because You are worthy of:

Love, devotion, and praise;
Honor, respect, and commitment;
Thanksgiving, tribute, and treasures.

I will therefore:
Lift up my eyes in recognition of Your majesty;
Lift up my hands in spiritual surrender and visible praise;
Lift up my voice in songs of admiration and words of deep devotion.

Today I will worship with a spirit of wonder and expectation!

MY PRAYER NOTES FOR TODAY

____

____

____

____

____

BIBLE READING

❑ **Day 179 – Psalms 143–150**

DAY 180 — I'M BLESSED!

I woke up this morning with the sun shining and a spirit of expectation. **I'm blessed!**

I looked at myself in the mirror and thought about "Christ in me, the hope of glory." **I'm blessed!**

I reflected on my home life—a wonderful companion and talented children. **I'm blessed!**

I will be honored to go to work today to use my God-endowed skills and to be compensated with a salary and a feeling of significance. **I'm blessed!**

I will have the glorious privilege in many ways to meditate on God's Word, feel His presence, and share His love. **I'm blessed!**

I am a person made in the image of God and today He will walk with me and talk with me and tell me that I belong to Him. **I'm blessed!**

MY PRAYER NOTES FOR TODAY

____

____

____

____

____

BIBLE READING

❑ **Day 180 — Proverbs 1—3**

DAY 181 — IMMENSE GENEROSITY

Father, Your nature shows loving kindness and immense generosity. You give abundantly and richly! You bless with grace and beauty! You guide with care and compassion! You challenge with clarity and rewards. In my daily life, I want to represent You with these same characteristics.

Touch me to be GODLY. Open my life to the marvelous in-filling of Your nature and the infusion of abilities to work righteousness. I will depend on Your provisions and protection to represent You scripturally with honor and integrity.

Touch me to be a GIVER. Share Your love with my family, friends, and associates. You freely give salvation, hope, peace, and significance. I will depend on Your grace and glory to follow Your example by giving financially, in friendship, and in service.

Touch me to be GRACIOUS. I will display a gentle, kind, understanding, and supportive spirit. The unchurched are looking for these virtues in believers. I will depend on Your tenderness and kindness to empower me to influence my surroundings and to make a difference in the thinking and actions of others.

MY PRAYER NOTES FOR TODAY

BIBLE READING

❑ **Day 181 — Proverbs 4—6**

DAY 182 — MAKING AN IMPACT

A day filled with breathtaking adventure and unlimited opportunities in my career is before me. I have the opportunity to make an impact in the lives of others at home, work, and church.

I want to impact my family through **CHARACTER** and **CONDUCT.** Teach me so that my conduct is in total harmony with my character. **I want to be a model of Christlikeness.**

I want to impact the people I work with through **COURTESY** and **CONVICTIONS.** Teach me today to be kind, considerate, and to show a thankful spirit. Let me live my convictions about serving You and living a holy life. **I want to demonstrate in words and deeds the love of Christ.**

I want to impact the church I attend through **COMMITMENT** and **COURAGE**. Teach me to be active, visionary, and accountable. **I want to be a cheerful giver and a dependable worker.**

MY PRAYER NOTES FOR TODAY

BIBLE READING

❑ **Day 182 — Proverbs 7—9**

DAY 183 — IMPACTING FAVOR

Lord of unlimited blessings, I want to live in Your favor today. I want to please You with my commitment, conduct, and conversation. I want to be pleasing in my influence and interaction with others. Guide me in having:

Favor in PRAYER. Power for a victorious life is anchored in prayer. I want my prayer life to be open to Your instructions and holy inspiration. I ask for Your favor to expand my faith, experience enriching fellowship, and achieve spiritual fulfillment.

Favor with PEOPLE. Friends, church members, and work associates offer opportunities to join hands and combine talents, to experience character development, and to explore ways to learn and grow together. I ask for Your favor to have impactful interactions with others.

Favor with my PASTOR. I want to be a trustworthy partner with my pastor in ministry. He or she is Your representative and deserves honor and respect. I ask for Your favor in being dependable, productive, and delightful in service with my pastor.

MY PRAYER NOTES FOR TODAY

____

____

____

____

____

BIBLE READING

❑ **Day 183 — Proverbs 10—12**

DAY 184 — IN PRAYER TODAY

I am truly thankful for the gift of communication with You, Father. I am never alone! You are always near to hear my voice and my supplications. I will honor this gift and will not abuse it or misuse it. In prayer today, I will:

TOUCH Your throne. Through Christ, my Intercessor who sits by Your side, Father I will touch Your throne. From Your throne flows abundant grace, Holy Spirit anointing, and answers to my prayers. You rule in righteousness and oversee the affairs of Your children with tenderness and stabilizing truth.

TRACE Your blessings. Master, as I talk with You today, I will recall and review the magnificent ways You have blessed me. You have given me sound health, affirming hope, and undiluted happiness. I ask You today to receive my gratefulness and thanksgiving.

TALK About Challenges. I have both positive and negative challenges. Give me guidance in accepting the positive challenges and grit in facing the negative challenges. I will place my faith in You and move forward in praise and spiritual growth.

MY PRAYER NOTES FOR TODAY

____

____

____

____

____

BIBLE READING

❑ **Day 184 — Proverbs 13—15**

DAY 185 — IN THE WINNER'S CIRCLE

Being a winner in Christ is wonderful, inspiring, nurturing, ennobling, enriching, and refreshing. What a way to begin each day! I am grateful! I am thankful! I am awestruck! I am a winner because of:

WORTH. You have made me worthy by instilling Your Spirit in me. You have transformed me into the likeness of Your Son, Jesus Christ, so I can walk in newness of life exhibiting the holy characteristics of purity, devotion, and creative power. **I'm a winner!**

WORK. You have made me valuable and invested power in me to work and to be productive. Thank You for the privilege to work to earn a living, to work in the church, and to obey Your design for mankind. Today I want to apply myself in work, to be fruitful and personally fulfilled. **I'm a winner!**

WORSHIP. You have made me valuable, instilling in me the ability to walk with You in grace and to worship You in honor and with a wholehearted commitment. I draw strength from You through worship which gives me security and significance. **I'm a winner!**

MY PRAYER NOTES FOR TODAY

BIBLE READING

❑ **Day 185 — Proverbs 16—18**

DAY 186 — IN TUNE TODAY

Father of sight and sound, I want to be in tune with You today, singing from the same page and in the proper key. I can do this through worship, reading Your Word, and prayer. I begin today with prayer.

I want to know the meaning of the TUNE. What does closeness to You mean? How can I join in what You are doing? How can I train myself to be in harmony with You? Give me answers today.

I want to stay in TUNE. I don't want to be distracted today by busy work or faith fatigue. I want to open my mouth and sing praises and choruses of thanksgiving.

I want to share the TUNE. Sharing begins with a happy attitude and a congenial spirit. Let me share Your warm love, kind words, friendliness, helpful disposition, and encouraging insights. According to Your Word, "let me sing a new song today" (Ps. 144:9).

MY PRAYER NOTES FOR TODAY

____

____

____

____

____

BIBLE READING

❑ **Day 186 — Proverbs 19—21**

DAY 187 — INCREASE MY FAITH

Today, vision-inspiring Father, I want my faith to increase, to feel closer to You, and to see more of Your majesty. I want to do my part by reading Your Word, a consistent prayer life, and reviewing past experiences of Your grace and glory. I ask You to inspire me with an empowerment of faith:

For FULFILLMENT. I realize, Holy Father, that I cannot fulfill Your ideal will for my life without a growing, glowing faith. I want to hear, read, and practice Your Word so my faith will be strong, vibrant, and contagious.

To FIGHT. I want to engage in the good fight of faith and to advance the cause of Jesus Christ. Fortify my faith so I can stand against the attacks of Satan and lead assaults against his strongholds.

To combat FRICTION. Satan wants to cause friction in the church to divide the body and destroy trust. Let my faith bring church members together in affirming each other and in focusing on the mission of the church. Let my faith show forth in understanding, reasoning, and in coming together.

MY PRAYER NOTES FOR TODAY

BIBLE READING

❑ **Day 187 — Proverbs 22—24**

DAY 188 — INCREASING MY VALUE

Master of mercy, You have made me valuable through Your redeeming grace. I belong to You. I am a member of Your family and I am a part of Your church—the bride of Christ! I want to increase my value today in three specific ways:

By SEEKING Your will, guidance, and empowerment. My value increases as I know Your will, follow Your leadership, and utilize Your power. I bow before You in obedience, seeking Your touch to transform my attitude, actions, and activities.

By SPEAKING words of kindness, goodwill, and hope. My value increases as I share Your love, Your promises, and Your willingness to forgive and set free. I will speak in Your name words that uplift, motivate, and point to Jesus as Savior and Lord.

By SERVING in my church, city, and neighborhood. My value increases as I demonstrate Christian character by establishing relationships with the unchurched, participating in community projects, and assisting those in need. I will serve to show the caring nature of Christ.

MY PRAYER NOTES FOR TODAY

____

____

____

____

____

BIBLE READING

❑ **Day 188 — Proverbs 25—27**

DAY 189 — INFLUENCING MY WORLD

As a believer I am to be a light in a world of darkness! Father, You are my power source to generate liberating and contagious love. In my walk and talk I purpose to influence my surroundings as I receive affirmation and anointing from You through:

SHINING hospitality. Jesus on the inside will shine on the outside, visible in my pleasing disposition, pleasant smile, and purity of purpose. I desire to win friends and influence people with my life as a committed, compassionate, and caring follower of Jesus Christ through love, laughter, and cheerfulness.

SHARING dreams. Father, inspire me to paint a picture of tomorrow with my life by sharing hope, showing God's plans, and sharing ways to dream and achieve. Today I will be upbeat, inspiring, and demonstrate leadership.

SHOWING innovation. I am thankful for the creative spirit You have birthed in me. Each day offers new ways to accommodate, achieve, and advance. Each day promises adventure and holy excitement. You have changed my life totally and completely, and I want to influence my surroundings today!

MY PRAYER NOTES FOR TODAY

____

____

____

____

____

BIBLE READING

❑ **Day 189 — Proverbs 28—31**

DAY 190 — INSPIRATIONAL THOUGHTS

Mighty Master, fill my mind with thoughts that honor You and undergird Your mercy, majesty, and manifold blessings. Inspirational thoughts from You will keep me on the track of truth and steadfastness. I ask you to give me:

GODLY thoughts. Father, without Your intervention, my thoughts will be self-centered, selfish, and short-lived. Satan desires to sabotage positive, inspirational thoughts. Encircle, enrich, and empower my thoughts to focus on the nature of Christ—goodness, mercy, peace, and prosperity.

CREATIVE thoughts. I don't want to get into a rut of sameness. I don't want to be bound by unproductive patterns. Make my thoughts creative, filled with newness, color, and challenge. I will seek the mind of Christ and observe His methods of creative action.

CHURCH vision thoughts. Satan and his forces cannot stand against the conquering forces of the Church. Fill my mind with visions that see the Church structure sanctified, church personnel dedicated, and church members unified in fulfilling the Great Commission.

MY PRAYER NOTES FOR TODAY

BIBLE READING

❑ **Day 190 — Ecclesiastes 1—3**

DAY 191 — INTENSE APPRECIATION

Heavenly Father, when I think about intense love, I think about Your unconditional love, sacrificial, and unlimited love. I want to express my appreciation to You for salvation, security, and significance. My heart overflows with joy today and I want to convey appreciation for:

Expressions of LOVE. I am surrounded by Your love, Father, and the giving, supporting, and understanding love of my family and friends. I express intense appreciation for the expressions of love that enrich my life.

Adventures of LIFE. Father, my life is not dull or boring. You have set before me paths of adventure—exploring, discovering, and experiencing. I express intense appreciation for the adventures of life that generate daily excitement.

Opportunities to LEARN. Daily I have the privilege to gain insights from the Bible and communion with You. I want to be open to new ideas, concepts, and ways to be more effective in worship, witness, and work. I express intense appreciation for opportunities to learn and develop abilities and skills.

MY PRAYER NOTES FOR TODAY

____

____

____

____

____

BIBLE READING

❑ **Day 191 — Ecclesiastes 4–6**

DAY 192 — INTENSE WORSHIP

Lord, You are worthy of praise, glory, and honor. I am strengthened through worship at church. I am uplifted and molded through worship in my quiet time and daily communion with You. I want my worship to embody:

Forceful PRAISE that is powerful and energetic. I release my praise today with thankful words, creative thoughts, and soulful meditation. I praise You for Your worth in making my life valuable, significant, and successful.

Factual PETITIONS that are pure and honest. I offer up petitions today from my head and heart that are pointed and loving. I petition You for the health of my family, the success of my friends, and the unity of my church. I petition You for these things from the prospective of Your worth.

Focus on PARTNERSHIP that is personal and active. I pledge partnership in fulfilling Your will in kingdom ministry and in living victoriously. I will minister with partnership in focus, at all times drawing from Your divine energy, unlimited grace, and productive guidance.

MY PRAYER NOTES FOR TODAY

____

____

____

____

____

BIBLE READING

❑ Day 192 — Ecclesiastes 7—9

DAY 193 — IRRESISTIBLE INFLUENCE

Liberating Father, the world has been influenced by the birth, death, and resurrection of Jesus Christ, Your Son. He established a moral code for humankind, dismantled bondage, and created confidence to live an abundant life. I want to be an influencer that is:

ENABLED by truth. Your truth, Father, sets free, enables, and empowers me to influence my family, friends, and associates. They are able to see Christ in me and how He transforms and turns bad into good, darkness into light, and weakness into strength. **I thank You!**

ENCOURAGED by truth. Your truth serves as a solid platform for life. It shows me the way to avoid conflict and accept Your resources to influence the unchurched, the seeking, and the perplexed. **I honor You!**

ENGAGED in sharing truth. I want to be a sharer of hope, contentment, and happiness to inspire others to advance in trust and holy living. I cherish truth and will guard it and share it. **I praise You!**

MY PRAYER NOTES FOR TODAY

____

____

____

____

____

BIBLE READING

❑ Day 193 — Ecclesiastes 10—12

DAY 194 — JESUS ON THE INSIDE

My life has been cleansed and changed, Holy Father, through the indwelling of Your Son, Jesus Christ. He is on the inside and He works on the outside through my character, convictions, and commitments. Today I want Jesus to be revealed in my life:

Through a spirit of WORSHIPING. I want to worship You with a prayer on my lips, a song in my heart, and an attitude of thanksgiving. I want expressions of praise to flow freely at all times!

Through a spirit of WINNING. You have given me overcoming power! I want to stand straight and tall and display a winning disposition at church, home, and work!

Through a spirit of WITNESSING. I want to convey my love for Jesus Christ by the values I embrace and in verbal testimony. Keep my approach warm, prudent, and polite. Today I accept Your provisions to be spiritually productive!

MY PRAYER NOTES FOR TODAY

BIBLE READING

❑ **Day 194 — Song of Solomon 1—3**

DAY 195 — JOY TODAY

I am joyful today, cleansing Father, because I have been liberated from the suffocating stranglehold of the Evil One, Satan. I now breathe new life, energizing life, God-anchored life! Joy in Jesus is full, flowing, and foundational. I am thankful for:

JUSTIFICATION joy. Selfish acts. Sin. Stubborn spirit. Through the blood of Your Son I have been forgiven, cleansed, pronounced innocent. I'm free from condemnation, imprisonment. This gives me pulsating, life-directing joy. **I'm thankful!**

JUBILATION joy. Every day, overcoming Master, I face life with excitement and great expectations. I sing. I shout. I celebrate. I have a jubilant spirit because of Your love for me. I'm joyful! **I'm thankful!**

JOINT-HEIR joy. In Your kingdom I am a joint heir with Your Son, Jesus. Jesus joy! We walk together. We enjoy kingdom riches together. It's a wonderful daily experience of relating, discovering, sharing, and becoming. I will bask in Your goodness today. **I'm thankful!**

MY PRAYER NOTES FOR TODAY

____

____

____

____

____

BIBLE READING

❑ **Day 195 — Song of Solomon 4–6**

DAY 196 — KNOW MY HEART

I want my thoughts, relationships, and actions to be aligned with Your holy will, heavenly Father. Therefore, I need Your searching and evaluation so my life can be power-packed and productive. I ask You today to:

Search the flow of my SPIRIT. I want to be pure and pleasing in my thinking, attitude, and behavior. I want my spirit to convey these goals so others can see that I am real and authentic.

Search the direction of my STEPS. Am I on the right path? Am I following You close enough to fulfill Your will for my life? Steady my steps. Quicken them if I am falling behind. Let them lead me, by Your Spirit, to higher ground and higher experiences with You.

Search the level of my SERVICE. Can others see Christ in me by the way I serve those who need to be encouraged, lifted up, and delivered from bondage? Reveal weakness and inconsistencies so I can make adjustments. Thank You for the privilege of asking You for assistance.

MY PRAYER NOTES FOR TODAY

____

____

____

____

____

BIBLE READING

❑ **Day 196 — Song of Solomon 7—8**

DAY 197 — LAUGHTER TODAY

Father of life and laughter, You supply all my needs. I need food, water, and sleep—You meet these needs! I need happiness, joy, and laughter—You meet these needs! Today I will face life with a smile showing the Christian life is filled with laughter that springs from Your love and liberty.

Laughter REVEALS security. Salvation in Christ gives me security. I am not afraid of being intimidated or isolated. I can laugh during trying experiences. I have a merry heart from You that gives a bright countenance.

Laughter RELEASES energy. Laughter generates creativity and spontaneity. Father, You have opened the beauty of life to me—brightness, beauty, and boundless opportunities.

Laughter RELIEVES stress. Contentment in You refreshes, enhances wellbeing and produces laughter. Laughter enables me to loosen up, stimulates positive thoughts, and contains healing properties. I am thankful, Master, for the gift of laughter, and for the joy of a daily walk with You.

MY PRAYER NOTES FOR TODAY

___

___

___

___

___

BIBLE READING

❑ **Day 197 — Isaiah 1–3**

DAY 198 — LEAD AND SUCCEED

Lord, all creative ideas and resources come from You. You are the Creator of the universe and all that is good, pure, inspiring. Today I want to tap into Your creative energy and apply it to spiritual leadership and success. Lead me to:

Lead with LOVE. Father, You are the essence of love. All Your actions today, and in times past, are based on unrestricted and compassionate love. Let me lead with examples and demonstrations of Your love—seeking, sharing, and serving.

Lead with LONGSUFFERING. I will not agree with the attitude and actions of many of the people I will relate to today. They will not be in step with my values and lifestyle. Let me lead with patterns of longsuffering—understanding, embracing, and guiding.

Lead with LOYALTY. Loyalty is a test of character and a solid value system. Lord of Glory, I am committed to being a loyal believer and follower. But, I need Your instructions and inspiration so I can lead and succeed. Let me lead with unquestionable loyalty—faithfulness, dependability, and accountability.

MY PRAYER NOTES FOR TODAY

BIBLE READING

❑ **Day 198 — Isaiah 4—6**

DAY 199 — LEAD ME TODAY

God of the past, present, and future. God of grace, glory, and precious gifts. I ask You, standing on the foundation of faith in Your promises, to lead me today.

Lead me in understanding Your **PRESENCE** to protect me from the attacks and influence of the enemies of my soul.

Lead me in understanding Your **PROVISIONS** for both my spiritual and physical life and to receive them humbly and graciously.

Lead me in understanding Your **POWER** to enable me to be a shepherd to the searching, a soldier to defend the faith, and a servant-leader to achieve goals to advance Your kingdom on earth.

As You lead me, I will love You, enjoy You, adore You, and devote myself to You.

MY PRAYER NOTES FOR TODAY

____

____

____

____

____

BIBLE READING

❑ **Day 199 — Isaiah 7—9**

DAY 200 — LET GO TODAY

Faithful Father, I know I must let go in order to grow. I want to grow in spiritual understanding, in steadfastness in faith, and in sharing my faith with others. Today, I want to let go of anything that would interfere with my direct line of talking and walking with You.

I want to LET GO of negative thoughts and replace them with elevating thoughts about guiding values, inspiring visions, and unmatched victories.

I want to LET GO of past mistakes and focus on the great and wonderful things You want to do in my life today by the empowerment of Your Spirit.

I want to LET GO of standoff attitudes created by unkindness, betrayal, and poor communication and build stronger channels of connectivity, compassion, and care.

I want to LET GO so You can move in and take control so I can grow . . . grow . . . grow!

MY PRAYER NOTES FOR TODAY

BIBLE READING

❑ **Day 200 — Isaiah 10—12**

DAY 201 — LET LOVE FLOW

Loving Father, Your Word is filled with illustrations, quotations, and challenges about love. The greatest of these is Your love in sending Your Son, Jesus Christ, to provide salvation and hope for life and the future.

Let Your love flow in my life today in a way that reflects Your tenderness, understanding, and insight. I want others to see Jesus in me, and I want to love others as Jesus loved.

Let love direct my attitude so I can show faithfulness to friends, show love for my neighbors, show compassion for the hurting, and show urgency to reach the unchurched.

Let love be the rule for my pursuits, my practices, the prizes I strive to receive, and by doing what You have told me to do today.

Let my love be pure, authentic, and contagious. Let Your love flow through, in, and around me!

MY PRAYER NOTES FOR TODAY

____

____

____

____

____

BIBLE READING

❑ **Day 201 — Isaiah 13—15**

DAY 202 — LET MY LIGHT SHINE

Christ in me is the hope of glory (see Col. 1:27). I believe this, Father, and I want the light of His love to shine in and through me today. I do not want the light of my commitment to be veiled. I want it to be visible in all I do—illuminating, penetrating, and escalating. Let my light shine so I can show and tell:

GOOD works. Father, work works of righteousness, temperance, and holiness through me. This will honor You and give light to those who live in darkness. I also want to do good works of benevolence that relieve hunger, stress, loneliness, misfortune, and conflict.

GLORIFY You. When the works of Christ are reflected in my life, Your name, kingdom, and cause is magnified and glorified. Today I want to receive blessings from You, testify of Your blessings, and share Your blessings.

GAIN understanding. I want to show love today in a way that people will gain an understanding of what it means to be a Christ follower—freedom from bondage, blessings from above, and the beauty of wholeness.

MY PRAYER NOTES FOR TODAY

____

____

____

____

____

BIBLE READING

❑ **Day 202 — Isaiah 16—18**

DAY 203 — LIVING CONFIDENTLY

Your grace, Father, is all-sufficient, all the time, everywhere. Knowing that whatever I confront I can conqueror gives me confidence, courage, and control. I am thankful today and will go about my activities with an acute awareness of what Your presence and empowerment gives me.

SPIRITUAL confidence. "I can do all things through Christ" (Phil. 4:13 NKJV). I can mature in my Christian walk consistently, pray fervently according to Your will, and witness effectively about Your goodness.

SELF confidence. I do not want to act arrogantly in my spiritual posture and pursuits. I do want to act with confidence and boldness. I have confidence in Christ's completed work of redemption that gives me confidence to be positive in my speech, visionary in service, and consistent in spiritual discipline.

SOCIAL confidence. Mixing with others, believers and unbelievers, is important in being a total person and an influencer. I ask that "Christ in me" would show forth in my conversations, activities, relationships, attitude, and how I live out spiritual values.

MY PRAYER NOTES FOR TODAY

BIBLE READING

❑ **Day 203 — Isaiah 19—21**

DAY 204 — LIFE IN CHRIST

I have liberty, insights, faith, and energy in life today.

Father, thank You for the presence of Your Spirit that gives me **LIBERTY**. Liberty to think, plan and act according to Your will, Your Word, and Your works of grace.

I need **INSIGHT** today so I can recognize the traps of the Enemy, seize opportunities to share my faith, and perform Christian service that impacts lives.

I need **FAITH** today to see the invisible and to achieve the impossible. I know Your power is unlimited and I want to appropriate this power to honor You with acts of complete surrender and impacting service.

I need **ENERGY** today to overcome weakness in witnessing and slothfulness in working. I want to be delightful in personality, and different in conduct. I want to represent You with refreshing energy and zeal.

I believe. Amen!

MY PRAYER NOTES FOR TODAY

___

___

___

___

___

BIBLE READING

❑ **Day 204 — Isaiah 22—24**

DAY 205 — LIFE TODAY

Life-giving, holy Father, I want to experience life today in fullness and fruitfulness. I also want to be an example in life today. I am asking You to guide me and empower me to be an authentic example in four distinct areas of my life:

Living SACRIFICE. Keep me on Your altar of holy surrender and heavenly allegiance. Let my thoughts focus on Your will, not my self-interests or will but Yours.

Loving SERVANT. Keep me humble, showing true Christian love by serving others. Let my acts of service focus attention on Your goodness, not my personality or performance but Yours.

Learning STUDENT. Keep me in Your Word, learning, growing, sharing. Let me focus on Your plan for redemption and Christian responsibilities, not my reasoning or personal interpretation but Yours.

Leading SAINT. Keep me visionary and full of vitality in my walk with You. Let me focus on leading others, not my goals or skills but Yours.

MY PRAYER NOTES FOR TODAY

____

____

____

____

____

BIBLE READING

❑ **Day 205 — Isaiah 25—27**

DAY 206 — LIFT UP TODAY

I will lift You up today, Father, because You are holy, gracious, and worthy.

I will lift You up . . .

With soul-songs of praise;
With words of thanksgiving and witness;
With holy commitment and conduct;
With excitement about enlarging Your kingdom;
With robust faith to finish the course.

I will lift You up but I need You to fill me . . .

With Holy Spirit energy and authority;
With the power-packed promises of Your Word;
With binding relationships with other believers;
With heavenly sunshine that sustains.

I ask. I believe. Thank You, I receive!

MY PRAYER NOTES FOR TODAY

___

___

___

___

___

BIBLE READING

❑ Day 206 — Isaiah 28—30

DAY 207 — LIFTING YOU UP

Lord of all that is grand and glorious, I am humbled by the privilege to lift You up in my daily life. I want to represent You with dignity and honor by the way I talk and treat other people. By Your Holy Spirit:

I want to lift You up by my ATTITUDE. I want to be positive, cheerful, and helpful. I want people to see You in me by my gracious spirit, by my enriching words, and by my disposition of agreement.

I want to lift You up by my ACTIVITIES. I want to back my Christian posture and speech with activities that build Your kingdom, bring people to new life in Christ, and bless those suffering and in need. I want to back my testimony of commitment to Christ with words of faith that resemble the life of Christ.

I want to lift You up by my ADVANCEMENT. I want to grow daily in Christlikeness. I want to advance in discipleship maturity, in developing service skills, and in demonstrating vision in advancing the ministry of my local church. I ask You to cover, anoint, and direct me in fulfilling Your ideal will for my life today.

MY PRAYER NOTES FOR TODAY

____

____

____

____

____

BIBLE READING

❑ **Day 207 — Isaiah 31—33**

DAY 208 — LISTEN TODAY

Today, Father, I want my ears, mind and heart to be open to You. I want to hear from You. I must listen for Your voice through thoughts, ideas, and the revelation of the Holy Spirit. I will listen by:

Focusing on Your LOVE. As You show Your love to me through grace, guidance, and daily gifts, You speak to me about Your nature and will and how I should embrace Your example.

Understanding Your LONG-SUFFERING. I realize that I am a work in progress. Every day you are patient with me and gradually guide me into becoming a devoted disciple.

Yielding to the LANGUAGE of the Holy Spirit. Many times I am lost for words in carrying on a conversation with You. Let Your Spirit step in and speak to You for me in a heavenly language that conveys my needs, aspirations, and devotion. "Speak, for your servant is listening" (1 Sam. 3:10).

MY PRAYER NOTES FOR TODAY

____

____

____

____

____

BIBLE READING

❑ **Day 208 — Isaiah 34—36**

DAY 209 — LIVE IN GRATITUDE

Lord, You have crowned me with grace and goodness. I'm grateful! I'm thankful! My life is blessed, blessed, blessed! I want to live and shine with gratitude for Your hand of beauty and bountifulness on my life. I will show:

Gratitude for unrestricted GRACE. You give, Master, and keep on giving—abundant provisions, nonjudgmental affirmation, and anchors for my faith. I will show my appreciation by expressing my love with pure flowing praise.

Gratitude for unlimited GROWTH. Father, You give me the privilege to grow every day, following in the footsteps of Christ and learning how to obey and put into practice His instructions on how to trust Him and treat others. My heart overflows with thanksgiving.

Gratitude for unselfish GIVING. Lord, today I want to observe and follow Your practice of unselfish giving. I will give loyalty to my church. I will give love to my family and friends. I will give support to assist those who have lost their way in life and need hope and help. I'm grateful for Your goodness!

MY PRAYER NOTES FOR TODAY

____

____

____

____

____

BIBLE READING

❑ **Day 209 — Isaiah 37—39**

DAY 210 — LIVE IN LIGHT

I will say yes to light! Father, You are the Maker of light and I want to live in Your light—Your light of love, liberty, and learning. These three light gifts also represent opportunities and possibilities to grow, contribute, and achieve. In praise and thanksgiving I will live in the:

Light of LOVE. Master, Your love redeems, releases, and rewards. It redeems from the bondage of sin, it releases a new burst of creative energy, and issues rewards of peace, assurance, and spiritual and financial prosperity.

Light of LIBERTY. I deeply respect the liberty you give me, Father. Liberty to be a free thinker, to face uncharted waters, and to make bold decisions. I will cherish my liberty and commit to using it with calculated wisdom.

Light of LEARNING. Every day I have the privilege to learn more about You, Holy Father, Your nature, and how to walk in Your will. Thank You for this privilege. I will grow in Christian maturity as I utilize the privilege to acquire knowledge to live in light today.

MY PRAYER NOTES FOR TODAY

____

____

____

____

____

BIBLE READING

❑ **Day 210 — Isaiah 40—42**

DAY 211 — LIVE LIFE TODAY

Mighty Master, You are the source of life and I want to live life to its fullest today. Life is a precious gift and it represents Your love and grace.

I want to ENJOY life today. I am surrounded by problems and pitfalls, pain, and perplexities. I am also surrounded by possibilities, pleasures, and good people. Touch me to focus on the positive and Your presence to lift up and to uphold.

I want to EXPERIENCE new things today. I want to learn and grow. I want to examine and develop new thought patterns and new ways to be more effective in relationships, family life, and in my career.

I want to EXPAND Your influence today. May I be aware of witnessing opportunities and unique ways of assisting the seeking, hurting, and insecure. I want to be a bright light in my service to my local church and pastor. Let divine energy enable me to achieve these goals.

MY PRAYER NOTES FOR TODAY

___

___

___

___

___

BIBLE READING

❑ **Day 211 — Isaiah 43—45**

DAY 212 — LIVING LIFE TODAY

Father, You have set today before me. It is filled with beauty, potential, and opportunities to discover and experience. I want to live life today in its fullness under Your watchful eye. Let Your creative power flow in my life so I can:

Live in PRAISE—Display a positive spirit of thanksgiving for salvation and security; for family and friends; for faith and freedom. I will be thankful to You for opportunities to grow spiritually and for grace to overcome opposition. **I will live with a heart of praise today!**

Live my PASSION—Follow the path of the dreams You have placed in my heart to be a faithful follower of Jesus Christ, a witness of Your love for the lost, and to utilize my talents to be productive and successful. **I will live with a commitment to my passion today!**

Live in PARTNERSHIP—Join forces with You and others to achieve worthy objectives. Father, I will partner with You in walking the Christian walk, with my pastor in fulfilling the ministry of my church, and with family and friends in a fruitful lifestyle. **I will live a life of trustworthy partnership today!**

MY PRAYER NOTES FOR TODAY

___

___

___

___

___

BIBLE READING

❑ **Day 212 — Isaiah 46—48**

DAY 213 — LIVE OUTSIDE THE BOX

Creative Father, I do not want to be boxed in with my expressions of love to You, my experiences in kingdom ministry, and my spiritual expectations. In Your care I want to live outside the box of new beginnings every day. Give me a driving spirit:

To shun a life in ISOLATION. I want to live among the people, to mix and mingle. I don't want to be like them, but to show them better ways. I can't be a positive influence by standing back and not forming relationships. **I will learn, grow, and relate today!**

To avoid a life of IMITATION. Father, You have given me unique gifts. You have a distinct plan for my life. I do not want to copy, cope, cry, or confront. Let Your nature and goals for my life be reflected in my daily walk and talk. **I will be unique, creative, and innovative today!**

To live with INSPIRATION. Reading Your Word inspires. Praying to You inspires. Worship services inspire. Fellowship inspires. Every day I want these inspirational forces to be valuable and active in my life. **I will rejoice, sing, and let spiritual freedom reign in my heart today!**

MY PRAYER NOTES FOR TODAY

BIBLE READING

❑ Day 213 — Isaiah 49—51

DAY 214 — LIVING THE RESURRECTION

Behold He is alive and lives forever more! (see Rev. 1:18). The Resurrection message is a message of life to those dead in trespasses and sin. I rejoice, Father, because I have new, abundant, and eternal life in Your Son, Jesus. Today I will live the Resurrection message in full faith and in fellowship with Christ.

New LIFE. I am free from the binding force of sin and the grip of Satan. I am a new creation in Christ. My heart flows with praise, and I speak words of thanksgiving. Today I will exercise my privileges set forth in the Resurrection message.

Abundant LIFE. New life, abundant life in Christ. Father, You are all sufficient! You restored completeness through the Resurrection message—Jesus is alive and gives pardon, peace, and prosperity. You supply all my needs and I am grateful. Today I will enjoy and share the abundant life offered by Christ.

Eternal LIFE. Father, Christ is at Your right hand talking to You about me—my completeness, my contentment, and my companionship. He is also assuring me of eternal life with You. Today I will walk as a new creation with the confidence of eternal life.

MY PRAYER NOTES FOR TODAY

____

____

____

____

____

BIBLE READING

❑ **Day 214 — Isaiah 52—54**

DAY 215 — LIVING THE VISION

I am thankful for the vision You have birthed in my mind and heart—a vision of success, significance, and service. I want to live this vision every day in my attitude, activities, and actions toward others. I ask you to let Your Word and wisdom guide me in:

Maintaining CLARITY—Keeping the vision in focus. If I need to make adjustments in how I see, what I see, and how I respond to what I see, let Your Spirit lead me and order my steps.

Staying in CONTROL—Exercising discipline in Christian duties regarding my vision of success, significance, and service. I will face obstacles today. By Your power, Father, I will control my disposition, highlight characteristics of dependability, and model Biblical fortitude.

Counting the COST—Willingness to pay the price. Father, You have given me everything I have and the privilege to walk with You. I commit my all to You.

MY PRAYER NOTES FOR TODAY

____

____

____

____

____

BIBLE READING

❑ **Day 215 — Isaiah 55—57**

DAY 216 — LOVING CHILDREN

Father, children are a precious gift from You who deserve affirmation, attention, and continual love. Sometimes this is difficult because young people are in physical, mental, and educational transition. My aspiration is to be a model, a mentor, and a messenger for young people.

MODEL. I realize, Father, that adults influence the values and behavior patterns of children. I want to be a model at church by my love for Christ and people; at home by my fairness and caring spirit; and in relationships by showing concern and care.

MENTOR. I can teach and lead children! But I need insight and oversight from You. I need to take initiative and show that I am interested in their welfare, development, and future stability and happiness.

MESSENGER. I know children need daily encouragement and guidance. They need inspiring messengers. I want to be a messenger who inspires hope, generates enthusiasm, creates optimism, and builds self-esteem. Father, let Your Spirit teach me and empower me to be a supercharged messenger that makes a difference in the life of children.

MY PRAYER NOTES FOR TODAY

___

___

___

___

___

BIBLE READING

❑ **Day 216 — Isaiah 58—60**

DAY 217 — MAKE PLANS TODAY

Father of guidance, I want to know and perform Your will. I realize this requires making plans—plans that include studying the Scriptures, surveying possibilities, and stretching my vision and work ethic. As I understand Your will, empower me to make plans that are:

MAGNIFICENT. Father, You have set before me beautiful opportunities to influence, impact, instruct, and inspire. **I will make magnificent plans today!**

MANAGEABLE. Touch me to make plans in the framework of the gifts You have invested in me. I want to fully develop my gifts and use them for ministry, testifying of Your greatness. **I will make manageable plans today!**

MOTIVATIONAL. Powerful Master, I want to stay fired up, filled with zeal in carrying out the magnificent and manageable plans I make. I want my friends to see my excitement, feel my energy, and see my spiritual growth. **I will make motivational plans today!**

MY PRAYER NOTES FOR TODAY

____

____

____

____

____

BIBLE READING

❑ **Day 217 — Isaiah 61—63**

DAY 218 — MAKE LUKEWARMNESS HOT

Lord of new beginnings, I don't want to be lukewarm in my approach to total commitment and accepting new challenges. I want to be alert, visionary, aggressive, and to help make good things happen. I need Your oversight and insights to shine with:

FIRED-UP faith to grow stronger and improve performance. Father, I believe You have a specific plan for my life. I will not permit this plan to be lukewarm. **I will exercise fired-up faith to believe and achieve and to honor You.**

FIX-IT attitude to engage in positive action and attack problems. Master, through Your indwelling Spirit I do not have to sit back, stand aside, or fold up. I can take fix-it action. There will be emotional and spiritual things at church and in my life that need repair. **I will, by Your authority, take fix-it action.**

FUTURE-FOCUSED disposition to believe in tomorrow and to plan wisely. Lord, I ask You to direct my thoughts and spiritual strategy about the future by faith that I will see You at work in my life. **I will develop and maintain a future-focused disposition that creates a spirit of great expectations.**

MY PRAYER NOTES FOR TODAY

____

____

____

____

____

BIBLE READING

❑ **Day 218 — Isaiah 64—66**

DAY 219 — MANAGING EMOTIONS

Lord, You have given me emotions to express agreement, disagreement, delight, discouragement, heartache, and happiness. All these are good when managed discreetly, honestly, and in keeping with Christian character. I ask for wisdom to:

Manage LOVE. One thing is certain. I want to love You, heavenly Father, with all my heart, mind, and spirit. I want to manage this love with disciplined devotion and active expressions. I also want to reveal my love with words and actions to those close to me everyday, always.

Manage LAUGHTER. A jolly spirit indicates a contented heart. Laughter releases an inward energy of openness and aliveness. I want to be pleasant. I want to manage my laughter so that it will not distract from my testimony and lifestyle as a committed believer.

Manage LONELINESS. Father, Your promise is: "I will never leave you nor forsake you" (Heb. 13:5 NKJV). Sometimes pressure and problems create loneliness, and I feel isolated. Open my eyes during these times, and let the light of Your magnificent glory and grace surround me.

MY PRAYER NOTES FOR TODAY

BIBLE READING

❑ **Day 219 — Jeremiah 1–3**

DAY 220 — MARKS OF COMMITMENT

Lord, I know there are visible marks of commitment in relationship to my family, to You, and to my church. People understand my commitment to You as these marks are visible in expressions, the allocation of time, and the expenditure of resources. Bless me in:

LOVING my family. I will check my **TNT** today—time, nurture, **and** treasures! I want to give time to the members of my family and express Your love. This will nurture my relationship with them. I will share my treasures with them—my character, trust, and resources.

LEARNING Your ways. I will check my **TNT** today—talking to You, doing noble service, tithing. I will display marks of prayer, serving, and giving. Walk with me, Lord, so I can walk out these virtues.

LEADING in ministry. I will check my **TNT** today—toiling, noting opportunities, and testing. I will expend energy in seizing opportunities and will be accountable for consistency. Let the glow of Your Holy Spirit cover me so marks of commitment will be evident in my talk and walk.

MY PRAYER NOTES FOR TODAY

____

____

____

____

____

BIBLE READING

❑ **Day 220 — Jeremiah 4—6**

DAY 221 – MAXIMUM MOTIVATION

Master, I want to be motivated for ministry achievements. It is easy to sit back, enjoy blessings, and sing "Victory in Jesus." My desire is to also be motivated for maximum ministry participation, performance, and productivity. I will do this by:

PRINCIPLE-centered motivation. Your Word, Father, is the catalyst for vision and action. It contains the principles for living a life that honors You, advances Your kingdom, and establishes a platform for trust. Today, I will be motivated by the principles outlined in the Ten Commandments, the Beatitudes, and Your instructions to love.

POSITIVE-based motivation. Upbeat! Visionary! I will stand up, speak up, and show forth an attitude of optimism, courage, and expectation. I will be motivated by the positive promises You have given to me.

PRODUCTION-grounded motivation. I will dream and I will also deliver! I will be spiritually productive and achieve "inreach" and "outreach" goals. I will be a person of action. Today, I will be motivated by the assurance of creative oversight for maximum productivity in ministry.

MY PRAYER NOTES FOR TODAY

____

____

____

____

____

BIBLE READING

❑ **Day 221 – Jeremiah 7–9**

DAY 222 — MAY I SHOW DISCIPLINE

I know discipline is a part of discipleship—devotion, direction, determination. I also know that I need Your guidance, Father, to achieve the goals that will honor You.

DEVOTION. I want to be visibly devoted to You in my lifestyle, career, and involvement in ministry. **Guide me by Your grace.**

DIRECTION. I want to follow Your direction for my life and I want this attitude to be reflected in my Bible study, prayer life, and the sharing of my faith. **Guide me by Your Spirit.**

DETERMINATION. I want to consistently show forth my commitment to You, visible in discipleship, stewardship, and leadership. I will joyfully determine to live a disciplined life today! **Guide me by Your standards.**

MY PRAYER NOTES FOR TODAY

____

____

____

____

____

BIBLE READING

❑ **Day 222 — Jeremiah 10—12**

DAY 223 — MOMENTUM TODAY

I need momentum today in my walk with You, Master, so I can be alert, aggressive, and advance. I never want to be stationary or idle. I always want to be driven by a compelling, open-throttled vision. Clothe me with spiritual energy:

To GROW in faith. I will face mountains today that could thwart plans, peace, and progress. I can face and surmount these mountains with a growing faith. You give faith, mighty Father, in Your Word. **I believe!**

To GAIN confidence. Momentum gives me confidence to worship extravagantly, work enthusiastically, and witness effectively.You give confidence, mighty Father, through affirmation, anointing, and aspirations. **I believe!**

To GO Forward. I want to go forward in faith and be fruitful by planting, sowing, and reaping. You give power to go forward, mighty Father, through the guidance of Your Holy Spirit, supportive grace, and transforming love. **I believe!**

MY PRAYER NOTES FOR TODAY

BIBLE READING

❑ Day 223 — Jeremiah 13—15

DAY 224 — MOTIVATING PRESENCE

I realize that feelings and faith go hand in hand. Bold faith will sustain in times of trouble and temptation. Authentic feelings of Your presence always motivate and encourage. I want to feel Your presence today as I:

STUDY Your Word. Your Word brings energy and purpose in life. It lights my pathway with clear directions, an understanding of duties, and delightful experiences.

SPEND time in prayer. I want to talk openly, honestly, and sincerely with You in prayerful conversation. I don't want my prayer time to be limited to a brief session. I want a prayer message on my lips, a prayer song in my heart, and a prayer promise on my mind at all times.

SATURATE my life with holy promises. You will never fail me, desert me, or withdraw Your promises from me. I want to claim Your promises for me personally, for the protection of my family, and to be spiritually productive in my church.

MY PRAYER NOTES FOR TODAY

____

____

____

____

____

BIBLE READING

❑ **Day 224 — Jeremiah 16—18**

DAY 225 — MOVING MOUNTAINS

Fathomless Father, You have told me that I can move mountains if I have sufficient faith. I want to exercise mountain-moving, mobilizing, and motivating faith in my life today. I desire this caliber of faith because:

I will face disturbing MISERY in the lives of friends today. Friends will confront sickness, suffering, separation, salary adjustments, and strains in relationships. Touch me to touch them with uplifting words, support, and guidance.

I will face possible MISTAKES in my work and behavior today. Demands and circumstances will require me to make quick decisions. Touch me so I can be touched by Your Spirit to make correct decisions based on holy principles, honesty, and fairness.

I will face opposition to MINISTRY today. Satan will mobilize negative forces to reduce spiritual zest, vision, and advancement. Touch me by examples from Your Word so I can touch mountains before me and watch them move, paving the way for regrouping, renewal, rejoicing, and rewarding experiences.

MY PRAYER NOTES FOR TODAY

___

___

___

___

___

BIBLE READING

❑ **Day 225 — Jeremiah 19—21**

DAY 226 — MY ATTITUDE TODAY

Lord of new beginnings, You have told me that my attitude should be the same as that of Christ Jesus (see Phil. 2:5). Today, energize my spirit to comply with this admonition. As I look at the attitude of Christ, it reveals three things to me:

HOLY attitude—reverent toward You and divine things. You are above all—eternal, sufficient in grace, and understanding in relating to me. **I want a holy attitude today.**

HELPING attitude—gracious toward those in need. You are my supplier of peace, joy, and love. Let me forget myself long enough to lend a helping hand to others. Let me agree with others, love others, and be a deep-spirited friend (see Phil. 2:3). **I want a helping attitude today.**

HUMBLE attitude—thankful for God's grace and gifts and a willingness to represent Him without fanfare or an elevated position. Let me observe the example of Christ, who set aside the privileges of deity and took on the status of a slave (see Phil. 2:7). **I want to exhibit a humble attitude today.**

MY PRAYER NOTES FOR TODAY

BIBLE READING

❑ **Day 226 – Jeremiah 22–24**

DAY 227 — MY DESTINY TODAY

Today will be a delightful day! My final destiny is secure in Christ. Each day, however, is a part of my destiny—how I think, what I say, what I do, and how I exercise faith. Heavenly Father, I depend on Your leadership today!

My DESTINY is not down! Today I will not look down, feel down-and-out, or think down thoughts. I will not entertain negative people and will avoid negative conversations.

My DESTINY is up! Today I will look up because my strength comes from You. I will not be distracted by what is taking place around me but will stay focused on my privileges and the unlimited promises I have in Christ.

My DESTINY is secure! Today I know salvation is real, grace is real, and my destiny in heaven is real. I feel secure and will face life today with courage, optimism, and creative insight.

MY PRAYER NOTES FOR TODAY

BIBLE READING

❑ **Day 227 — Jeremiah 25—27**

DAY 228 — MY EYES ON THE GOAL

Father, I want to have challenging goals to intensify my vision and my daily walk with You. I must keep my eyes focused, my faith firm, and my communication with You fresh and flowing from my heart. I will keep my eyes on the goal of:

GROWING spiritually. Every day is an opportunity to grow in Christian experience. Let Your Holy Spirit lead me in understanding, internalizing, and practicing the precepts of Your Word. **This will empower me to keep my eyes on the goal of daily growth in Christlikeness.**

GIVING thanks. Every day You shower me with kindness, favor, and gifts. I am blessed! I am thankful! Let Your Spirit lead me in showing my thankfulness with praise and worship. **This will stabilize me in keeping my eyes on the goal of honoring You.**

GAINING influence. Every day You open doors for me to touch others with good news. Let Your Holy Spirit lead me to set the right example, to speak the right words, and to share truth. **This will position me to keep my eyes on the goal of influencing others for the cause of Christ.**

MY PRAYER NOTES FOR TODAY

BIBLE READING

❑ **Day 228 — Jeremiah 28—30**

DAY 229 — MY FAITH TODAY

Lord, I want to learn more about the faith You have birthed in my mind and heart. I pray that You will increase my faith. I want to recognize, amplify, and magnify my faith. I am open for teaching, training, and leading. I want my faith to be active and aggressive. I am committed to:

FULLNESS for faith that is powerful and explosive. Full faith is receiving what You have instructed and promised without hesitation, fear, or backwardness. I will approach life today with high-powered faith that sees, acts, and achieves.

FRESHNESS for faith that is bright, colorful, and cheerful. Fresh faith, Father, is enjoying new experiences with You every day and discovering new avenues of fellowship with You and new ways to convey love and admiration.

FRUITFULNESS for faith that believes, receives, and changes attitudes and situations. Fruitful faith is alive, active, and rewarding. Loving and life-giving Father, rock my faith today so I can show the wonders and fruit of following You—fruit that thrills, instills, and fills with strength and significance.

MY PRAYER NOTES FOR TODAY

____

____

____

____

____

BIBLE READING

❑ **Day 229 — Jeremiah 31—33**

DAY 230 — MY I WILLS FOR TODAY

Today I Will rejoice and be glad for You have created this day for Your holy purposes and my pleasure.

Today I Will look out and see the beauty of the people, places, and things You have set before me.

Today I Will relate to my family, friends, and co-workers with understanding, helpfulness, and an upbeat spirit about the opportunities of life.

Today I Will share my faith in Christ by being an example of integrity in relationships, modeling commitment to ministry, and openly talking about the blessings of being a believer.

Today I Will strive to perform meaningful service to others, increase my performance skills, and work to make a difference in my profession.

Today I Will keep a song in my heart and praise on my lips. I will be a winner in Christ.

MY PRAYER NOTES FOR TODAY

____

____

____

____

____

BIBLE READING

❑ Day 230 — Jeremiah 34—36

DAY 231 — MY JOURNEY TODAY

Adventure-sharing Father, my journey with You has been packed with renewed strength, new paths of learning, and a bold awareness of new beginnings. I believe it is Your will that every day with You be blessed, blessed, blessed! May my journey today be:

Directed by FAITH. Lord, I want my faith to grow stronger … and stronger … and stronger! In accordance with Your Word, I want mountain-moving faith to plan wisely, achieve goals, and enjoy the full benefits of Your kingdom.

FRUITFUL. I say yes to growing, harvesting, and sharing spiritual fruit. Love, joy, peace, long-suffering, gentleness, and kindness are spiritual fruit that make a difference.

Oriented FORWARD. Master, I will not become immobile in my walk with You. I will look forward to the new doors You are opening and new encounters You want me to experience. I praise You for the joy of the journey!

MY PRAYER NOTES FOR TODAY

____

____

____

____

____

BIBLE READING

❑ **Day 231 — Jeremiah 37—39**

DAY 232 — MY POTENTIAL TODAY

Lord of unlimited power, You have set before me today opportunities to live, learn, and lead with explosive potential. As I look at the word **po-TEN-tial** I see ten things You have set before me:

1. To be optimistic
2. To engage in prayer
3. To learn something new
4. To relate to friends
5. To share faith
6. To help the needy
7. To grow spiritually
8. To be productive
9. To spread smiles
10. To be trustworthy

Energized by Your Spirit, I will receive and practice the ten things in my **po-ten-tial** and make a difference in my world.

MY PRAYER NOTES FOR TODAY

____

____

____

____

____

BIBLE READING

❑ Day 232 — Jeremiah 40—42

DAY 233 – MY PRAYER LIFE TODAY

Prayer! What a wonderful, grand, and glorious privilege! You permit me to hold a conversation with You, ask questions, confess weaknesses, and seek guidance. I am blessed! I receive these blessings with a humble and grateful spirit. Today:

I want my prayer life to be SCRIPTURAL. Your Word, Father, outlines how I am to pray. The Lord's Prayer addresses Your will and Your plan for my life. I will pray without ceasing and embrace the guiding principles set forth in the pattern You have given.

I want my prayer life to be STRETCHING. Every day, Master, I want to draw closer to You. I can do this through stretching prayer. I ask You to stretch my faith in receiving from You, in giving to others, and in performing ministry.

I want my prayer life to be STRENGTHENING. You invite me to come to You believing with a big faith and with overflowing expectations. Let Your Spirit surround me and set me apart for influential service. My prayer today is that I will honor You in all I do and that I will be a walking witness of a winning life in Christ.

MY PRAYER NOTES FOR TODAY

____

____

____

____

____

BIBLE READING

❑ Day 233 – Jeremiah 43–45

DAY 234 — MY PRAYER TIME TODAY

As I pray to You, all-knowing Father, I want my communion to be open, honest, and sincere. I cannot do this in my own knowledge or understanding. I need help! I need Your help. So today:

I want to pray according to Your WILL. Your ways are perfect, Father. Teach me how to pray according to Your holy nature, Your plan for my church, and Your direction for my life. **I will seek Your will today!**

I want to pray to receive holy WISDOM. I understand that wisdom is the ability and insight to act appropriately in the situations I face. There will be both problems and opportunities that will surface before me. **I will seek Your wisdom today!**

I want to pray for power in my spiritual WALK. Many people will cross my path today. I want my walk with You to influence them to make a difference in their faith and future. **I will seek You for a holy anointing on my walk today!**

MY PRAYER NOTES FOR TODAY

____

____

____

____

____

BIBLE READING

❑ **Day 234 — Jeremiah 46—48**

DAY 235 — MY STAND TODAY

Within my own strength, Holy Father, I cannot declare anything or achieve anything. But, in You, by the power of the Holy Spirit, I can declare my dedication, my determination, and my discipleship intentions. And today that is what I want to do.

I declare my DEDICATION to God Jehovah. Lord, You are my life, my hope, and my future. Without You I am absolutely nothing. Today I want You to know I am totally dedicated to worshiping You, reading Your Word, and witnessing about Your loving grace.

I declare my DETERMINATION to live righteously. I will, Master, by Your guidance walk rightly, talk rightly, relate rightly, and rightly model Your love. I am set, determined to stand tall in embracing the truth of Your Word.

I declare my DISCIPLESHIP intentions. I understand a dedicated, determined disciple must practice consistent stewardship of time, tithe, and sharing truth. By Your infusion of zeal and strength I will display all three of these characteristics in my daily lifestyle.

MY PRAYER NOTES FOR TODAY

____

____

____

____

____

BIBLE READING

❑ Day 235 — Jeremiah 49—52

DAY 236 — NEW EXPERIENCES

God of benefits and blessings, You have set a new day before me, fresh, flowing with possibilities and opportunities to fulfill dreams. I want to be wide awake, ready to exercise faith, and be creative in my approach to life and work.

I want to SEE ways I can make a difference. I want to be a difference-maker in my relationship with my family, friends and coworkers. I want to add value to their lives.

I want to SEIZE opportunities to learn, grow, and reflect Your grace, giving Father. New experiences are before me and I want to fully capitalize on the adventure they offer.

I want to SANCTIFY my new experiences. Yes, and commit them to making me strong in You and more aggressive in sharing spiritual fruit and Your plan of salvation. Thank You for new experiences today to enliven my spirit and enrich my walk with You.

MY PRAYER NOTES FOR TODAY

BIBLE READING

❑ **Day 236 — Lamentations 1—3**

DAY 237 — NEW POWER

All authority and power comes from You, gracious Father. With spiritual authority promised by You comes power. Today I claim that power. In Your name I will reflect this power in many meaningful ways.

PARTNERSHIP power. I join with You as a partner in fulfilling the Great Commission and going with the good news of redemption in Christ.

PEACE power. You said You would give me Your peace. I accept this peace of mind, peace about my motivations, and peace about performing ministry.

PEOPLE power. By Your Spirit I will relate to the lost with love, to the hurting with compassion, and to the church with commitment.

PRODUCTIVITY power. In the name of Christ I will bear fruit today in my work and in my witness, maintaining a winning attitude with my family and others with whom I interact.

I accept Your power today with praise and thanksgiving.

MY PRAYER NOTES FOR TODAY

___

___

___

___

___

BIBLE READING

❑ **Day 237 — Lamentations 4—5**

DAY 238 — NEW THOUGHTS

Fill my mind with new thoughts today, Blessed Father. I know You are the source of creative energy. Let Your divine power flow through me in a way that I can represent You with respect and honor.

Fill me with THANKFUL thoughts. I am deeply appreciative of Your daily watch, care, and oversight. I am thankful for faith, food, and family. **Let my thoughts flow with expressions and acts of thanksgiving.**

Fill me with THRILLING thoughts. I want to see the "big picture" of how You want to work in me and through me. There is adventure awaiting me in walking with You and serving with You. **Let my thoughts flow with thrilling pictures and experiences of life in Christ.**

Fill me with TRIUMPHANT thoughts. I want to face evil enemies with power and boldness. I want to be a champion for Christ. **Let my thoughts flow with songs of victory and triumphant praise.**

MY PRAYER NOTES FOR TODAY

____

____

____

____

____

BIBLE READING

❑ Day 238 — Ezekiel 1—3

DAY 239 — NEW WAYS FOR NEW DAYS

Every new day has new opportunities to discover, develop, and deploy. Every new day is packed with promise and potential. Every day, Father, You give me the opportunity to be productive. I accept this and will use each day to:

DISCOVER new paths of adventure. I do not want to be locked into unproductive patterns, set ways to witness, and limited ways to express my love to You in worship. Lead me in paths of righteousness and new paths of spiritual adventure and advancement.

DEVELOP new skills for new days. For changing times I need advanced skills to be effective in kingdom ministry. I will read, study, pray, and grow. Lead me in paths that stretch my faith and that introduce me to new paths of advancement in Christlikeness.

DEPLOY spiritual gifts to assist others. Gifts from You, Father, are to be used to glorify You and to assist others in understanding Your love and compassion. Lead me in paths that connect with the unchurched and deploy Your DNA through me.

MY PRAYER NOTES FOR TODAY

____

____

____

____

____

BIBLE READING

❑ **Day 239 — Ezekiel 4–6**

DAY 240 — NEW ZEST FOR TODAY

Father, I don't want to be locked into the norm, the expected. I want to ring the bell of new zest every day. You have set open doors of discovery, development, and dedication before me. All these doors are open to me and I want to walk through them by:

VIEWING things differently. I want to see the good, positive, and progressive. I want to look beyond the expected and see the views of individuals and groups different from mine so I can understand or stand against radical concepts. Give me wisdom in evaluating the views and values of others.

VOICING positive feelings. You voice positive feelings and say, "I want you to have life in all its richness and fullness and I will show you how." I want to add richness and fullness to others by speaking words that validate, instruct, and inspire.

VIBRATING with adventure. Father, there are so many things You want me to see, feel, experience, and achieve. I want to vibrate with adventure, release energy, and shine with expectation. I will face today with new zest to reach my potential in Christ and recognize Your gifts of love that surround me.

MY PRAYER NOTES FOR TODAY

____

____

____

____

____

BIBLE READING

❑ **Day 240 — Ezekiel 7—9**

DAY 241 — NO ANGER TODAY

I have observed, heavenly Father, that anger surfaces when discipline is not monitored. Anger indicates the lack of focus on values and the lack of self-control. In my Christian walk and in my relationships I want to be spiritually and mentally discipled so I can be a true testimony of Christ in my convictions, conversations, and conduct.

My CONVICTIONS. Your Word provides standards to follow in living my faith and responding to insults, confrontations, and forces of evil. I will depend upon the Holy Spirit to guard my convictions and guide me in maintaining control over anger.

My CONVERSATIONS. Through strength from You, Master, I will not respond with negative words or actions to hostile encounters. There will be a tendency to flare up and show anger. I will respond with positive action that reveals character and control.

My CONDUCT. I always want to act and react with compassion and yet with spiritual discipline and authority. I will use the instructions in Your Word, Father, as the standard for my conduct so that my words and walk will be acceptable to You.

MY PRAYER NOTES FOR TODAY

BIBLE READING

❑ **Day 241 — Ezekiel 10—12**

DAY 242 — NO CRYING TODAY

Changeless Father, You are always the same—receptive, dependable, and understanding. I do not want to be labeled as a complainer or faultfinder. I want to be recognized as an encourager who enriches the life of others. Overshadow me:

To **TRUST.** I will not cry—I will trust You for devotion and directions in all situations of stress, strain, decisions, and actions. I will embrace Your Word and I will not rely on my own strength and decision-making. **I will look to You in total trust!**

To **TRY.** I will not cry—I will act boldly and try new methods of service, personal spiritual growth, and wholesome relationships. According to Your Word I can do all things in Christ. I will not sit down. **I will stand up and try new approaches in living victoriously!**

To **TURN**. I will not cry—I will be decisive and turn around habits and nonproductive spiritual routines, no longer ignoring opportunities to learn and grow, permitting tension to develop among family members and friends, and failing to be alert to share Christ. **I will engage in turn-around action!**

MY PRAYER NOTES FOR TODAY

____

____

____

____

____

BIBLE READING

❑ **Day 242 — Ezekiel 13—15**

DAY 243 — NOBLE INFLUENCE

Father of light, love, and liberty, I want to point others to You by the life I live. I want to be an influencer today—a noble influencer of integrity and inspiration. Empower me to be an influencer:

By my **ACTIONS.** Let Your Spirit shape my actions so my steps will be in line with Your will. I want my actions to demonstrate my commitment to Jesus Christ and to His command to love the lost and to care for the needy.

By my **AFFIRMATIONS.** Let Your grace cover my affirmations so I will walk in Your perfect will. I want to affirm the truth of Your Word, the power of prayer, and the tenderness of Your care. Let my life reveal the true essence of Your nature and Your openness to give good gifts to those who believe.

By my **ADVOCATIONS.** Let Your truth guide my advocation so I will stand for what You stand for. I will advocate fairness in transactions, holiness in conduct, biblical standards in judgment, compassion in service, and a spirit of purity in worship.

MY PRAYER NOTES FOR TODAY

BIBLE READING

❑ **Day 243 — Ezekiel 16—18**

DAY 244 — OPEN DOORS TODAY

Lord of glory, I want to be ready to walk through every open door You set before me—opportunities to learn and grow. I also want my life to be an open door—ready to share and to serve. Opportunities and readiness require willingness to yield. I'm ready! I will walk through open doors:

To REVEAL truth. Anoint me to reveal the truth of Your Word. I will study, practice, and share Christian principles. Father, let Your Spirit open the door of my understanding and open doors for me to impact and influence both believers and nonbelievers.

To RECEIVE friends. I want to be a true friend at all times. I want my time and home to be an open door for friends to receive affirmation, fellowship, inspiration, and trust.

To REFUEL faith. An ever-growing faith—establishing, empowering, and equipping. That's me! That's what I want. In my church activities and in associating with other believers, I want to demonstrate faith that is strong and active and that lifts You up, Father, and advances Your kingdom.

MY PRAYER NOTES FOR TODAY

BIBLE READING

❑ **Day 244 — Ezekiel 19—21**

DAY 245 — OPEN DOUBLE DOORS

Mighty, holy, heavenly Father, in Your Word You talk about opening double doors—doors of refreshing worship, doors of challenging opportunities, and doors of uplifting relationships. I want to walk expectantly through these doors with You today.

Doors of refreshing WORSHIP. In Your presence there is spiritual completeness and fullness of joy. I worship You because You are my Creator, Provider, and Protector. As I stand before You, lift me to higher realms of thrilling joy.

Doors of challenging OPPORTUNITIES. Today I want to seize opportunities to grow in grace, to learn new ways of utilizing my skills, and to show integrity in taking giant steps in reaching the next level.

Doors of uplifting RELATIONSHIPS. There are people who need me and there are people that I need. Let me be honest in my relationships so that I can both give and receive with a spirit of caring, selfless love.

MY PRAYER NOTES FOR TODAY

BIBLE READING

❑ Day 245 — Ezekiel 22—24

DAY 246 — OPEN MY EYES

Lord of heaven and earth, I want to see You today in all Your magnificent glory. Keep my eyes wide open to see Your handiwork in the beauty of nature, Your transforming power in the hearts of believers, and the preparations You have made in heaven for the true and faithful. Open my eyes to see the:

Vastness of Your PROTECTION. Thank You, Father, for surrounding me with heavenly protection. I feel safe and secure in You. You have given me faith, washed away failure, and eliminated fear. **I rejoice in Your peace and protection.**

Scope of Your PROMISES. Thank You, Master, for Your promises of help, hope, and healing. Every day Your promises are the same—fresh, full, faithful, and fulfilling. **I rejoice in Your unlimited and unrestricted promises.**

Durability of Your PROVISIONS. Thank You, Lord, for Your unfailing provisions. Every day I receive from Your hands—care, clothing, comfort, and career skills. **I rejoice in the flow of Your unstoppable and undeniable provisions.**

MY PRAYER NOTES FOR TODAY

____

____

____

____

____

BIBLE READING

❑ Day 246 — Ezekiel 25—27

DAY 247 — OVERCOMING STRENGTH

Almighty God with unlimited vision and vitality, I come to You requesting overcoming strength to deal with, and defeat, the enemies of righteousness and peace.

Give me strength to RECOGNIZE. Don't let me be ignorant of Satan's schemes and devices. Open my eyes so that I can see clearly his traps and techniques. Give me the power to know, understand, and perform valiantly.

Give me strength not to RETREAT. I want to face the Enemy head on. Fortify my faith to stand boldly. Give me staying power to trust and obey, stand my ground with Your Word in my hand, and advance gallantly.

Give me strength to REDOUBLE. I want to be visionary in kingdom ministry, aggressively moving forward in the might of Your Holy Spirit. Give me ambitious power to eagerly reach new goals and to claim new territory for spreading the good news of life, victory, and significance in Jesus Christ Your Son.

MY PRAYER NOTES FOR TODAY

____

____

____

____

____

BIBLE READING

❑ Day 247 — Ezekiel 28—30

DAY 248 — OVERFLOWING LOVE

Father, Your love is the foundation for life, faith, and the future. You loved . . . You gave . . . You set the example! Your love fills, thrills, seals, and overflows. I want Your love to be visible, active, overflowing, in my life. This calls for me:

To SERVE. Christ came to serve, not to be served (see Matt. 20:28). I desire the overflowing love of Christ in me to flow outward in Christian service—uplifting, assisting, encouraging, and supporting. **I want to serve with love, joy, and gladness.**

To SACRIFICE. Christ sacrificed everything to provide overflowing love—power, prestige, and popularity. Others will know that I am a follower of Christ if I am willing to serve and sacrifice. **I will sacrifice intentionally, scripturally, and thankfully.**

To SUSTAIN. Christ sustained abuse, criticism, and humiliation. Father, He did this willingly because He knew Your plan and He knew His major role in the plan. He stood the test! He was totally victorious! He provided the strength for His followers to stand against the assaults of Satan. **Through Christ, I will stand and shine spiritually.**

MY PRAYER NOTES FOR TODAY

____

____

____

____

____

BIBLE READING

❑ **Day 248 — Ezekiel 31—33**

DAY 249 — OVERSIGHT TODAY

Lord of glory, I will depend on Your oversight today—ownership and leadership. I want to take part in meaningful activities—to influence and to inspire. Today I will set forth three goals in my relationship with You:

OFFERING daily sacrifice. In the Bible I am challenged to offer my body as a living sacrifice to You (see Rom. 12:1). I am to confess You as Lord and Savior, to commit my energies to serving You, and to depend upon Your Spirit to control my behavior. **I will do this!**

ORIENTATION for daily supervision by the Spirit. In the Bible I am instructed to be led by Your Spirit (see Rom. 8:14). I am to trust You for guidance to reveal the truths of Scripture, and to talk with You about plans and activities. **I will do this!**

OPPORTUNITIES found in daily surveillance. In the Bible I am told to open my eyes and see the ripe harvest fields (see John 4:35). I am open to developing spiritual skills, serving in the church and community, and being a shining authentic witness of Your love and Your plan of salvation. **I will do this!**

MY PRAYER NOTES FOR TODAY

____

____

____

____

____

BIBLE READING

❑ **Day 249 — Ezekiel 34—36**

DAY 250 — PASS THE PEACE

Lord, Your peace brings calmness to my spirit and enables me to live life without fear or anxiety. I praise You for peace that surpasses understanding. I enjoy peace because it was passed to me by You through godly, dedicated individuals. I want to pass the peace to others by:

SHARING good news. I am surrounded by bad news—conflict, corruption, bickering, and battling. Father, work in and through me to share good news and pass the peace of faith and forgiveness, service and success, hope and happiness.

SHOWING a better way. Jesus Christ shows a better way to live, work, worship, and be a good neighbor. He passes the peace! I also want to pass the peace by sharing a bright, optimistic attitude, pointing out the good taking place, and sharing uplifting reports.

STANDING for peace. By Your strength, Father, I will not entertain bad news. I will stand and live on a foundation of faith, truth, love, and cheerfulness. I will pass the peace! I rejoice and honor You because I can face life with a smile and a victorious song.

MY PRAYER NOTES FOR TODAY

BIBLE READING

❑ Day 250 — Ezekiel 37—39

DAY 251 — PATIENT ENDURANCE

In times of conflict and confusion, You are always there, Father, to defend and support. I must be patient, stand firm, and wait for You to complete Your work. This requires courage and dependence on Your promises. I will patiently endure!

Supported by Your WORD. I will examine Your Word, apply Biblical principles, claim Biblical provisions, and depend on Biblical guidance. Father, allow me to rightly interpret and relate to Your Word.

Authenticated by WITNESSES. Lord, I am surrounded by witnesses of Your keeping, healing, and restoring power. Today I will rejoice with these witnesses and will find fortifying and enduring strength in their testimony.

Directed by WISDOM. I need to know when to act and when to react, when to be patient and polite, and when to press and push. The impartation of Your wisdom is my only source. I open my mind to You, protecting Father. Fill it with Your wisdom—ability to discern, faith to stand, and skill to execute. I will endure and advance today according to the guidance of Your Holy Spirit.

MY PRAYER NOTES FOR TODAY

____

____

____

____

____

BIBLE READING

❑ **Day 251 — Ezekiel 40—42**

DAY 252 — PEACE OF MIND

Peace from You, Father, settles my spirit, issues significance, and shows me the steps to take to achieve fulfillment. Worldly and wicked forces seek to create stress and nullify peace. You are my Protector and You safeguard my peace. I look to You today for:

Peace in MEMORIES. Lord, I want to remember Your goodness, guidance, and grace today. These things give me peace of mind and create a calm mood. I will build landmarks that remind me of Your miracle-working power and protective oversight.

Peace in MINISTRY. Christ set the pace, "I must be about My Father's business" (Luke 2:49 NKJV). Today, Master, I want to be about Your business—teaching, demonstrating care, and showing trustworthy allegiance. Equip me and energize me to be a faithful servant.

Peace in MIGHT. Your Holy Spirit provides overcoming, devil-defeating power. I will not fear or be fainthearted. Today, Father, I will worship, witness, and work with the peace of mind that You give.

MY PRAYER NOTES FOR TODAY

____

____

____

____

____

BIBLE READING

❑ **Day 252 — Ezekiel 43—45**

DAY 253 — PENETRATING SUNSHINE

Heavenly sunshine—warming, refreshing, penetrating. I rejoice today in Your liberating sunshine. Regardless of politics or pressure, perplexities or pitfalls, heavenly sunshine dispels overcast skies and brings rays of belonging, hope, and security. Today, Father, let me receive:

SOUL sunshine. Illuminate my soul with Your refreshing, revealing, and cleansing sunshine. Today I will face dark circumstances, turn dark corners, and meet individuals with a dark outlook on life. Let Your penetrating sunshine guide, grace, and guard me.

SCRIPTURE sunshine. Your Word, Master, is a light that leads and enlightens. As I read and study, give me insight and understanding so I can relate to, and apply, Your message to my life and ministry.

SANCTIFYING sunshine. Your sunshine warms, but it also cleanses and sets apart. I want to walk a pure path with You—devoted, determined, and dedicated. I respond to, receive, and rejoice in Your penetrating sunshine.

MY PRAYER NOTES FOR TODAY

BIBLE READING

❑ **Day 253 — Ezekiel 46—48**

DAY 254 — PERSONAL POWER

Lord of unlimited strength, creative power, and dynamic action, I need Your oversight and empowerment today as I yield to You with an open mind and heart.

I need Your power to PLEASE You. I want to stand sturdy, walk straight, and work enthusiastically. I cannot do this without Your uplifting, infilling, and life-directing enabling! **I wait on You!**

I need Your power to be PRODUCTIVE. I want my life to make a difference today. I want to experience good things and I want to make good things happen. Touch me to be wide awake and aggressive. **I trust You!**

I need Your power to be prudent in PLANNING. Enlarge my vision. Let me see possibilities. Let me make action plans, discipline myself, and hold myself accountable. **I will plan with YOU!**

MY PRAYER NOTES FOR TODAY

BIBLE READING

❑ Day 254 — Daniel 1—3

DAY 255 — PERSONAL SUCCESS

Thank You, Father, for giving me the resources to be successful—physical, spiritual, mental, and emotional strength, energy, and insight. In Your care I have everything I need to advance, achieve, and:

SET goals. I want to set **FAT** goals—faith-based, attainable, transforming goals. Faith in You is the foundation. Prayer is the force. The Holy Spirit is the transforming agent. My goals for today are to model Christlikeness, exhibit a positive attitude, and stress excellence in ministry.

STAY on course. Father, Satan wants to distract my attention and get me off course. He wants to sabotage my influence and dilute my convictions. By grace, I will not bow or bend. I will stay on the course that leads to favor with You and a future with You.

SALUTE Achievements. I want to show loyalty to the commitments I have made and the path I have taken. I want to relax, enjoy achievements, and feel good about the gifts You have entrusted to me. Today I will celebrate victory through my Lord and Savior Jesus Christ!

MY PRAYER NOTES FOR TODAY

BIBLE READING

❑ **Day 255 — Daniel 4–6**

DAY 256 — PERSONAL VICTORY

God of thunder and majesty, I ask You for personal victory today. Every day is a new adventure with You—new open doors, new relationships, new experiences. I yield to Your victorious movement in my life today.

Give me victory in my VISION. Open my eyes to see opportunities to grow spiritually and to serve compassionately. Let me visualize the good, honest, and decent.

Give me victory in my VALUES. Let me focus on my relationship with You, my love for my family, and my loyalty to the church. Let my emphasis and focus be on things of true value and worth.

Give me victory in VITALITY. I want to be awake, active, and alert. Let spiritual and physical energy flow so I can arise and build up your kingdom, build bridges of hope and happiness, and help build people into Your likeness through encouragement and training.

MY PRAYER NOTES FOR TODAY

____

____

____

____

____

BIBLE READING

❑ **Day 256 — Daniel 7—9**

DAY 257 — PLEASING PERSONALITY

Inspiring Father, walking with You motivates me to look up to achieve, to look around to advance, and look down to assist. Today I want the way I think and act to be progressive and pleasing to You and to those I am around. I will display a:

Warm SMILE. Lord, how I relate to others reveals to them how I relate to You. A warm smile connects and shows acceptance and openness. A smile makes a statement. I'm valuable, others are valuable, and today is a valuable day God has given us.

Positive SPIRIT. My positive spirit today will be based on Your presence, promises, and provisions. I will look for, expect, and help the good things happen today. I will speak with positive words, act with positive intentions, and perform positive ministry.

Internal SONG. A pleasing personality begins with my self-esteem and the song I sing inside. You have set me free, made me a new creation in Christ, and placed a song of love, security, and peace in my heart. I want my light of love from You to shine through a pleasing personality. I'm a winner and a witness of the empowering work of the Holy Spirit.

MY PRAYER NOTES FOR TODAY

____

____

____

____

____

BIBLE READING

❑ **Day 257 — Daniel 10—12**

DAY 258 — POSITIVE CHANGE

Father, I know You never change in Your wisdom, righteousness, holiness, goodness, and justice. You also want me to maintain these virtues in my daily walk with You. I realize, however, that changes in approaches and activities are necessary. Change my:

Frame of **MIND.** Don't let my thinking be governed by surroundings or situations. Give me "the mind of Christ" so I can entertain thoughts of purity, spiritual productivity, and partnership with You in kingdom ministry.

Faith for **MINISTRY.** Father, I desire an audacious faith for ministry. Break me out of sameness and routine. Let me see and seize the opportunities that surround me. Touch me to look up, and then to look out to seek and to serve.

Future and **MOTIVATION.** Master of mercy, a bright future in Christ is before me. By Your Spirit I want to stay motivated to test the new, stand tall for the right, and tell of the good news of salvation, hope, and happiness. Charge me to serve you.

MY PRAYER NOTES FOR TODAY

____

____

____

____

____

BIBLE READING

❑ Day 258 — Hosea 1—3

DAY 259 — POSITIVE RESPONSE

Today, hope-giving Father, I want to be positive! I want to be positive in my scriptural stand and positive in my speech. I want to see the good, the beautiful, and the beneficial. I want to say yes to:

God's LOVE. Love covers and cares for me. Love controls conflict! Love brings together and binds! Father, I say yes to Your love today and will demonstrate it in my decisions and relationships.

Christ's LIBERTY. I am thankful for my liberty and freedom in Christ. Father, I say yes to the liberty I have in Christ. I want to use this liberty today to be a committed Christian, a devoted church member, and an honorable citizen.

Holy Spirit's LEADERSHIP. I will depend upon the Holy Spirit to guide me in understanding and applying truth to my attitude and actions. Father, I say yes to the leadership of the Holy Spirit. I will depend upon the Holy Spirit to guide me in developing and applying my spiritual gifts for service and successful living.

MY PRAYER NOTES FOR TODAY

BIBLE READING

❑ **Day 259 — Hosea 4—6**

DAY 260 — POWER AND RESOURCES

Open my eyes, mind, and heart today so I can see, understand, and embrace with love Your unlimited power and Your all-sufficient resources.

PRIVILEGES. I do not want to live below the privileges and the spiritual power You have extended to me. Today, let me stand on Your promises and exercise biblical authority to defend the faith, defeat negative advances, and achieve.

POWER. Whatever the task, whatever the temptation, let me boldly stand up and stand out for the cause of Christ. Let me reflect His likeness—love, tenderness, forgiveness, and sacrificial care—with meekness and sincerity.

PERFORMANCE. Today I want to **FACE** life with faith, ambition, confidence and excitement. I accept Your power and resources today to make this happen.

MY PRAYER NOTES FOR TODAY

____

____

____

____

____

BIBLE READING

❑ **Day 260 — Hosea 7—9**

DAY 261 — POWER FOR TODAY

Today I will **RELY** on Your power to proclaim the good news of life in Christ.

Today I will **TRUST** Your power to protect me from the temptations and traps of Satan.

Today I will **EMBRACE** Your power to achieve goals that will make me strong and stable.

Today I will **ACT** in the realm of Your power to meet the needs of those who are suffering and struggling.

Today I will **SHARE** Your power with words of hope, encouragement, and assurance.

Today I will **TRUST** Your power to dream big and to act positively to accomplish them.

Today I will **MOUNT** up on eagles' wings by Your power to new heights and to soar victoriously.

MY PRAYER NOTES FOR TODAY

____

____

____

____

____

BIBLE READING

❑ **Day 261 — Hosea 10—12**

DAY 262 — POWER FROM YOU

God of wisdom and energy, I need personal power from You today. I need power to lift You up in praise and to live abundantly in Your love. Grant my requests today and give me:

Power to be PERSONABLE so I can be an inspiring light, a holy example of a life overflowing with God's grace. I will be a living testimony of freedom, faith, and fun-filled experiences in Christ.

Power to be PRAYERFUL so I can experience enriching and rewarding communication with You. I will worship in times of confession and direction, walking the path of righteousness.

Power to be PRODUCTIVE so I can make a difference in my world and in the work of my church. I will grow personally in Christ and share the good news with others for positive, life-changing results.

MY PRAYER NOTES FOR TODAY

____

____

____

____

____

BIBLE READING

❑ **Day 262 — Hosea 13—14**

DAY 263 — POWER-PACKED LIVING

Today is the first day of the rest of my life. Father, I want to take full advantage of the joy and opportunities that are set before me today. With Your strong arm of support and Your divine strength …

I will offer PRAISE triumphantly. Through praise, I connect with You, commit to You, and receive counsel to walk resourcefully with You. I praise You for Jesus Christ, for the joys of sins forgiven, and for the jubilant empowerment of freedom and faith that flows from Your Spirit.

I will think POSITIVELY and boldly. Today I will look for the best in every situation. Instead of judging, I will think positively about the actions and expressions of coworkers, believing they have good intentions and the best interest of the project or problem at heart.

I will treat PEOPLE kindly. My actions can build bridges of friendship or erect walls that will block openness and communication. I will walk uprightly, treat others with dignity and respect, and verbally witness about the transforming love of Christ.

MY PRAYER NOTES FOR TODAY

BIBLE READING

❑ Day 263 — Joel 1—3

DAY 264 — POWER TODAY

All-powerful, mighty God, Father of all fullness, You have given me power for today through the indwelling of the Holy Spirit. Let the Holy Spirit work in my life mightily and marvelously. Release power through me today.

Release **POWER** to trust You in all situations, knowing You will work out the best thing for me in relationship to Your divine plans for my life.

Release **POWER** to treat others with respect and dignity so I can make a difference in my relationships in all areas of life.

Release **POWER** to tame the wild beasts of jealousy, anger, depression, anxiety, fear, and frustration so I can live a balanced and blessed life.

Release **POWER** to tread on evil opposition, shortsightedness, self-centeredness, and stubbornness so I can think progressively, be productive, and impact Your kingdom.

Release **POWER** to testify of Your love manifested in the life of Christ so I can live a fruitful, abundant life today.

MY PRAYER NOTES FOR TODAY

____

____

____

____

____

BIBLE READING

❑ **Day 264 — Amos 1—3**

DAY 265 — POWERFUL WORDS

Today is a fantastic day packed with potential to explore, acquire, and adore. I want to explore new avenues to grow, acquire skills to glow, and use sparkling words to adore You, Father. I want to use powerful words to express my fullness in You.

REJOICING words. In all my conversations, I want my words to ring with the merits of my relationship with Jesus Christ—freedom, contentment, peace, security, companionship, guidance, gifts, glory, and a bright future. **I will speak rejoicing words!**

REVEALING words. I will meditate on words that illuminate possibilities—opportunities, adventure, discovery, change, cooperation, creativity, effectiveness, teamwork, and new methods to be more productive. **I will speak revealing words!**

REFRESHING words. In my relationships today I will convey words that underline wonderful privileges—nature, beauty, friendship, church, conversations, giving, receiving, fellowship, compliments, values, and talents. **I will speak refreshing words today.**

MY PRAYER NOTES FOR TODAY

BIBLE READING

❑ **Day 265 — Amos 4—6**

DAY 266 — POWERFUL RELATIONSHIPS

First of all, affirming and loving Father, I press for a personal, intimate, and powerful relationship with you today. A powerful relationship with You issues energy to conceive, believe, receive, grow, and glow. **Therefore, I will:**

Reflect Your **GLORY** in my relationships with others, living in purity and peace, giving testimony of Your mercy and miracles, and testifying of personal faith and fulfilment.

Revere Your **GRACE** in my relationship with You, abiding by the standards of Your Word, studying to conform to Your image, yielding in the full force of Your presence.

Respond to Your **GIFTS** in kingdom service, discovering my spiritual gifts, developing my gifts to their fullest potential, and utilizing my gifts to honor You, advance the mission of the Church, and function with maximum Holy Spirit enabling.

MY PRAYER NOTES FOR TODAY

____

____

____

____

____

BIBLE READING

❑ **Day 266 — Amos 7—9**

DAY 267 — PRAYERS OF BLESSING

Giver of eternal life, You have blessed me to bless others. Today I want to pray prayers of blessing on my friends, relatives, associates, and neighbors. I will pray for:

PEACE in their hearts. Your Son, Jesus Christ, is the Prince of Peace. I pray that my associates and neighbors will know Him through a personal experience, commit to following Him, and be overflowed with peace of mind and heart that exceeds understanding.

POWER in their witness. I pray that my Christian friends will be powerful witnesses of Your extraordinary love. May they be blessed with joy that is contagious, words that instruct, and a positive attitude that encourages.

PROSPERITY in their pursuits. I ask You to bless my family and friends with material blessings. Bless them today with hope that gives assurance, vision to see their potential, determination to achieve value-based goals, and a heart that overflows with thanksgiving.

MY PRAYER NOTES FOR TODAY

____

____

____

____

____

BIBLE READING

❑ **Day 267 — Obadiah 1**

DAY 268 — PRESSING FORWARD

Father, I am told to press forward in response to Your high calling in Christ Jesus (see Phil. 3:14). My spirit is willing but my flesh is weak! I look to You for what I need to be obedient and acquire the skills and power to press forward. Under Your authority:

I will BREAK OUT of restraining ropes. It is Your will for me to be aggressive, not stalled, in my walk with You. Policies, procedures, platforms, and personal agendas of others can be ropes that restrain creative thinking. **Today**, in the name of Jesus, I will experience freedom from any restraining force.

I will BREAK UP hindering habits. I recognize some habits can hinder my spiritual growth. Habits hinder me from pressing forward in a closer relationship with you. **Today**, I will set forth a detailed plan to form healthy habits to support spiritual growth.

I will BREAK THROUGH blinding barriers. Schemes of Satan, unmotivated church leaders, and personality conflicts can block my view of the path You have set before me. **Today**, with spiritual armor and weapons, I will destroy any barriers that would limit me from pressing forward with Your favor.

MY PRAYER NOTES FOR TODAY

____

____

____

____

____

BIBLE READING

❑ **Day 268 — Jonah 1—4**

DAY 269 — PREVAILING GRACE

Master, mighty God, I know You have grace for me today. Your grace is complimentary, full, free, abundant. Thank You! Thank You! Thank You!

I know Your grace is a gift of goodness, "glad tidings of great joy," and generous blessings.

I know Your grace is restoration, renewal, and rewards.

I know Your grace is comfort, control, commitment, and contagious joy.

I know Your grace is excitement, expectation, holy experiences, and eternal life.

I accept Your grace today with a humble heart, holy pleasure, jubilation, and great anticipation.

MY PRAYER NOTES FOR TODAY

BIBLE READING

❑ **Day 269 — Micah 1—3**

DAY 270 — PROSPERITY TODAY

I believe You will prosper me, trustworthy Father, because You already have! My life is filled with acts of favor, grace gifts, and divine guidance from You. Prosperity from You comes in many different forms. I am thankful for each one of them.

PEACE of mind. You allow the "mind of Christ" to work in my mind. This is creative prosperity, allowing me to see people, possibilities, and problems differently. You give me peace of mind because I see that every person is unique in Your sight, that I am surrounded by possibilities, and that You provide answers to every problem.

PERSONAL health. You provide physical wholeness and healing. This is life-giving prosperity! I praise You for strength to live a full life. I praise You for spiritual prescriptions for healing and happiness.

PRODUCTIVE performance. You have given me skills to work and earn wages. This is financial prosperity! What a wonderful blessing. Today, Father of grace, I want to earn, spend, save, and give wisely in honor and respect for the abilities You have invested in me. You are all-sufficient in all of Your ways.

MY PRAYER NOTES FOR TODAY

BIBLE READING

❑ **Day 270 — Micah 4—7**

DAY 271 — PROTECTING FRIENDSHIPS

Faithful Father, Your Son, Jesus Christ, is a Friend that stays closer than a brother—steadfast, dependable, and supportive! I want to follow His example and protect my friends from slander, selfish acts, and Satan's attacks. I can do this through:

UNITY OF PURPOSE. This calls for walking in agreement, serving together, and a solid trust relationship. Empower me today to reflect and practice these characteristics.

UNDERSTANDING OF POSTURE. My friends have particular thought-provoking patterns, personality traits, and techniques. I want to understand what makes my friends click and tick so I can enjoy them and work hand-in-hand with them in ministry. Empower me today to do this.

UPHOLDING IN PRAYER. I want to bring my friends to You in prayer—their spiritual journey with You, their needs, and their personal goals. Empower me today to bless them! Let Your love warm their spirit, Your power equip them for service, and Your grace sustain them in living a fruitful, victorious, Christ-exalting life.

MY PRAYER NOTES FOR TODAY

____

____

____

____

____

BIBLE READING

❑ **Day 271 — Nahum 1–3**

DAY 272 — KEPT FROM MISDIRECTION

Lord of deliverance, I need Your guiding hand to protect me from going in the wrong direction. Many paths are before me. I want to walk the path You have designed for me—closeness and commitment to You, obedience, and ministry vision. Protect me from being:

OFF-COURSE. Father, Your Word contains directional signs to keep me on course. I will study, relate, and apply Your Word today so I will not stray and go off-course in my devotion and duties to You.

OFF-KEY. I want to stay on key as I listen to Your voice and sing songs of victory and praise. I will not attempt to create my own tunes or compose my own songs. Master, I yield to your directions and am dependent upon Your protection.

OFF-COLOR. I want my conversations to be filled with colorful words that uplift, inspire, motivate, and encourage. I ask You, Father, to protect me from being negative, misleading, or undignified in my work and tasks. I want my words to be laced with truth; truth that points to Your holiness and my life of purity in Your protective care.

MY PRAYER NOTES FOR TODAY

____

____

____

____

____

BIBLE READING

❑ **Day 272 — Habakkuk 1—3**

DAY 273 — PROTECTION TODAY

Father of unlimited power and resources, I lift You up with overflowing praise. I know You will protect me and I depend on You.

You will protect me from falling into the evil traps of temptation the devil has set before me.

You will protect me from the physical dangers that lurk on the highways and byways of life.

You will protect me from becoming complacent in my prayer time with You and my personal growth in Your love.

You will protect me from being caught up in selfish ploys and pursuits that sidetrack me from the mission You have designed for my life.

I will relax. I will be refreshed. I will rejoice. You have issued a protective policy on my life today.

MY PRAYER NOTES FOR TODAY

BIBLE READING

❑ **Day 273 — Zephaniah 1—3**

DAY 274 — PROVIDE KNOWLEDGE

Father of all wisdom, I know knowledge is necessary to live successfully. I want knowledge and I need Your guidance. Guide me to acquire knowledge by:

LOVING Your precepts and promises. Your Word is true and everlasting and relates to all aspects of my life. I love Your Word and today, I want to store it in my heart so I will know how to conduct myself, make grounded decisions, and fulfill Your plan for my life.

LEANING on Your Holy Spirit to receive the power necessary for a convincing witness and performing Your work with boldness and authority. Your Spirit will guide me in all truth (see John 16:13). This is the foundation for knowledge.

LISTENING to you in prayer and through Spirit-filled teachers and leaders. Let me stay close to those who stay close to You. Let me learn from those who have stood the test and modeled the spirit of Your Son Jesus Christ. Let me gain knowledge today.

MY PRAYER NOTES FOR TODAY

____

____

____

____

____

BIBLE READING

❑ **Day 274 — Haggai 1–2**

DAY 275 — READY FOR TODAY

Every day is a new beginning with new challenges, experiences, and avenues of adventure. Lord, I recognize this and I stand ready to respond.

I'm ready to RESPOND to Your love, leadership, and methods of getting things done.

I'm ready to ENGAGE the skills You have placed within me to complete the tasks at hand.

I'm ready to ADVANCE in my relationship with You and to reflect Your positive attitude and gracious kindness.

I'm ready to DEMONSTRATE faith to believe, conviction to act, and courage to stand steadfast.

I'm ready to YIELD to Your will for my life and to show that I am ready through a yielding mind, heart, and hands to perform Your work.

I'm READY in the name of Jesus Christ and I step forward into this day with great zeal and holy anticipation.

MY PRAYER NOTES FOR TODAY

____

____

____

____

____

BIBLE READING

❑ **Day 275 — Zechariah 1–3**

DAY 276 — RECOMMITMENT TODAY

I get bogged down in routine and responding to external pressure. This type of action leads me away from my commitments to You and to ministry. I want back on the straight path that leads to Your ideal will.

Today, I recommit my VALUES. The most important thing in my life is communion with You, connecting in consistent and open communication. Talk to me. I'm listening, ready to receive and to respond.

Today, I recommit my VISION. I do not want my vision of a Christian lifestyle to fade. I want to maintain a clear vision of walking in step with Christ and serving others like He did.

Today, I recommit my VITALITY. Enthusiasm! Excitement! Exuberance! I want my love for You and my church to be visible, elaborate, and uninhibited. I ask You to touch me with holy energy and teach me to stay close to You, demonstrating my dedication openly in worship and in work.

MY PRAYER NOTES FOR TODAY

____

____

____

____

____

BIBLE READING

❑ **Day 276 — Zechariah 4–6**

DAY 277 — RELAXATION TODAY

Father, stress and strain surround me. I do not want to be caught in the web of uptightness and tension. You provide peace of mind, physical and spiritual peace, and peace in performing ministry. Today I will:

RESIST negative thoughts. Father, I will embrace the positive and turn my back on negative projections and thinking. I will do this because the gospel is good news, positive news, productive news. I will resist, relax, and rejoice in the open doors of life You set before me.

REFOCUS on priorities. My priorities, Master, are abiding in Your presence, living under Your protection, and claiming Your promises. I will refocus, resist, and relax in walking closely with You today.

RESPOND to available opportunities. Today I will look up, look around, and survey the challenging opportunities that surround me. These opportunities include the development of new skills, strengthening relationships, and embracing new ways to serve. I will respond, resist, refocus, and relax in Your soothing grace.

MY PRAYER NOTES FOR TODAY

BIBLE READING

❑ **Day 277 — Zechariah 7—9**

DAY 278 — RELEASE FAITH TODAY

Father, I realize the power and privileges of faith. Faith highlights Your love, leads me in Your paths, and directs me in learning about Your righteousness and laws! I am thankful for Your gift of faith and I want to maximize its benefits.

ENLARGE my vision. Every day, every hour, I want to see You high and lifted up. I want to see You, Master, in all of your magnificent glory! This requires active, growing, and expressive faith. Today, lead me in enlarging my vision of the expansive nature of Your kingdom.

EXPERIENCE new vitality. I want to increase my vitality in walking with You, and in expressing my Christian values. I will make it a point every day to count my blessings and to reflect my joy and happiness in Christ.

EXPOSE Satan's vices. Through faith, Father, let me visualize the traps and vices of Satan so I can avoid them and warn others of them. I will renew, release, and honor the results of faith today!

MY PRAYER NOTES FOR TODAY

____

____

____

____

____

BIBLE READING

❑ **Day 278 — Zechariah 10—12**

DAY 279 — RELEASE STRUGGLING

I realize I don't need to struggle, heavenly Father, but I do. I come to You today aware that Your grace is sufficient to release me from doubt and indecision, allowing me to think like Christ.

Release me from DOUBT. Let me trace what You have said, done, and promised; You have loved and lifted me in times past. Doubt creeps in when I fail to remember Your ways and works. **I claim victory over doubt today.**

Release me from INDECISION. I want the Christian path that I walk to be straight and my actions Christ-centered, deliberate, and bold; performing the truth I know to do. **I claim guidance to avoid indecision today.**

Release FAITH in me to think like Christ. I want to employ the mind of Christ, to be motivated by His love, and to utilize His methods. **I claim faith to remove barriers that hinder maturity in Christ today.**

MY PRAYER NOTES FOR TODAY

____

____

____

____

____

BIBLE READING

❑ **Day 279 — Zechariah 13–14**

DAY 280 — RELIEF FROM ANXIETY

God, I know You are always in control of circumstances and situations, but sometimes feelings and friction cause me to forget. Today, I trust You for relief from the inner turmoil and anxiety that pins me against the wall and reduces positive thinking and positive steps of action.

I accept relief through REDEMPTION. I have been redeemed, set free from bondage through Jesus Christ! I claim victory over stress, strain, and the evil influences of Satan.

I accept relief through REFRESHING. I will claim the refreshing flow of the Holy Spirit. The Holy Spirit will direct my steps, separate me from negative situations, and issue me strength to remain calm and to conquer.

I accept relief through RESTRUCTURING. I know I must accept responsibility in how I spend my time and what my priorities are. Guide me, Father, in restructuring my schedule so that it will reflect commitment to You, to my family, and to my church.

MY PRAYER NOTES FOR TODAY

____

____

____

____

____

BIBLE READING

❑ **Day 280 — Malachi 1—4**

DAY 281 — RIGHTEOUS PURSUITS

Sinless Father, I want to walk the right way today, say the right things, and do the right things, to be righteous in my relationship with You. I trust You for strength to develop skills and for grace to demonstrate holy standards. Direct me in the:

Pursuit of PURITY. I want to be pure in my commitment to You, with no hesitation in taking a stand, performing services, or financial matters. Empower me to walk a pure path and model righteousness that conforms to Your image.

Pursuit of PURPOSE. My purpose in life is to love and enjoy You forever without hidden motives or negotiating behind closed doors, and with total integrity in striving to expand Your kingdom and in ministry performance.

Pursuit of PRODUCTIVITY. Lord, I want to be productive in living the Christian life, cultivating the fruit of the Spirit, sowing seeds of personal evangelism, and harvesting an abundant crop that glorifies You and shows the extent of Your compassion and tenderness.

MY PRAYER NOTES FOR TODAY

____

____

____

____

____

BIBLE READING

❑ **Day 281 — Matthew 1—3**

DAY 282 — SALT AND LIGHT

As a member of Your family, adopted and affirmed, You have instructed me to be "salt and light" in my world—to impact, illuminate, and illustrate Your compassion and care. By Your grace and guidance I will obey your instructions today.

I will IMPACT the lives of those around me. I will be salt by demonstrating the value and taste of a life totally committed to Christ. I will stress the daily benefits of membership in Your family, significance, and security.

I will ILLUMINATE love to those around me. I will be light by revealing God's plan of becoming a new creation in Christ! I will show the daily joy of Your transforming grace, beauty, and blessings.

I will ILLUSTRATE the Christian life to those around me. I will model Christlikeness in my pursuits, relationships, and disposition. I will provide examples of daily fellowship with You in duties and delights.

MY PRAYER NOTES FOR TODAY

BIBLE READING

❑ **Day 282 — Matthew 4—6**

DAY 283 — SCRIPTURAL INSIGHT

Your Word, the Holy Scriptures, reveal to me, Holy Father, Your will and how I can realize it in my life. I receive light, love, and liberty as I search the scriptures and open my mind and heart to Your guidance. Today:

Give me insight for spiritual GROWTH. Every day I want to grow stronger in You, to please You, and to be an effective witness of Your love. Your Word provides the path to follow to do this. **I will follow Your path!**

Give me insight to share GRACE. Your grace is sufficient for salvation, healing, comfort, and fortification against Satan. Your Word provides guidelines to do this. **I will embrace Your guidelines!**

Give me insight for worshiping GLORY. Your glory, nature, characteristics, and name are to be honored, respected, and lifted up in praise and worship. Your Word provides directions to do this. I **will safeguard Your directions!**

MY PRAYER NOTES FOR TODAY

____

____

____

____

____

BIBLE READING

❑ **Day 283 — Matthew 7—9**

DAY 284 — SEARCH ME

God of everlasting and unconditional love, search me today. I want my heart to be holy, my thinking to be Christ-centered, and my attitude to be governed by Your grace and gifts.

I request of You today, don't let questions block my view of the open doors You have set before me to experience new horizons, to go deeper into the mysteries of biblical doctrine, and to grow stronger and taller in exercising spiritual gifts.

I request of You today, anoint me with the "oil of gladness" that I might glow and show Your nature in my dedication, my deeds, and my declarations of faith in You.

I request of You today, a song of praise on my lips, open ears to hear from You, and helping hands to serve and show Your love.

MY PRAYER NOTES FOR TODAY

BIBLE READING

❑ **Day 284 — Matthew 10—12**

DAY 285 — SECURITY IN YOU

My hope, my security is in You, Father of unlimited power. Today I claim my security in You.

Check my STEADFASTNESS. I don't have to sway in my commitment. I can be steady because of the strength You give to me. I will work and minister today standing secure in You.

Check my SPIRIT. I want to be positive in facing the challenges of life and show a spirit of trust and optimism. I want to exhibit an upbeat attitude and convey self-confidence by the indwelling of the Holy Spirit.

Check my SOURCES. Am I drawing daily power from Your Word? I know Your Word will guide me into all truth and equip me with wisdom to make wise decisions. Strong relationships, service to others, and heart-anchored worship are sources that build me up and that make me effective in kingdom ministry.

MY PRAYER NOTES FOR TODAY

BIBLE READING

❑ **Day 285 — Matthew 13—15**

DAY 286 — SELF-LEADERSHIP

Under Your oversight, Father, I am responsible to practice self-leadership. I cannot take a back seat and let emotions, the opinions of others, and circumstances lead me. I must take the lead in my own life by trusting You, fostering great expectations, and developing skills. Guide me to:

Release POWER. I am open and ready to receive. Release Your power in my life. Your strength will enable me to practice self-leadership, to be disciplined, stand firm, and move forward in Christian growth and service. **I will take control by Your power.**

Recognize POTENTIAL. Master, I am thankful for the gifts You have placed in my life. I want to fully recognize, develop, and maximize them for personal fulfillment in following Your Son, Jesus Christ. **I will take the lead by honoring You with my potential.**

Respond to PROBLEMS. I will face and solve problems by employing self-leadership. I will lead by controlling my tongue, putting down temptation, and utilizing my talents. Father, I want to lead by self-control and by example. **I will depend on You to lead me so I can lead in fulfilling Your will.**

MY PRAYER NOTES FOR TODAY

____

____

____

____

____

BIBLE READING

❑ **Day 286 — Matthew 16—18**

DAY 287 — SEND DELIVERANCE

Many forces attempt to distract me from seeing and following Your will for my life. Bondage-breaking heavenly Father, send deliverance today so I can be a motivating influence in my life at home, work, and church.

Deliver me from SMALL thinking. I want Your creative spirit to flow in my life. I want to see clearly my potential to grow in grace, to be a loving leader in my home, and to be a vision-caster in my church. **Let me think big, bold thoughts today!**

Deliver me from SPIRITUAL lukewarmness. I want to be a fire-spreading believer. I want to radiate a contagious spirit of love for the Lord and His Church. **Let me show love for the needy and the unchurched.**

Deliver me from SENSELESS acts. I want to be disciplined in my conduct. I want to reflect dependability and to let my friends and coworkers know they can trust me to be open-minded, honest, and accountable. **Let me maintain a sparkling reputation.**

MY PRAYER NOTES FOR TODAY

BIBLE READING

❑ **Day 287 — Matthew 19—21**

DAY 288 — SETTING GOALS

I realize, Master, that goals serve as a guide and a gauge for outlining productive paths and measuring progress. It is vital that I set spiritual goals to motivate involvement in ministry and measure discipleship maturity. I will set goals to:

REENERGIZE dreams. Father, You have given me sparkling dreams of expanding my Christian testimony, advancing my career, and drawing closer to my family and friends. I want to achieve all of these goals, but I need Your energizing power to keep them fresh and to maintain daily discipline. **I look to You for this!**

REACH out. Today I want to reach out and explore new possibilities and paths of self-improvement. You have created a wonderful world. I will cherish it, learn more about it, and develop the resources it offers me. **I ask for Your guidance to do this!**

RESPECT achievements. I will show appreciation for the fruitful growth, family harmony, and financial gain you work in my life. I will respect achievements because they come from You. **I praise You for Your glorious gifts of love and care!**

MY PRAYER NOTES FOR TODAY

____

____

____

____

____

BIBLE READING

❑ **Day 288 — Matthew 22—24**

DAY 289 — SHAPING HOPE

Hope brings comfort and confronts a defeatist attitude. I want to share and spread hope. The backbone of hope is the transforming power of Your Son, Jesus. Equip, enable, and empower me to be an effective distributor of Your good news. I want to:

STAND for hope. I am surrounded by people who have lost hope, who look and live on the negative side of life. Let my ways testify that I have strong convictions about hope, health, happiness, and wholeness.

SPEAK words of hope. I want to model hope, but I also want to speak words of hope. I want to point people to the positive change that can take place, gold mines of solutions and strength that can be discovered, and creative thinking that can rule the mind.

SHARE ways of hope. Hope begins with faith in, and commitment to, Jesus Christ. Supportive hope can be found in Christian fellowship, seeking new avenues to develop personal skills, and examining career and financial values. Father, I will share the hope You have given to me with others today.

MY PRAYER NOTES FOR TODAY

____

____

____

____

____

BIBLE READING

❑ **Day 289 — Matthew 25–28**

DAY 290 — SHAPING ENVIRONMENT

My environment, Father, can lift me up or let me down! I have a responsibility to help shape my environment to be conducive to happiness and health. I need Your Spirit working within me to help make this happen. I will:

RECOGNIZE the contributions of others. I do not live in isolation. Many individuals contribute to my security, service, and significance. I want to affirm their value in making my life fulfilling and complete. I will do this today in conversation and prayer.

RESTORE confidence in teamwork. Master, my church family is a team. As we work together in fulfilling the Great Commission, You are honored, the church influences the community, and young people are trained to live godly lives. I want to be trustworthy and to build strong teamwork loyalty.

REVIEW opportunities to serve. My vision is to serve You, my church, and others. I will carefully review opportunities, possibilities, and practices I can adopt and develop. I ask for wisdom today to trust and obey, to act with courage, and to be dedicated and dependable.

MY PRAYER NOTES FOR TODAY

____

____

____

____

____

BIBLE READING

❑ **Day 290 — Mark 1—3**

DAY 291 – SHARING RESOURCES

In times of hardships and crisis among friends and neighbors, it is my duty to share resources with them. Not only is it a duty, it is also an opportunity to showcase the love and compassion of Jesus Christ. I need supernatural strength to meet the challenge. Equip me, empower me to:

PROVIDE support. Father, You have blessed me. I want to bless others in their time of need with food, clothing, shelter, counseling, and encouragement. I want to do this with a humble spirit, helping hands, and a heart of compassion. I ask You for a covering of grace and guidance.

PARTNER in a relationship. Your Word tells me that a true friend "loves at all times." Food lasts only for a short period of time, but friendship is ongoing. Help me to build relationships through understanding and interaction to lay a foundation of trust.

PROCLAIM the truth. Truth sets free. I will provide support, partner in a relationship, and share the good news of new life in Jesus Christ. Let me know, Father, when the time is right. Let me move with You to bring about repentance, renewal, and restoration.

MY PRAYER NOTES FOR TODAY

BIBLE READING

❑ **Day 291 – Mark 4–6**

DAY 292 — SHARING THE FAITH

Faith is a beautiful virtue. Faith is hooking my life to Your promises. I praise You, Master, for birthing faith in my heart. It frees me, keeps me, and issues internal and external fulfillment. Faith is free, and it can transform the lives of my relatives and friends if I share it with them. Anoint me to:

Tell about faith and the FUTURE. Faith paints a picture of future acceptance, achievements, and advancement. Your plan for humankind is intimate fellowship with You. **Today I will tell about faith that gives meaning to life!**

Tell about faith and FORGIVENESS. Father, people are perplexed, burdened with guilt, and searching for meaning. Your forgiveness requires only asking and accepting by faith. **Today I will tell about forgiveness that gives new directions in life!**

Tell about faith and FAVOR. Through faith I can walk in Your favor with divine protection, surplus provisions, and performance power. You send Your favor to those who embrace the future and accept Your forgiveness. **Today I will tell about the wonder and splendor of Your favor!**

MY PRAYER NOTES FOR TODAY

____

____

____

____

____

BIBLE READING

❑ **Day 292 — Mark 7—9**

DAY 293 — SHINING INTEGRITY

Father of consistent holiness, my desire is to follow Your example in my daily modeling of purity, trust, and temperance. I want to shine as Your child, as a servant, and as a soldier of hope and freedom.

I want to be STEADFAST in faith. I want to trust You in all circumstances. I also want my family and friends to be able to trust me in all circumstances. I want to be a person who stands by his or her word and who shows faith by works.

I want to SERVE with humility. Thank You for the privilege to serve You, to serve in my church, and to serve as a power point in Your kingdom. Touch me to serve effectively, with enthusiasm, and with a spirit of thanksgiving.

I want to STAND up in witnessing. I want to be bold and positive, yet tactful in sharing the good news of love, liberty, and life in Jesus Christ. I want to stand up, stand steady, and stand tenaciously for the unchanging precepts of Your Holy Word.

MY PRAYER NOTES FOR TODAY

____

____

____

____

____

BIBLE READING

❑ **Day 293 — Mark 10—12**

DAY 294 — SHOWING APPRECIATION

It is an extraordinary privilege to live in a land where I can worship, work, and witness about my faith without persecution or intervention from the government. I am thankful that we still print "In God We Trust" on our currency. I want to be a model citizen and show appreciation for the:

Land of LIBERTY. My country is not in bondage. There is no dictator, no slavery, no persecution. There is freedom to pursue goals, raise a family, and contribute to the good of the nation. I am thankful for spiritual liberty and to live in a land of liberty.

Land I LOVE. I love my country because I live in freedom and can express my faith freely. I want to show this love by accepting civic responsibilities, respecting leaders, and participating in community projects. I pray for national, state, and local leaders.

Land to show LOYALTY. Father, when I am loyal to You, I will show loyalty to my country. When I serve You, I help build a healthy society. When I am a dedicated Christian, I display the characteristics of a model citizen. Today I want to walk with You in liberty, love, and loyalty.

MY PRAYER NOTES FOR TODAY

____

____

____

____

____

BIBLE READING

❑ **Day 294 — Mark 13—16**

DAY 295 — SHOWING HOSPITALITY

Showing hospitality reveals positive self-esteem, a keen appreciation for the value of others, and Christian character. Father, I want to represent You by maintaining scriptural convictions, a calm disposition, and courteous manners. Guide me, Master, to show hospitality:

At WORK. I spend a major portion of each day at work. I desire to be productive. More importantly, however, I desire to be a personal witness of a Christ-like lifestyle. This calls for me to be punctual, dependable, efficient, and to show caring hospitality.

In WORSHIP. Hospitality reveals love, appreciation, confidence, and praise. I desire to be fervent in worship and to inspire others to express themselves reverently and freely. This calls for me to yield spiritually, to be prayerfully alert, and to be obediently focused in exalting You, wonderful Father.

While WITNESSING. In representing you, Father, I must be polite, respectful, and tactful in explaining Your plan of repentance and forgiveness. I will depend on the Holy Spirit to be my guide so I can be an influential witness through holy hospitality.

MY PRAYER NOTES FOR TODAY

BIBLE READING

❑ **Day 295 — Luke 1–3**

DAY 296 — SHOWING YOUR LOVE

Father of all goodness, You have set a wonderful day before me bristling with opportunities to relate, create, and facilitate. Your love is the foundation for all of these and I want to show Your love today. I want to show:

Your love CURES broken hearts, strained relationships, and unfulfilled dreams. Your love provides a new start, new directions, and new goals for every person, regardless of surroundings or situations.

Your love expresses COMPASSION for the needy, hungry, and homeless. You work through Your Church to demonstrate that love is action, feeding, restoring, and stabilizing.

Your love builds CONVICTIONS that are firm and instill faithfulness. Your love is the same yesterday, today, and forever. It doesn't change. I want to show Your love in my life by practicing the true elements of divine love. Anoint me with your love today!

MY PRAYER NOTES FOR TODAY

____

____

____

____

____

BIBLE READING

❑ **Day 296 — Luke 4—6**

DAY 297 — SPEAK POWERFUL WORDS

Words have power to condemn or comfort, insult or inspire, injure or inform. Lord of love, I want "to speak the truth in love" and to use words to create connectivity and wholeness. I will speak:

WORSHIPING words. I will keep words of thanksgiving and praise on my lips. I will express thanksgiving to You for life in Christ, for family and friends, and for heath and happiness. I will praise You, Father, and the fruit of the abundant life You provide.

WINNING words. I will purpose to speak positive, nurturing, uplifting, and strengthening words today. I will talk about excellence, dignity, and the acceptance of challenging goals. I will purposefully lace my conversations with words that center on the creative and strengthening force of the Holy Spirit.

WITNESSING Words. I will share words that convey my love and devotion to Your Son, Jesus Christ. I need your guidance to speak the right words at the right time. I also need power to represent You with appealing grace, pure motives, prevailing prayer, a pleasing personality, and influential sincerity.

MY PRAYER NOTES FOR TODAY

____

____

____

____

____

BIBLE READING

❑ Day 297 — Luke 7—9

DAY 298 — SPECIAL GRACE

Today, God of grace, be with me. Grant me

In my **work**, Your **wisdom**.

In my **difficulties**, divine **direction**.

In my **opportunities**, the **touch** of the Master, Jesus Christ.

Today, let Your love flow like a river in me and through me

Changing my attitude and actions.

Touching others with warm care and heavenly wisdom.

Illuminating my path so I can walk with steady steps and guided by the Holy Spirit.

Today, I will show forth grace that

Encourages the weak and weary.

Stimulates faith to attempt great things for God.

Builds confidence to witness with authority.

MY PRAYER NOTES FOR TODAY

BIBLE READING

❑ **Day 298 — Luke 10—12**

DAY 299 — SPIRITUAL GROWTH

Growth is a grand and glorious privilege. Yet it can include pain and reworking plans. Father, I want to be ready for all that positive growth entails. But I need Your undergirding support and strength. Equip me, empower me, to grow:

In APPRECIATION. I want to grow in my appreciation of Your love, the promise of heaven, and the guidance of the Holy Spirit. I also want to show a greater appreciation for my faith, my family, and my friends. And I will!

In APPEARANCE. I want my appearance to symbolize strength of character, dependability, and honorable intentions. I want people to see in me that I am open, honest, and unpretentious. Enable me to appear calm, confident, and committed to You!

In AGGRESSIVENESS. I want to step out in visionary ministry that magnifies You, elevates the cross of Christ, and brings the Church together in harmony and holy hunger to reach the lost. Clothe me with a spirit of Bible-based aggressiveness. I lift up willing hands to receive Your anointing for continual growth in the image and nature of Christ!

MY PRAYER NOTES FOR TODAY

BIBLE READING

❑ **Day 299 — Luke 13—15**

DAY 300 — SPIRITUAL INTEGRITY

Lord, I want to be open and honest before You today. No cover up, confusion about facts, or doubts about faith. I want to be a person of integrity.

I want integrity in INFORMATION—facts I share with others. I do not want to color information so that it will appear to be something that it is not; I want to be gracious, but truthful.

I want integrity in INSPIRATION—compliments I share with others. I do not want to say things that I really do not feel in order to gain attention or acceptance. I want to bless and encourage, based on true feelings.

I want integrity in INTERCESSION—requests I share with You. I do not want to pray superficially and simply go through the motions. I want to commune with You sincerely, respectfully, and openly. I want to be an agreeable, accountable, and dependable person of integrity.

MY PRAYER NOTES FOR TODAY

____

____

____

____

____

BIBLE READING

❑ **Day 300 — Luke 16—18**

DAY 301 — SPIRITUAL POWER

I realize, protective Father, that the forces of evil are around me and want to rip apart my faith and separate me from Your protection and care. I need spiritual power to live a life of balance and beauty in Christ. Today I claim Your power:

To PARTNER with You. I am not alone in my fight against Satan. I am a partner with You and all Your resources are available to me. Today I will take authority to stand tall and speak of Your unlimited power.

To be PRODUCTIVE in You. I can exercise the gifts of the Spirit and produce the fruit of the Spirit. Today I will look out, look in, and then I will look up to You. My strength and security comes from You.

To be PERSUASIVE in You. I want to model a Christ-centered life and be a witness that makes a difference. Today I will put on Your promised armor, fight the good fight of faith, and broadcast the good news with confidence.

MY PRAYER NOTES FOR TODAY

BIBLE READING

❑ **Day 301 — Luke 19—21**

DAY 302 — SPREADING CHEER

Father, I want to spread cheer today, encouraging, lifting up, and motivating. I can only do this by the infusion of Your love and the inspiration of the Holy Spirit. I ask You to anoint me to spread cheer by:

RELIEVING strain. There will be strain in my home, at work, and even in the church. I will relieve strain by creating a relaxing, open atmosphere. I will talk about the peace of Christ that relieves, lifts up, and issues calmness.

RESTORING confidence. Pressure and pitfalls weaken personal confidence and cause doubt and confusion. Father, You restore confidence by focusing on possibilities. Make me Your messenger who builds spiritual pride, dignity, and honor.

REVIVING vision. My vision of Your glory, Father, sometimes becomes fuzzy as a result of negative surroundings. Revive my vision of Your glory, grace to overcome, gifts to receive, and guidance to excel. Thank You, Master, for resisting strength and for the confidence and vision to live a high and holy life.

MY PRAYER NOTES FOR TODAY

____

____

____

____

____

BIBLE READING

❑ **Day 302 — Luke 22—24**

DAY 303 — STANDING TALL

Lord of unlimited power, I want to stand tall today in my commitment to You—firm, fruitful, inflexible in faith and Christian loyalty. I want my friends and associates to know where I stand, the principles I stand for, and the source of my ability to stand. Touch me to:

Stand tall in SPEECH. Let my walk support my talk. Empower me to speak positive, encouraging words of faith, hope, trust, and dependability. Let me speak words of truth and life in Jesus Christ.

Stand tall in SEPARATION. I realize I must live a separated and sanctified life in order to please You and to positively influence my friends and neighbors. I ask You for inward fortitude to be disciplined in prayer and Bible study, and to abstain from the very appearance of evil.

Stand tall in SERVICE. I want to serve You with freshness and zeal, to be spiritually aglow. I want to serve my church through participation in outreach projects that minister to the searching, lonely, confused, and unchurched. Today, standing by Your side, overshadow me with Your all-sufficient grace.

MY PRAYER NOTES FOR TODAY

____

____

____

____

____

BIBLE READING

❑ **Day 303 — John 1—3**

DAY 304 – STANDING AGAINST SATAN

A believer should spread peace. There is also a time to stand up and fight against the sin and wickedness in society. I ask you today, heavenly Father, to guide me in knowing when and how to spread peace and when to fight. There is:

A time for FELLOWSHIP. I know that I am in the world but I am not a part of the world's system. Teach me how to have fellowship with people in the world so I can invest in them through a wholesome relationship and show the love of Christ that liberates and issues a sustained flow of inward peace.

A time for FREEDOM. There is a right time to share a verbal witness, to speak out against wrong doings, and to stand up for godly principles. Teach me to be in tune with Your Spirit so my witness will make a difference. I need Your wisdom to be prudent and persuasive.

A time to FIGHT. You will bless me as a peacemaker. I also believe You will bless me as a fighter. Teach me to be bold in defending truth and fighting against enemies who attempt to destroy unity and growth. I will be both a faith-giver and a faith-fighter today!

MY PRAYER NOTES FOR TODAY

____

____

____

____

____

BIBLE READING

❑ Day 304 – John 4–6

DAY 305 — STAY FOCUSED

Father, I want to stay focused and move with Your mission. I want to do seven things:

1. **Realize** that my work today will impact my FUTURE—**Mission.**
2. **Realize** my attitude will contribute to a positive OUTCOME—**Objectives.**
3. **Realize** that sharing my vision will foster CONFIDENCE—**Self-image.**
4. **Realize** my connection with others will create UNITY—**Purpose.**
5. **Realize** that my approach will create a bonding SPIRIT—**Teamwork.**
6. **Realize** that my ministry will revolve around ETERNITY—**Values.**
7. **Realize that** my efforts will be undergirded by DEITY—**Empowerment.**

I will stay focused today!

MY PRAYER NOTES FOR TODAY

BIBLE READING

❑ **Day 305 — John 7–9**

DAY 306 — STEADFAST AND SECURE

Eternal Father, You are steadfast in all of Your ways. You do not change in Your divine nature, acts of kindness, or care for those who are a part of Your family. I have security and a solid foundation for work, ministry, and relationships. I want Your steadfastness to shape my life. I want to be steadfast in my:

EXPERIENCE with You. I want to be dependable and accountable in my walk with You, in my work at church, and in my witness in daily life. I want Christ to be constantly reflected in my life.

EMOTIONS with others. I want people to have confidence in me to be balanced, agreeable, and co-operative. I can only do this by the inner strength You provide by the equipping power of the Holy Spirit.

EXCITEMENT about life. I want to live a full life every day! Walking with You is filled with adventure, experiencing new things, and witnessing the wonders of Your love. My mind and heart are open today to the flow of Your glorious miracle-working presence and power.

MY PRAYER NOTES FOR TODAY

BIBLE READING

❑ **Day 306 — John 10—12**

DAY 307 — STICKABILITY

Stickability! Unchangeable heavenly Father, I want to be known as a believer with concrete values and credibility. I want to be dependable and influential. In order to lift up these goals and live by these aspirations, I need a daily infusion of divine initiative and inspiration. Empower me:

To stick with spiritual STANDARDS. Lord, abiding by Your standards gives strength and stickability. I want Your Word to be active in all areas of my life. Your Word is my foundation for firm, guiding principles and standards. I will stick with them.

To stick with spiritual SUCCESS. Achievement and victory! Father, You have promised overcoming power to be "more than a conqueror." This means total victory, success! In both my home and church life, let me focus on spiritual success.

To stick with spiritual STRENGTH. In victory and success, let me always remember that it comes from You. I want to maintain a humble and submissive attitude, always lifting You up in praise for spiritual strength to achieve, obtain, and advance.

MY PRAYER NOTES FOR TODAY

____

BIBLE READING

❑ **Day 307 — John 13—15**

DAY 308 — STICKING FAITH

Father, You are faithful in all Your ways. I want to be faithful in my relationship with You in all my ways—Christian ethics, career, and conduct. I need "sticking" faith to do this. Give me faith today to:

Stick with STANDARDS. In Your strength I will stick with biblical standards of personal surrender to Your will, to being an example in Christian service, and to sincere worship in spirit and truth. I **ask for steadfast, "sticking" faith!**

Stick with SCRIPTURE. Your Word, Father, is my guidebook for devotion to You. I will stick with it for making decisions and for outlining directions for my life. I will keep it in my heart so I can stay close to You. **I ask for sound, "sticking" faith!**

Stick with SUCCESS. By Your flow of faith I will experience uplifting and significant success. I will not give in, give up, give over, or give out. I will maintain a clear view of my self-worth in You, achieve worthy goals, and claim victory on every front in Jesus Christ, my Lord and Savior. **I ask for rejoicing, "sticking" faith!**

MY PRAYER NOTES FOR TODAY

____

____

____

____

____

BIBLE READING

❑ **Day 308 — John 16—18**

DAY 309 — STIMULATING ZEAL

Father, I have new life in Jesus Christ, Your Son. I want to demonstrate this new life with stimulating, glowing zeal. Your Spirit prompts me to explore, experience, and expound. Today, I do want to release these "zeal" forces.

Zeal to EXPLORE. Lord of grace and glory, there is adventure all around me—spiritual adventure, career adventure, and discovery adventure. I want to explore new possibilities in loving You and in leading others in understanding Your nature and new creation plans.

Zeal to EXPERIENCE. Father, every day You open new doors and set before me new things to experience. I do not want to hesitate or contemplate. I want to walk briskly and directly through the open doors, experiencing new revelations, thought patterns, and spiritual models.

Zeal to EXPOUND. Today, Master, I will talk about my new life and new experiences in walking with You. I want to fervently expound the beauties of life in Christ, the joy of faith, forgiveness, and the fruit of the Holy Spirit.

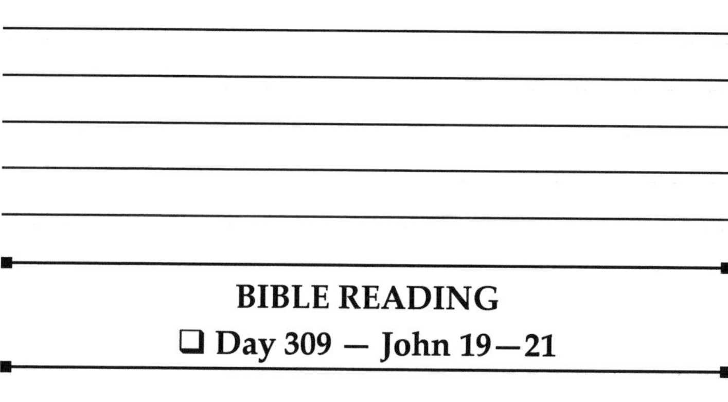

MY PRAYER NOTES FOR TODAY

BIBLE READING

❑ **Day 309 — John 19—21**

DAY 310 — STRENGTH FOR TODAY

I am grateful for the gift of physical strength. I also need Your gift of spiritual strength. I need a flow of holy energy.

I need strength to SURRENDER. I want Your will to be my will. Correct my course if I stray into paths of personal interests and desires. I seek Your directions. Give me strength to stand firmly on Your purposes for my life.

I need strength to SHINE. I do not want to hide my light of commitment to You under a bushel by being spiritually bashful. I want to reflect Your graciousness and goodness in my daily routine and in my relationships.

I need strength to SERVE. I want to serve You, Your Church, and Your family within the Church. Let me display an attitude of gratitude by performing ministry that lifts up and aids those in need of encouragement, financial help, or a faith partner to deal with strained situations.

MY PRAYER NOTES FOR TODAY

BIBLE READING

❑ **Day 310 — Acts 1—3**

DAY 311 — STRENGTH IN HIM

You, O Lord, have ordained hope. Many times I feel hopeless, helpless, useless, powerless, and visionless.

You rescued me. I can dwell in Your house (see Ps. 15:1-2) because You empower me to

walk blameless—***perfection***;
do what is righteous—***purity***;
speak the truth from my heart—***proclamation***.

You renew hope; eliminate helplessness; give vision to be useful; restore power; and clarify vision.

Thank You! Glory and praise to Your name!

MY PRAYER NOTES FOR TODAY

BIBLE READING

❑ Day 311 — Acts 4–6

DAY 312 — STRENGTHENING WORDS

My priority, heavenly Father, is to have a holy, honorable relationship with You that is evident in communion with You and commitment to the cause of Christ. My daily communion with You will connect me with others in harmony and holy health. Equip me to build relationships that show:

RESPECT. Father, the gifts You have given to me are different from the talents You have invested in others. All gifts are vital to the balanced function of Your body, the Church. I want to show respect for every person, gift, and talent in my church. **This pattern will build powerful relationships!**

RAPPORT. I know it is important to establish honest rapport with people around me in order to develop authentic relationships. I ask You for favor to create a framework to do this. **Guide me in cultivating a compassionate attitude and a caring spirit.**

RENEWAL. Relationships can become distant as a result of tension and conflicting views. Let me take positive steps to renew relationships that have become weak and fragile. **Let me be bold enough to admit my shortcomings and turnoff characteristics.**

MY PRAYER NOTES FOR TODAY

___

___

___

___

___

BIBLE READING

❑ **Day 312 — Acts 7—9**

DAY 313 — STRETCH ME TODAY

Father of superior grace, I want to experience new things with You every day. To do this I realize I must be stretched in my devotion to You and in the direction of my pursuits. So, today, I ask You to:

Stretch my MIND. Let me be creative in my thinking. I want to entertain new avenues of fellowship with You, new approaches in my prayer life, and new ways to be more effective in influencing the unchurched.

Stretch my MOTIVATION. I want to face everyday with great expectations, stirring excitement, and captivating vision. I want to see the possibilities You have set before me and act decisively and devotedly. Touch me with the Spirit of fire so I can stay fired-up for impacting service.

Stretch my MINISTRY. I want to fully utilize the gifts You have entrusted to me. I want to use them wisely, daily, meaningfully, and effectively. I ask You to anoint me by Your Spirit in developing them and in using them to lift You up in praise and to expand and fortify Your kingdom.

MY PRAYER NOTES FOR TODAY

BIBLE READING

❑ **Day 313 — Acts 10—12**

DAY 314 — CLOSER COMMUNICATION

Communicating with You, Holy Father, is a wonderful, unprecedented privilege. I honor and praise You for this glorious privilege. I will cherish it, safeguard it, seek harmony in it, and strengthen it through:

CONFESSION. Lord, thank You for forgiveness. I confess my faults, shortcomings, and need for complete integrity in communicating with You. I always want to confess my true feelings, aspirations, and needs with You.

CLARITY. You know my thoughts, Master, before I speak. However, You want me to express myself clearly, openly, and fervently. This is what I want to do and will do by the inspiration of the Holy Spirit.

CONNECTION. Father, I want my spirit to connect in relationship to Your will, purposes, and nature. I want to walk the path You have set before me in perfect harmony with Your divine plan and connect with You in worship, serving, and witnessing.

MY PRAYER NOTES FOR TODAY

____

____

____

____

____

BIBLE READING

❑ **Day 314 — Acts 13—15**

DAY 315 — THANK YOU FOR STUFF

Lord of all resources, I thank You for stuff today—things I don't absolutely need but You give them to me anyway.

Giver of all resources, You have promised me food, shelter, and clothing. These things are great gifts from You! I don't take these great gifts for granted. I daily lift my eyes upward, "for my help comes from the Lord" (Ps. 121:2).

Master of all resources, You don't stop with my daily needs. You go far beyond food, shelter, and clothing. You give me things that are not necessities. But, I enjoy them; they are "from above" also.

God of all resources, thank You for stuff—new household items, fishing equipment, trendy clothing, vacations, sporting items, dining out, jewelry, and attending enjoyable events. I am so thankful, grateful, and appreciative for stuff. But above all, I am thankful for salvation!

MY PRAYER NOTES FOR TODAY

____

____

____

____

____

BIBLE READING

❑ Day 315 — Acts 16—18

DAY 316 — SUCCESS TODAY

Your Son, Jesus Christ, was successful because He knew, followed, and proclaimed Your will.

I want to follow His example in living Your will today in my **spirit**, my **speech**, and my **service** with You and for You.

My SPIRIT—upbeat, outgoing, Christ-exalting, friendship-building.

My SPEECH—enthusiastic, encouraging, Christ-honoring, soothing, integrity-based.

My SERVICE—joyful, unpretentious, Christ-centered, grateful, kingdom-building.

Today is a gift from You, a package filled with grace that reveals the way of truth, light, holy experiences, and supernatural joy. Let me receive sunshine from You and spread sunshine about You in love.

MY PRAYER NOTES FOR TODAY

____

____

____

____

____

BIBLE READING

❑ **Day 316 — Acts 19—21**

DAY 317 — SUNSHINE IN MY SOUL

Sunshine warms, purifies, and gives light. Sunshine refreshes, invigorates, and inspires. Father, thank You for the favor and flow of divine sunshine. My soul flourishes on the energy from sunshine. I want sunshine in my soul to be:

Scripturally SOUND. I trust the Bible to be my guide. All my actions and activities must have scriptural roots. Your Word comforts, corrects, outlines a secure course, and generates sunshine in my soul.

Relationally SEASONED. My friends and associates can be a source of sunshine in my life. I want to be mature and trustworthy in my relationships and how I demonstrate respect. Father, let the joy of my relationship with You overflow and touch those I am around today.

Prayerfully SERVING. In my conversation with You, I want to be instructed on how to serve with an unselfish spirit and with glowing happiness. May Your sunshine in my life warm and refresh those I interact with today.

MY PRAYER NOTES FOR TODAY

BIBLE READING

❑ Day 317 — Acts 22—24

DAY 318 — SUPPORTING LEADERS

Lord of heaven, You are above all nations, rulers, and armies. You are all-powerful, all-knowing, and omnipresent. You set up or put down as You see fit. In Your wisdom You have instructed me to honor and support those in authority. In obedience to You, I want to do this. I will support:

CHURCH leaders. My Father, You have appointed and anointed church leaders to feed Your flock, to guide in becoming mature disciples, and to direct in Christian service. I want to be a model follower and supporter. I will consistently support church leaders with prayer, encouragement, and stewardship.

COUNTRY leaders. My president is required to make decisions that affect the health, wealth, and welfare of the people. I will pray that He will seek You for guidance and utilize Your Word as a standard for behavior and operational policies.

COMMUNITY leaders. My community leaders represent the values and living standards of the people. I will work with them by participating in support activities. I will undergird them with consistent prayer for vision and integrity in performing duties.

MY PRAYER NOTES FOR TODAY

____

____

____

____

____

BIBLE READING

❑ **Day 318 — Acts 25—28**

DAY 319 — SUPREME PEACE

I want to experience Your peace today, life-giving Father. You want to give me daily peace and I want to accept it, apply it, and live by it.

Today, I accept Your peace for my MIND. I will be free, creative, and positive in my thinking. I will let the mind of Christ be my model and guide—pure, kind, considerate, compassionate, and heaven-focused.

Today, I accept Your peace for my MINISTRY. I will be content with, develop, and maximize to the fullest degree the spiritual gifts You have invested in me. I will minister with confidence, joyfulness, boldness, diplomacy, and Spirit-powered energy.

Today, I accept Your peace for MOTIVATION. I will look for ways to grow spiritually, to relate effectively, and to perform professionally. I will be visionary, enthusiastic, pro-active, and success-oriented.

MY PRAYER NOTES FOR TODAY

BIBLE READING

❑ **Day 319 — Romans 1–3**

DAY 320 — SUSTAINING STRENGTH

Today I can face the test, whatever it might be, through the sustaining strength You provide, mighty Father. This assurance creates courage and gives me a conquering disposition. Your sustaining strength will empower me to:

Recognize POSSIBILITIES. Father, You will set opportunities before me to explore new paths of self-improvement, of expanded faith to achieve, and high levels of expressing thanksgiving to You. Clear my eyes so I can see and seize the privileges and possibilities You set before me.

Face PROBLEMS. There will be problems today. I will face them with biblical optimism, bold belief, and heaven-sent strength. I will grow stronger by solving them through the guidance of the Holy Spirit.

Bypass PITFALLS. Satan will set pitfalls before me. You will steer me around them. I will go forward unhindered to achieve spiritual goals. I will also be a ministry model to help others bypass pitfalls and understand the deep dimensions of Your sustaining strength.

MY PRAYER NOTES FOR TODAY

____

____

____

____

____

BIBLE READING

❑ **Day 320 — Romans 4—6**

DAY 321 — TAKE CHARGE TODAY

Father, I know You have all power; that You are in charge of Your kingdom. I am aware, however, that I must release my will, goals, and desires to You. Take charge of my aspirations, activities, and action.

Let Your **love** shine in my life.

Let Your **grace** form my relationships.

Let Your **Word** stabilize me.

Let Your **Spirit** empower me.

Let Your **church** disciple me.

Take charge of my life. Be in control of where I go and what I do. I release myself to Your care and keeping.

MY PRAYER NOTES FOR TODAY

BIBLE READING

❑ **Day 321 — Romans 7—9**

DAY 322 — TALKING WITH GOD

What a grand and glorious privilege! The privilege to talk with You, joy-giving Father, to talk one-on-one, personally, confidentially. Thank you! When I talk with You, I think about the composition of my prayer time:

The TRUTH of talking with You. You invite me to talk with You and You give me the assurance that You will listen and respond. I can talk openly without fear of rejection or condemnation. **I honor You for this!**

The THRILL of talking with You. I feel Your presence. It stirs my soul, giving assurance, courage, and laughter. I feel strong and significant when I commune with You. **I praise You for this!**

The TURNAROUND possibilities in talking with You. Prayer-power can turn around individuals, projects, and situations. Today I will pray, trust, and believe. Nothing is too hard for You. **I exalt Your name for this!**

MY PRAYER NOTES FOR TODAY

____

____

____

____

____

BIBLE READING

❑ **Day 322 — Romans 10—12**

DAY 323 — THANKFUL FOR GIFTS

Loving Lord, I am thankful for spiritual gifts that You have ordained to guide Your people in fulfilling the Church's mission. Guide me in recognizing and respecting the gifts you have given to different individuals in the Church, and in developing and demonstrating the gifts You have invested in me.

INDIVIDUAL gifts. Father, the Church is one body with many members. Each member is essential to biblical evangelism and effectiveness. I embrace each member with affirmation and prayer. May we all come together as a team to advance the mission of the church.

INSPIRATIONAL gifts. Included in Your gift package are gifts that inspire for aggressive, visionary daily living. I want to walk in the full range of these gifts today, experiencing, exploring, and enjoying them.

INSTRUCTIONAL gifts. Thank You, Master, for gifts that inform and instruct. I need coaching! I need companionship to keep me in "the way." Today I will listen and learn as You lead me. I have a heart of love and thanksgiving, and I honor and praise You!

MY PRAYER NOTES FOR TODAY

BIBLE READING

❑ **Day 323 — Romans 13—16**

DAY 324 — THANKFUL FOR CARE

Dependable, divine Father, I am so thankful You watch over me every day and care about my wholeness and happiness. I go about my daily activities with the assurance of your nearness to give peace, guarantee protection, and supply provisions. I am grateful! My life is secure because of:

Your PEACE. No stress or strain today! I have peace from You, Master. You give me peace of mind. I will think holy, constructive, and peaceful thoughts. You give me peace, soundness, wholeness, wellness, pleasantness, and happiness. **I am super thankful!**

Your PROTECTION. No fear or isolation today! I have protection from You, Lord. You stand guard over me and protect me from the traps and advances of the Evil One, the devil. This gives me security and boldness. **I am richly thankful!**

Your PROVISIONS. No want or shortage today! I have provisions from You, Father. You prepare a table before me and I am sufficiently fed. You clothe me with righteous raiment. You provide shelter, security, and family happiness. **I am super, richly blessed!**

MY PRAYER NOTES FOR TODAY

____

____

____

____

____

BIBLE READING

❑ **Day 324 — 1 Corinthians 1—3**

DAY 325 — THE ABUNDANT LIFE

I have glorious, challenging dreams about tomorrow that you have placed in my mind. You have also assured me of an abundant, beautiful life today.

Today I will **LIFT** up my eyes and faith to You to understand, discuss, and receive Your abundant presence, power, and promises.

Today I will **LOVE** others in a way that will reveal Your abundant, forgiving, and providing love.

Today I will **LEAN** on You and Your invitation to receive affirmation, assurance, and divine energy to advance Your cause.

Thank You for abundance today!

MY PRAYER NOTES FOR TODAY

BIBLE READING

❑ **Day 325 — 1 Corinthians 4—6**

DAY 326 — THE GIFT OF LIFE

Today I rose early and embraced the gifts of love and life directly from you.

Joy awaits me in the world of people and beauty You have created. New adventures to experience, new people to greet, **new gifts to receive from You.**

I will express my love to my companion. I will convey love and appreciation to those close to me and to those who need a touch of kindness. I will tell about **Your gift of salvation in Jesus Christ.**

I recognize, like Enoch, You will walk and talk with me, revealing Your nature in a more detailed manner and bestowing **unique gifts, inspiration, and revelation.**

I will look up with holy anticipation, look in with self evaluation, look around to sense possibilities, and look ahead to **future gifts You have in store for me.**

MY PRAYER NOTES FOR TODAY

BIBLE READING

❑ **Day 326 — 1 Corinthians 7—9**

DAY 327 — THE GREAT COMMISSION

Lord of the harvest, You have given the church a holy mandate to go everywhere and tell everyone that Jesus Christ is the hope of the world (see Matt. 28:19). I have a responsibility in this task, a responsibility to act! I will act positively. I will:

Understand the MISSION and be an ambassador of love and truth. The mission given by Your Son, Jesus Christ, must be given priority attention by the church and by me. I will show my love for Christ! I will share what He means to me. I will lift high the name of Christ as Savior and Lord!

Stay MOTIVATED to be an example of trustworthy commitment. Father, every day I want to wake up with enthusiasm and start the day with great expectations of receiving from You, representing You with dignity, and responding to the opportunities to talk about Your kingdom.

Develop METHODS to be an effective witness. There are many ways to represent You. I want to develop the ways that are natural, nonthreatening, and inviting. Bathe me with a Christian fragrance that attracts and influences the surroundings.

MY PRAYER NOTES FOR TODAY

BIBLE READING

❑ **Day 327 — 1 Corinthians 10—12**

DAY 328 — IN THE NAME OF JESUS

I will speak the name of Jesus today! It is a name above every name—eternal, powerful, and energizing. Father, thank You for the ministry of Your Son, Jesus Christ, and the power in His name. I will recognize and rejoice in what His name represents and provides:

REGENERATION. I am a new person, recreated through the power of the name of Jesus Christ. I praise You, Father, that old things are in the past and new, intriguing things are before me. **I will live in newness of life today!**

REJOICING. I am filled with joy, happiness, and contentment today through the power of the name of Jesus Christ. I honor You, Father, that You fill every day with excitement and opportunities for new adventure. **I will live with refreshing joy today!**

RELEASING. I have authority, boldness, achievement, and zeal today through the name of Jesus Christ. I look to You, Father, to release Your energy and will through me in performing kingdom ministry. **I will live with victory power released from Your throne today!**

MY PRAYER NOTES FOR TODAY

____

____

____

____

____

BIBLE READING

❑ **Day 328 — 1 Corinthians 13—16**

DAY 329 — THE POWER OF TODAY

Yesterday's actions are valuable for insight and learning experiences. Tomorrow's thoughts build dreams and inspire hope. Today's activities give significance, structure for success, and power for life.

Today gives power to make a difference through productivity, relationships, and creativity.

Today gives power to become a stronger person through learning, exploring, and experiencing.

Today gives power to grow in Christlikeness through sincere prayer, Christian service, and sharing the good news of new life in Christ.

Today I will rejoice in my opportunities, seize my opportunities, maximize my opportunities, exalt Christ in my opportunities, and become a better person through my opportunities.

MY PRAYER NOTES FOR TODAY

____

____

____

____

____

BIBLE READING

❑ **Day 329 — 2 Corinthians 1—3**

DAY 330 — THE POWER TO SAY YES

All-wise Father, I thank You for the privilege to say "yes" or "no" to the many questions and challenges I face every day. You give me wisdom to make right choices, courage to confront evil, and strength to stay committed. Today:

I will say YES to majestic miracles. You always do the unusual and the extraordinary. You make a way in the wilderness and You open doors that seemingly cannot be opened. **I will look for Your miracle hand of action today!**

I will say YES to mission motivation. You permit me to personally participate in kingdom work. You give me assignments that call for vision and fortitude. **I will show excitement and enthusiasm in mission today!**

I will say YES to moving ministries. You want me to support ministries that move people to know You and walk with You and that make a difference in all aspects of their life. **I will promote local church programs and activities with sparkling faith today!**

MY PRAYER NOTES FOR TODAY

BIBLE READING

❑ Day 330 — 2 Corinthians 4—6

DAY 331 — THE PROMISE OF HEAVEN

I am thankful, Holy Father, for the promise of heaven. It is a promise that is definite, secure, and permanent. As I meditate on heaven today, it provides me with an overflowing spirit of thanksgiving and expectation. I praise You for the assurance of heaven and what it stands for.

Heaven is a place of HOLINESS. There will be no evil there. Satan will be bound forever. Purity will reign. All thoughts and activities will stem from God-inspired motives. Thank You, Father, for preparing such a place for me!

Heaven is a place of HAPPINESS. You have told us, Father, that You will wipe away all tears. The reasons for tears will be eliminated. There will be no burdens to bear and no problems to solve. Thank You, Father, for preparing such a place for me!

Heaven is a place of HEALTH! No sickness, no dying there . . . the cruel monsters of affliction and disease will be eradicated. There will be eternal life and energy to praise You and to enjoy the fruits of Your love. Thank You, Father, for preparing such a place for me!

MY PRAYER NOTES FOR TODAY

____

____

____

____

____

BIBLE READING

❑ **Day 331 — 2 Corinthians 7—9**

DAY 332 — THINK NEW THOUGHTS

Thoughts are a powerful force, Lord; and I want my thoughts today to focus on Your holiness and my spiritual health. I want to honor You with thoughts of love, thanksgiving, and appreciation. I want to maintain spiritual health with thoughts of, "You in me, the hope of glory," and that I am a champion by Your strength and oversight. Today I will think positive thoughts:

Truth. Your truth, forever settled, is a beautiful gift that sets free, settles, and stabilizes.

Hope. Your plans for me include a bright future with peace and prosperity.

Influence. Your Spirit will empower me to be an effective and enriching witness.

New. Your energy will renew my spirit and give me new insights and inspiration.

Knit. Your love will connect me with other believers and we will become one in You.

Today I will think on purity, love, and the power of the Gospel of Jesus Christ and the beauty of life in Him.

MY PRAYER NOTES FOR TODAY

____

____

____

____

____

BIBLE READING

❑ **Day 332 — 2 Corinthians 10—13**

DAY 333 — THINKING BIG

I stand in amazement, Father, when I survey the wondrous, creative works of Your hands. Everything is big—the clouds, the oceans, the vegetation. You are a big God without boundaries or limitations. As Your child, I want to think big.

I want to think BEAUTIFUL thoughts that are colorful and creative. Life is full of joyful events and great opportunities. I am committed to thinking about Your unlimited love, Your unlimited power, and Your unlimited grace today. I will think beautiful, uplifting, and intriguing thoughts in all situations.

I want to think without BOUNDARIES. I want thoughts that are mighty and mind-expanding. I do not want to be trapped by doubt, fear, or laziness. Today, I will think "out of the box," kingdom-advancing thoughts.

I will think about BLESSINGS, both heavenly and personally. You are a God of wonder and majesty. Your storehouse of gifts never runs low and is always running over. I will think about blessings from You—care and wisdom, and physical and spiritual wealth.

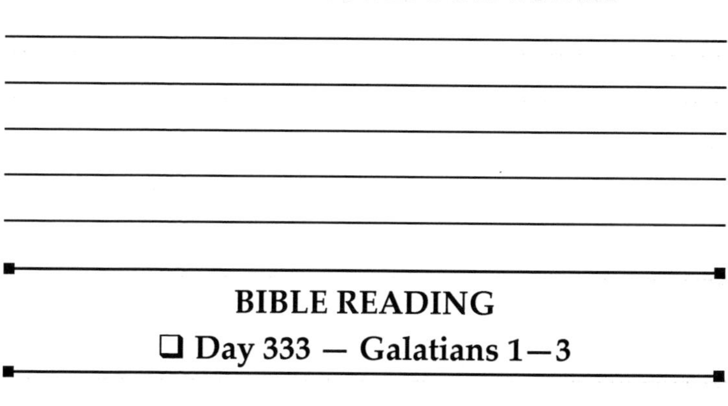

MY PRAYER NOTES FOR TODAY

BIBLE READING

❑ **Day 333 — Galatians 1–3**

DAY 334 — TOTAL ACCOUNTABILITY

Giving Father, I want to be thankful and accountable for the gifts You give me. You shower me with abundant gifts every day. My life is truly blessed! I want to show forth my appreciation by:

GROWING strong through obedience. I want to be obedient in open communication with You, by living the truth I profess, and by sharing the love of Your Son, Jesus Christ, in words and works of compassion.

GAINING understanding through obstacles. I do not want to be a complainer or whiner. I will face obstacles placed in my path by Satan and the circumstances of life with faith to learn from them. Father, direct me in being a daily learner, acquiring wisdom, learning new techniques, and demonstrating acute awareness.

GIVING praise for overcoming. Master, I do not want to look at praise for grace and gifts as a duty. It is a delight! A distinct privilege! A posture of respect, honor, and thanksgiving! As I grow, gain, and give, let me illuminate faithfulness, the fruit of the Spirit, and the virtues of spiritual accountability.

MY PRAYER NOTES FOR TODAY

____

____

____

____

____

BIBLE READING

❑ **Day 334 — Galatians 4—6**

DAY 335 — TOTAL AFFIRMATION

Lord of plenty, I affirm You are the God of unlimited resources to meet my needs in every area of life. I do not want to falter in faith to believe and receive Your bountiful provisions for—finances, food, facilities, and family life. Today I affirm Your:

SUFFICIENCY every day, in every way. Wisdom for every decision. Oversight for every activity. Support for every task. Insight for every project. Fortitude for every encounter. Might for every ministry. I will rely, trust in, and depend on Your sufficiency for a pleasing and productive life.

SENSITIVITY in every situation, every setting. When I feel lonely. When faced with financial pressure. When goals are not being achieved. When my faith seems to be weak. When beset by tests and trials. I will look to You because I know You are sensitive to my needs and will love me and lift me up.

SECURITY every day. When I face Satan's attacks, when I walk in the valley, when I am misunderstood, when I must stand alone, I will stand out and stand up because I have ultimate security in You. This security provides peace and overcoming power.

MY PRAYER NOTES FOR TODAY

BIBLE READING

❑ **Day 335 — Ephesians 1–3**

DAY 336 — TOTAL HEALING

Healing is prominently set forth in Your Word. Every member of Your family needs healing in some way. This includes me! Healing, I realize, takes on many different forms—divine intervention, medicine, and encouragement.

Today give HEALTH healing. Guide me in taking care of my "temple" through rest, diet, and exercise. I also bring my friends to You that need physical healing. Some are in desperate need of a divine visit from You. **Make a personal visit to them!**

Today give HEART healing. I thank You, Father, that my heart is fixed on You. It has been cleansed, filled with compassion, and committed to You. Some of my friends, however, have been hurt, wounded through betrayal, divorce, or abuse. **Make a personal visit to them!**

Today give HAPPINESS healing. Doubt and pressing circumstances can squeeze out contentment. Wisdom from You is a sure cure. Some of my friends are perplexed and discouraged. **Make a personal visit to them!**

MY PRAYER NOTES FOR TODAY

____

____

____

____

____

BIBLE READING

❑ **Day 336 — Ephesians 4–6**

DAY 337 — TOUCH MY MIND

Lord of the present and the future, touch my thinking today—let me have the mind of Christ. When I consider the mind of Christ I think about three things—obedience, a caring spirit, and a servant's heart.

1. **OBEDIENCE.** In His life on earth, Christ was totally given to performing Your will, Father. It was foremost in His attitude and activities. His attitude was to honor You. His activities centered on expanding Your kingdom. I want these same principles to characterize my life.

2. **A CARING spirit.** Christ was committed to caring and loving children, the sick and bruised, the hungry and the outcasts. To reflect the mind of Christ, I must be concerned about these things also.

3. **A SERVANT'S heart.** Christ said He came to serve, not to be served. Today let me convey a heart that serves, to be a helper, healer, and hope-giver. Let me know the mind of Christ today.

MY PRAYER NOTES FOR TODAY

BIBLE READING

❑ **Day 337 — Philippians 1—4**

DAY 338 — TOUCH MY SPIRIT

More than anything, I want my spirit to bear witness with Your Spirit. Infuse my thinking with wisdom so I can think holy, healthy, helpful thoughts of spiritual partnership, Christ-exalting prosperity, and internal peace.

Today, I will be SENSITIVE to Your grace and guidance, believing and receiving. I will also be aware of the faith and feelings of those around me, serving and encouraging.

Today, I will SURROUND myself with the music of praise and expressions of love to You. I will receive Your warm and gracious energy to look up with faith and to look around with a positive attitude.

Today, I will SERVE You in the beauty of wholeness and holiness by seeking to lift up the weary and by living in agreement with Holy Scripture and holy conduct.

MY PRAYER NOTES FOR TODAY

BIBLE READING

❑ **Day 338 — Colossians 1—4**

DAY 339 — TOUGH TIMES

Father of sustaining strength, I am surrounded by people facing tough times—trials, tests, and temptations. Only You, Father, have the authority and influence to prepare me, and those around me, to confront tough times with overcoming faith and solutions that work.

I will pray for those facing TROUBLES. You are a compassionate, loving Father. You want to help people in times of distress. I pray for those facing difficult times in finances, in family affairs, and in questions about faith. Lift them up! Liberate them!

I will embrace those shedding TEARS. Many of my friends are crying as a result of difficulties—the death of a loved one, marital complexities, career challenges, and disturbing personality clashes. Comfort them! Caress them! Care for them!

I will rejoice with those experiencing TRIUMPHS. Faithfulness results in victory! I praise You for victories in my life, victories in my church, and victories among my believing friends. I am an overcomer and a conqueror through Jesus Christ. I praise You! I honor You! I exalt You!

MY PRAYER NOTES FOR TODAY

BIBLE READING

❑ **Day 339 — 1 Thessalonians 1—3**

DAY 340 — TRIPLE BLESSED

What a wonderful day. I am blessed, blessed, blessed! I have Your supreme love, Heavenly Father, salvation in Your Son, Jesus Christ, and power for service and witnessing through the infilling and indwelling of the Holy Spirit. Yes, I am triple blessed today!

I am blessed with a loving FAMILY. Thank You for my family. They provide an atmosphere of love, care, and significance. Today I will respect the members of my family and will practice fairness and tenderness in my relationships.

I am blessed with a bright FUTURE. Thank You for my future. Christ gives me grace for each day and reveals what it will look like and feel like to spend eternity with Him.

I am blessed with caring FRIENDS. Thank You for friends. They surround me with excitement and experiences of sharing, learning, and growing. I want to be a friend that is trustworthy and exhibits the characteristics of a dedicated Christ follower.

MY PRAYER NOTES FOR TODAY

BIBLE READING

❑ **Day 340 — 1 Thessalonians 4—5**

DAY 341 — TRUST AND OBEY

Sometimes times get tough! During these times there is tension and my faith is tested. Father, in every situation, however, when tough times surface, I want to trust and obey—trust You to see me through and obey You to follow through. My desire is to:

Grow strong through OBEDIENCE. As I obey You and do the truth I know to do, I will grow stronger in spiritual power moves, in conveying Christian disciplines, and in expressing acts of generosity. **Trust and obey is the way!**

Gain understanding through OBSTACLES. I must face obstacles for what they are—opportunities to trust and obey. When I face the obstacles of life and the obstacles Satan sets in my path, I will trust and obey. **Because to trust and obey is the only way!**

Give praise for OVERCOMING. I praise You for the blessings of overcoming the trap of the Tempter, the rock and ruts that hinder spiritual maturity, the tendencies to procrastinate action to enhance my fellowship with You and to exercise a positive faith. To trust is foundational. To obey is relational. **I will trust and obey because there is no other way!**

MY PRAYER NOTES FOR TODAY

BIBLE READING

❑ **Day 341 — 2 Thessalonians 1—3**

DAY 342 — TRUST TODAY

Father, You have instructed me to trust You with all of my heart and not to depend on my own ability and skills (see Proverbs 3:5). If I will do this, You have promised to provide for my needs and to protect me from the traps and tricks of the devil.

Today, I trust You to guide me into all TRUTH. As I pray and read Your Word, show me the path to follow that leads to pleasing You, to soul peace, and to spiritual prosperity.

Today I trust You to empower me to be a TEACHER, to teach others by words and example of Your ways and works, and how to worship You in spirit and in truth.

Today I trust You to make me a TAKER, to take back those things that the devil has stolen from me: a bold faith, daring convictions, and aggressive kingdom service. Today, I will trust and obey for this is Your way to a victorious life.

MY PRAYER NOTES FOR TODAY

____

____

____

____

____

BIBLE READING

❑ **Day 342 — 1 Timothy 1–3**

DAY 343 — TRUSTWORTHY TODAY

Steadfast Father, I trust You without any doubt or hesitation. History reveals Your total dependability in all situations—fears, trials, temptations, and triumphs. Today I will walk with You in total confidence. I will show forth a trustworthy attitude in my:

TESTIMONY. I will testify of Your graciousness and goodness. I will share experiences from Your Word, and from my personal life, about mercy, miracles, and mighty acts that changed the world. **I will back my testimony with trust.**

TRANSACTIONS. I will engage in business today—perform assignments, make purchases, and promote activities. In all of these activities I will be open, honest, and perform with integrity so my transactions will blend with my testimony. **I will back my transactions with trust!**

TEAMWORK. I will respect the talents and skills of my friends and coworkers. I will cooperate with them and compliment them for achievements. At church I will emphasize teamwork in living out divine truths. **I will back my teamwork with trust!**

MY PRAYER NOTES FOR TODAY

BIBLE READING

❑ Day 343 — 1 Timothy 4—6

DAY 344 — UNDERSTANDING SCRIPTURE

Father, Your Holy Word—the Bible—is the foundation for knowing You, observing Your will, and performing Christian service. I need guidance in understanding Scripture today. As I study, pray, and meditate, I ask Your Holy Spirit to quicken my insight and comprehension so I can identify with:

PROPHETS. You ministered through prophets to give messages of instruction to Your people. They were submissive, yet bold. They were tender, yet tough. **Today, let me learn from their character and how they responded to Your leadership.**

PRIESTS. You called priests to represent You to the people. They were men of integrity who devoted their lives to You and the people, in intercession, instruction, and inspirational counseling. **Today, let me grow in respect from their disciplined devotion and dedication.**

PEOPLE. You were tolerant, yet loving, with people in the Bible. You dealt with them where they were, the conditions they faced, and how they responded to You. **Today, let me benefit in my Christian walk from both their strengths and their weaknesses.**

MY PRAYER NOTES FOR TODAY

____

____

____

____

____

BIBLE READING

❑ **Day 344 — 2 Timothy 1—4**

DAY 345 — UNWINDING TODAY

Father, I do not want my thoughts to be tough, tied up, or tangled today. I desire to be free in my feelings and to believe for liberating, overcoming, and achieving faith. I will unwind by:

LOOKING up for sunshine. I will open my eyes and my heart to Your warm sunlight of love. The rays will purify and energize. They symbolize divine oversight, divine protection, and divine enabling.

LEAVING off anxiety. Master, You have told me You will block danger and harm from my path. Therefore, I will not worry or fear. I will not let anxiety drain my joy, or dilute my inner peace, or distract my attention from looking up.

LETTING go of hurts. I have a tendency to harbor hurts—scathing accusations, wounded relationships, and unscrupulous dealings. I will unwind by letting go of hurts and fostering forgiveness. As You have forgiven me, I will forgive those who have caused me pain or grief. Thank You, Father, for guiding me in unwinding today and accepting Your plan for a rich life in Jesus Christ.

MY PRAYER NOTES FOR TODAY

____

____

____

____

____

BIBLE READING

❑ **Day 345 — Titus 1–3**

DAY 346 — USING MY GIFTS

Thank You, holy Father, for the gifts You have entrusted to me. I want to utilize them to the fullest to honor You. Today I want your leading in developing, dedicating, and demonstrating these gifts.

Give me knowledge to DEVELOP my gifts. Your Word, I realize, revealing Father, is the bedrock for understanding spiritual gifts and how to develop them. As I study, let the illuminating insight of the Holy Spirit reveal the course of action I should take.

Give me discipline to DEDICATE my gifts. I want to constantly develop and deploy the gifts You have assigned to me. Touch both my thinking and my timing in exercising gifts to worship, to witness of amazing grace, and to engage in fulfilling the Great Commission.

Give me strength to DEMONSTRATE my gifts. Faithfulness, loyalty, and tenaciousness are characteristics I want to model to others, revealing the nature of my gifts. I want to be a model that motivates my family and friends to understand Your love and Your plan for abundant life in Christ.

MY PRAYER NOTES FOR TODAY

BIBLE READING

❑ **Day 346 — Philemon 1**

DAY 347 — VISION FOR TODAY

Personal vision for each day is the force for productivity and work satisfaction. The following standards will guide me in experiencing super success. I pray for:

Vitality for the day. Choose to be upbeat.

Insight for the day. Determine what is important.

Strategy for the day. Outline a plan of action.

Impact for the day. Focus on how to make a difference.

Operation for the day. Purpose to work with integrity.

Nurture for the day. Include time for enrichment.

I will embrace these guidelines with uncompromising trust in You, with a tenacious disposition, and with assertive, aggressive, and Spirit-supported action.

MY PRAYER NOTES FOR TODAY

BIBLE READING

❑ **Day 347 — Hebrews 1—3**

DAY 348 — VIBRANT VISION

Father, You desire that I have a vision that motivates and activates the skills You have placed in me. That's what I want also! I want a sizzling, nonstop vision that leads to my best in demonstrating the qualities of a convinced, twice-born believer. Today I will focus on a:

VIRTUOUS vision. I want my thoughts and staked-out goals to be pure, honorable, Scripture-anchored, and Christ-exalting. Only through You, Master, can I exercise the discipline to maintain integrity, goodwill, and trust.

VIGILANT vision. Wide-awake, on duty, ready to serve. Your watchcare will engulf me and fortify me to be vigilant. I also want to be wide-awake in claiming Your provisions. Your storehouse has unlimited supplies ready for my acquisition.

VICTORIOUS vision. Victory in Jesus! I believe it! I claim it! I rejoice in it! Today, I will wear a crown of victory in serving You. I will wear it with a spirit of dependence, with thankful joy, and with the understanding You want me to experience victory in my walk with You every hour of every day.

MY PRAYER NOTES FOR TODAY

____

____

____

____

____

BIBLE READING

❑ **Day 348 — Hebrews 4—6**

DAY 349 — VICTORY TODAY

Lord of love and divine leadership, I claim victory today through Your Son, Jesus Christ.

Let my thoughts be **virtuous.**

Let my plans be founded on **values.**

Let my attitude reflect **vitality.**

Let my actions lead to **victory.**

Above all, let whatever I do denote that I am:

Connected to a divine source.

Committed to teamwork with my heavenly Father.

Controlled by the guidance of the Holy Spirit.

Convinced that You provide an anchor for my life by Your love and leadership.

MY PRAYER NOTES FOR TODAY

BIBLE READING

❑ **Day 349 — Hebrews 7–9**

DAY 350 — VISIONARY SERVICE

Kind Master, I want to serve with You and for You today. I want my service to be innovative and creative. I want it to be deeply personal and guided by sincere passion. I ask You to guide me in achieving these objectives.

I want to serve You in LOVE. I do not want my service to be forced or of a routine nature. I want it to flow freely, briskly, and purely from my heart. With humble gratitude I bow in holy praise in Your presence.

I want to serve You with bold LOYALTY. I want You to be able to count on me regardless of conditions or circumstances. I want to stand up and step out with courage in performing ministry.

I want to serve You with a LONG-SUFFERING spirit. I want to exercise patience in working with those who are slow or sluggish in their performance. Let me model vision and vitality that will influence them. Let my vision be a torch to ignite a fire in the service of others.

MY PRAYER NOTES FOR TODAY

___

___

___

___

___

BIBLE READING

❑ **Day 350 — Hebrews 10—13**

DAY 351 — WAKE UP TO OPPORTUNITIES

Mighty Master, every day is a new day filled with glowing opportunities. I do not want to sleep away these opportunities. I want to wake up, get up, stand up, and seize the day. This calls for changes in perception and practices. Therefore I will:

REFOCUS priorities. Lord, I want the things that are important to You to be important to me. There are three things that are very important to You: closeness in worship; communication through prayer; and commitment in service. **Today, I will refocus my attention on these priorities.**

REMOVE clutter. There are some things in my life that are not important. I want to use my time wisely and give my attention to fruit-producing activities. **Today, I will remove things that weaken spiritual and intellectual growth.**

REFINE values. I want my values to be based on Your Word. Lead me to check where I spend my time, how I treat other people, and share my testimony of my relationship with You. My goals and aspirations must be hooked to eternity. **Today, I will refine what is valuable based on Your will for my life.**

MY PRAYER NOTES FOR TODAY

____

____

____

____

____

BIBLE READING

❑ Day 351 — James 1—3

DAY 352 — WALKING A POSITIVE PATH

Lord of creation and adventure, I want to walk an exciting spiritual path today. I realize this will require a motivated mind and active, forward steps. I ask You to anoint both my spiritual body and my physical body for aggressive action. I want to:

Walk a path of PURITY. Overshadow me with insight to have a pure thought life by thinking, reading, and meditating. Let me dwell on the purity of Your love and how it can direct my life.

Walk a path of PEACE. Overshadow me with inner strength to reflect contagious peace in my life in relationships, witnessing, and working. Let me show that stabilizing peace comes from You.

Walk a path of PARTNERSHIP. Overshadow me with awareness of joining my pastor as a partner in ministry in my church life by supporting, praying, and encouraging. Let me display an attitude of appreciation, cooperation, and anticipation in ministering with my pastor and in honoring You.

MY PRAYER NOTES FOR TODAY

___

___

___

___

___

BIBLE READING

❑ **Day 352 — James 4—5**

DAY 353 — WALKING WITH YOU

What a joy! I have the privilege to walk with You today, life-giving Father. I will enjoy the close communion and the beauty of Your handiwork as we walk in the brightness of Your glory. On the journey I will:

Walk with the WORD—the Holy Bible! You have given Your Word as a road map to guide, strengthen, and fortify. I will respect it, embrace it, and use it both to move forward and to defend the faith.

Walk with "above" WISDOM—divine enablement! As I pray today, I ask You to touch my mind and spirit so my behavior and my decisions will match my testimony and keep me on the course you have set before me.

Walk with spiritual WINNERS—people who walk the talk! I want to be an example of Christlikeness and I want to walk with those who are a proven example of faithfulness and fruitfulness. Togetherness in ministry honors You and expands Your kingdom on earth.

MY PRAYER NOTES FOR TODAY

BIBLE READING

❑ **Day 353 — 1 Peter 1–3**

DAY 354 — WHAT'S IMPORTANT?

Lord, there are many things calling for my attention today. Guide me in sorting out what is important, the things that will make a difference in my relationship with You, my family, and those around me.

My FAITH is important. Keep me focused on how you want me to love and live according to Your Word. Let my steps be guided by Your will and my walk reflecting Your oversight.

My FAMILY is important. Keep my family together—sound, secure, spiritually grounded. Give me patience and tenderness toward my companion and children.

My FUTURE is important. I want to grow spiritually. I want to be a good steward. I want to advance in my career. The Holy Spirit will guide me in every area of my life. I know this! However, I also know that I must be responsive and yield totally. Let my spirit blend with the Holy Spirit today.

MY PRAYER NOTES FOR TODAY

____

____

____

____

____

BIBLE READING

❑ **Day 354 — 1 Peter 4—5**

DAY 355 — WHAT'S NEXT?

Every day with You, Father, is fascinating, full of opportunities flowing with grace from Your throne. You have surrounded me with privileges to discover, demonstrate, and develop. I look forward to what is next! Anoint my eyes to see, to size up, and to seize the beauty of belonging to Your family.

I have fantastic FRIENDS. I am blessed with friends who believe in me. They share with me, pray for me, and add value to my life. I ask You to shower them with heavenly blessings. I ask You to help me be a true and trusted friend.

I desire to be a fruitful FOLLOWER. Father, I want to be a fruitful follower—a positive, productive pattern of a dedicated disciple. Cultivate the fruit of the Spirit in my life. I am ready to do my part but I need Your oversight and overcoming enabling.

I enjoy first-class FULFILLMENT. Thank You for the infilling of the Holy Spirit that equips and empowers me to be victorious in my worship, in my work, and in my witness of Your care and control. What's next today! You fill my life with "wonder" and first-class experiences. I am thankful!

MY PRAYER NOTES FOR TODAY

____

____

____

____

____

BIBLE READING

❑ **Day 355 — 2 Peter 1—3**

DAY 356 — WHY NOT TODAY?

Today is a great day! Father, I will rejoice, express thanksgiving, and sing songs of praise. I will also look at the opportunities You have set before me and say, "Why not today?" I have thought about trying new methods in performing ministry, so "Why not today?" Make it happen in my life today by the creative energy of the Holy Spirit. I will:

Seek high ADVENTURES, follow new paths, perform with a clearer vision, and view from atop new ministry mountains. Every day You set new challenges before me. I will recognize them, embrace them, and capitalize on the releases of energy from them.

Strive for excellent ACHIEVEMENTS, set new goals, perform with stretching standards, and maintain a glowing attitude of optimism. I want to be excellent in my work ethic. More importantly, I want to be excellent in witness and modeling the Christ life.

Study for holy ADVANCEMENT, discover new truths, and gain illuminating insight as I study Your Word. I want to take the right steps, follow the right paths, and make the right decisions so I can advance in spiritual knowledge and advance Your kingdom.

MY PRAYER NOTES FOR TODAY

____

____

____

____

____

BIBLE READING

❑ **Day 356 — 1 John 1–3**

DAY 357 — WIDE-OPEN EYES

Creative Father, You have surrounded my life with glorious, glowing beauty. I'm thankful! I want to show my thankfulness by keeping my eyes wide open to see, by faith and trust, opportunities, obstacles, and outsiders.

OPPORTUNITIES to seize and serve. Master, motivate me to seize opportunities to advance my skills, capitalize on open doors, and focus on the magnitude of the work of Christ. Also, may my eyes be open to see the needs of people around me and to serve with compassion and sincerity.

OBSTACLES that hurt and hinder. Reveal to me the crafty work of Satan and the obstacles he has set in my path. Today, I will respond to the guidance of the Holy Spirit to sidestep obstacles and follow the path of liberty and freedom You have set before me.

OUTSIDERS who need hope and healing. People without You are without hope and need spiritual healing. I want to see them and respond to their needs with solid truth and a message of transforming grace. Equip me and empower me to see with my eyes, love with my heart, and work with my hands.

MY PRAYER NOTES FOR TODAY

BIBLE READING

❑ **Day 357 — 1 John 4–5**

DAY 358 — WORSHIP TODAY

Today I want to worship You. I want to worship You …

By **surrendering** my will to You;

In **spirit,** giving myself to You;

Through **serving**, revealing Your nature by giving, by going, and by sharing grace.

I want to worship You …

By lifting my **voice** in praise;

By clapping my **hands** in joy;

By opening my **heart** to express love.

I want to worship You …

Through **fellowship** with other believers;

By practicing **faithful** stewardship;

In pledging to be a **walking** witness of Your promises.

I want to worship You, Lord, and …

I will, **humbly** and sincerely;

I will, **graciously** and gloriously;

I will, **consistently** and righteously.

MY PRAYER NOTES FOR TODAY

____

____

____

____

____

BIBLE READING

❑ **Day 358 — 2 John; 3 John; Jude**

DAY 359 — "YES" TO YOUR WILL

Wonderful Master, "yes" is a positive and powerful word. Today I say, "yes" to Your will for my life. Embrace me, strengthen me, renew me as I proclaim a loud "yes" to life in Christ.

I say "yes" to Your WILL. You have a divine plan for my life. Don't let nagging doubt or busyness distract or detour me. I will seek Your will through Bible study, persistent prayer, and inward meditation. **I am committed to following Your plan.**

I say "yes" to You in WORSHIP. I will strive to have the "mind of Christ" in reverence to You, in praise to You, and in honoring You in spirit and with my substance. **I am committed to worshiping You according to Your Word.**

I say "yes" to You in spiritual WORK. Like the example set by Your Son, Jesus Christ, "I must be about my Father's business." **I am committed to being a keeper of the faith, a source of blessing to the needy, and a guiding light to the struggling and searching.**

MY PRAYER NOTES FOR TODAY

____

____

____

____

____

BIBLE READING

❑ **Day 359 — Revelation 1—3**

DAY 360 — YIELDED TO YOU

Lord of faith and forgiveness, I want to yield to You today. I want to lay myself on Your altar and ask You to supervise my life and direct my actions.

Today, I yield my SPIRIT. I want my attention focused on You and Your work of redemption and recruitment. I want my attitude to be positive, my witness to be impactful, and my disposition to be honorable and reflect priority values.

Today, I yield to SANCTIFICATION. I want to be totally set apart and committed in mind, body, and spirit to You, and to ministry. I want the mind of Christ in humility, the love of God in my heart, and the power of the Holy Spirit in witnessing with boldness.

Today, I yield my SERVICE. I want to be a true servant in attitude, vision, and labor. I want to stand by my pastor and let him or her know that I pray for church leadership, that I respect the calling and position, and that I will serve with my pastor as a faithful, dependable coworker.

MY PRAYER NOTES FOR TODAY

____

____

____

____

____

BIBLE READING

❑ **Day 360 — Revelation 4–6**

DAY 361 — YOU ARE MY REWARDER

Your Word clearly states, wonderful Father, that Your resources are unlimited. You freely give "all things" as an expression of Your love and character. I am not deserving. I realize this, but You reward me with blessings on top of blessings. You are my rewarder.

Because I believe, You ARE a rewarder of those who seek after You and serve You. I believe You are good and gracious in all Your dealings with humankind, especially to me! **I honor You for this!**

Because I believe, I AM a member of Your family with full benefits and privileges. You have adopted, accepted, affirmed, and rewarded me. **I praise You for this!**

Because I believe, You Will remove every obstacle that hinders or limits me from receiving and enjoying every aspect of Your kingdom power, gifts, and rewards. **I renew my commitment to You for this!**

MY PRAYER NOTES FOR TODAY

BIBLE READING

❑ **Day 361 — Revelation 7—9**

DAY 362 — YOUR PLAN TODAY

Lord of the past and of the present, I honor You today! I know You have a plan for my life that is challenging, honorable, and rewarding. Today, I need Your instructions and inspiration to understand and fully endorse the plan.

I will PARTNER with You in your plan, loving Father. I will give myself to You in mind, heart, and strength. I will embrace Your plan and partner with You in fulfilling it. I will write it down, pray over it, and exercise positive faith in making it a reality.

I will PRACTICE Your plan, guiding Father. I commit to assembling all of the gifts and talents You have invested in me. I will give one hundred percent in the pursuit of abiding in Your ideal plan for my life by cultivating, protecting, and honoring it.

I will accept the PROVISIONS of Your plan, giving Father. With the details of the plan comes spiritual equipment—Guidebook, armor, training, support, coaching, and watchcare. Your provisions, all-sufficient Father, will enable me to **partner** with You, **practice** Your plan, and receive and enjoy Your **provisions.** I lift You up in praise and thanksgiving.

MY PRAYER NOTES FOR TODAY

____

____

____

____

____

BIBLE READING

❑ **Day 362 — Revelation 10—12**

DAY 363 — YOUR WORD FOR MY LIFE

Lord of Glory, I want Your Word to be my guide. I know it is a lamp that provides light and a compass that will keep me on the right path of inward peace and outward prosperity.

Today I embrace the Bible, Your life-giving Word:

I believe its teachings;

I claim its promises;

I depend on its guidance;

I endorse its judgments;

I delight in its provisions;

I accept its standards.

Today I pledge allegiance to the Bible, Your Holy Word:

I will study it;

I will store it in my heart;

I will stand on its authority;

I will share its message of salvation in Christ.

Today I will let Your Word be my guide.

MY PRAYER NOTES FOR TODAY

____

____

____

____

____

BIBLE READING

❑ **Day 363 — Revelation 13—15**

DAY 364 — ZIP FOR TODAY

Lord, put zip in my life today! Give me zip, Father, so I can zap any force or circumstance that would hinder my joy of walking with You.

Empower me to be ZEALOUS of good works. I will have to work today on the job, at home, and many other different ways. In the midst of all this activity, let me do good work— studying your Word, seeking You in prayer, and standing by my church and pastor.

Equip me to INSPIRE others. I need burning, driving, contagious enthusiasm for myself and to influence people that I associate with today. I open my mind and heart for a flow of energy and inspiration from You. Let me inspire others, spread positive sunshine, and stress adventure in both work and play.

Engage me in PARTNERSHIP with You. Like Enoch, I want to walk with You today in partnership. Let me feel Your presence and power so I can keep my blessings in view—release from the bondage of sin, adoption into the family of God, and the gifts of a new beginning in life.

MY PRAYER NOTES FOR TODAY

___

___

___

___

___

BIBLE READING

❑ **Day 364 — Revelation 16—18**

DAY 365 — MY FUTURE

Lord of the present and future, my trust is in You. I know You have a plan for my life—a plan to prosper, protect, and partner with me in ministry for You. My mind and heart are open today to embrace Your plan as a guide for my future. I will:

Exercise FAITH. I will approach the future today with a positive attitude, believing that Your grace is sufficient for me to live an influential life that honors You. I will release life-building faith today!

Display FORTITUDE. I will stand firm today on the solid ground of Holy Scripture. I will depend on the Holy Spirit for strength to wage successful warfare against Satan and the forces of evil. I will display faith-based fortitude today!

Produce FRUIT. I will show forth the fruit of a Christ-centered life today. The fruit of love, acceptance, patience, and kindness will validate my commitment and serve as a testimony of the transforming nature of Christ in me. I will show forth the inspiring gift of heaven-sent fruit today!

MY PRAYER NOTES FOR TODAY

BIBLE READING

❑ **Day 365 — Revelation 19—22**

PERSONAL REVIEW

You have engaged in 365 days of personal prayer encounters with the Lord of glory—times of prayer in weeping, in worship, and in spiritual warfare.

How has your life been impacted? Have you advanced in Christlikeness? Is your vision for service larger, stronger, wider, and deeper?

Take time now to reflect. Jot down your thoughts, experiences, and victorious achievements.

— Personal Memories of My Prayer Journey —

PRAYER

The Heartbeat of the Church

The Church of God has placed a major emphasis on the priority of prayer and its transforming power. This churchwide prayer initiative is a major emphasis for three reasons:

- **To enrich** your personal life as well as the health of your congregation by making prayer a priority.
- **To enable** you and your church to break out of the paralyzing cycle of dullness and sameness.
- **To provide** materials and resources for God's people to teach, discuss, and share genuine prayer renewal.

Prayer—The Heartbeat of the Church was the initial emphasis in the church's three-pronged initiative for *Forward Together in Changing Times*. However, it was designed to be an ongoing emphasis and can be studied by any local church at any time.

To order support materials for *Prayer—The Heartbeat of the Church*, contact:

Pathway Press
1080 Montgomery Avenue
Cleveland, TN 37311
1-800-533-8506
www.pathwaypress.org
www.pathwaybookstore.com

THE GREAT COMMISSION

The Solution

The Great Commission is the solution to reaching the unchurched, developing mature disciples, and expanding the kingdom of God.

The Great Commission—The Solution was the second emphasis of the church's three-pronged initiative for *Forward Together in Changing Times.* However, it was designed to be an ongoing emphasis and can be studied by any local church at any time.

To order support materials for *The Great Commission—The Solution,* contact:

Pathway Press

1080 Montgomery Avenue

Cleveland, TN 37311

1-800-533-8506

www.pathwaypress.org

www.pathwaybookstore.com